The Autumn of Dictatorship

Stanford Studies in Middle Eastern and Islamic Societies and Cultures

The Autumn of Dictatorship

FISCAL CRISIS AND POLITICAL CHANGE
IN EGYPT UNDER MUBARAK

Samer Soliman

Translated by Peter Daniel

Stanford University Press
Stanford, California

Stanford University Press
Stanford, California

Library of Congress Cataloging-in-Publication Data

Sulayman, Samir, 1968- author.
    [Nizam al-qawi wa-al-dawlah al-da'ifah. English]
    The autumn of dictatorship : fiscal crisis and political change in Egypt under Mubarak / Samer Soliman ; translated by Peter Daniel.
        pages cm.—(Stanford studies in Middle Eastern and Islamic societies and cultures)
    Translated from the Arabic.
    Includes bibliographical references and index.
    ISBN 978-0-8047-6000-3 (cloth : alk. paper)—ISBN 978-0-8047-7846-6 (pbk. : alk. paper)
    1. Finance, Public—Egypt.   2. Egypt–Politics and government—1981-   3. Egypt—Economic policy.   4. Egypt—Economic conditions—1981-   I. Daniel, Peter (Peter Otto), translator.   II. Title. III. Series: Stanford studies in Middle Eastern and Islamic societies and cultures.
    HJ1456.S85   2011
    336.62—dc22   2011003140

Designed by Bruce Lundquist
Typeset by Westchester Book Group in 10/14 Minion

To my life companion
Mary Mourad

CONTENTS

FIGURES

TABLES

PREFACE

THE COUNTRYWIDE PROTESTS of January and February 2011 are the largest uprising in Egypt since the 1919 revolution against the British occupation. The country is finally reaching the autumn of its patriarch, Hosni Mubarak. When Mubarak first came to power in 1981, few Egyptians would have believed that Mubarak, the ex-commander-in-chief of the Air Force, would become the country's longest ruling leader in the twentieth century. It was not that the man was without abilities. Indeed, Mubarak had had an excellent career in the armed forces. Well known for his discipline and hard work, he had a reputation as a good officer and a discreet man with matters of national security. Yet compared to his three predecessors, Muhammad Naguib, Gamal Abdel Nasser, and Anwar Sadat, he had a much lower political profile and much less direct political experience. Naguib, Nasser, and Sadat, all military officers themselves, had gained political experience within the ranks of the many political movements that swept Egypt in the 1930s and 1940s. Nasser and Sadat could ably address the public and frequently appeared in the media. They showed an ease in public speaking, with both prepared and extemporaneous remarks. As for Mubarak, he could barely face the public except with the aid of a prepared written text.

The story of how Mubarak would go on to impose his rule for thirty years over the most populous and strategically important country in the Arab world deserves to be told. It is almost a universal law that authoritarian regimes live by the carrot and the stick; that is, by distributing some material benefits to select segments of the population and using harsh repression whenever necessary. This book analyzes how the Mubarak regime did just this, efficiently using public money to impose political stability. This was not done without consequences, and Egypt has literally been paying the price over the decades of Mubarak's rule. The regime's security logic that underpins their management of public finance has had disastrous effects on the Egyptian state.

I have had a long-standing interest in the state, mainly due to my concern with the various problems facing Egypt that are centered on or related to the state; namely the problems of the failing economic development, the endurance of political authoritarianism, the deep social inequality, and the increasing level of sectarian conflict between Muslims and non-Muslims, especially Copts. I am convinced that in order to deal with these problems, it is vital to reform the Egyptian state. A strong state capable of enforcing the law and public order, ruled by a democratic regime and subjected to its society, and accessible to all its citizens regardless of their gender, social origin, and religion is the main path to overcome these issues. Egypt has one of the oldest, if not the oldest, state in history. Founded in 3200 B.C. with political borders similar to those that exist today, the state in Egypt is almost unavoidable. It is both a mark of Egyptian civilization and one of the major sources of Egyptian malaise.

Today in Egypt, one cannot help but notice that the state is weakening. One does not need to be a specialist or to have empirical knowledge to observe this. It is sufficient to pass by Egypt to note the deterioration of its public transportation, public hospitals, and public schools. In fact, the word *public* in Egypt today is synonymous with *mediocrity*. The weakening of the Egyptian state and its consequent failure to deal with many challenges facing the country has been the main driver behind my choice of that state as an object of research. While this study focuses on the fiscal crisis of the state, the issue of public finance is only a window through which the state is dissected and analyzed.

This book started as a scholarly publication written in French.[1] However, it was never meant to be material for social scientists and academics only. My intention from the beginning was to offer intellectuals who are interested in Egyptian public affairs a tool to understand the functioning and the problems of the Egyptian state. Thus, I was keen to put it in the hands of the Arabic reader.[2] The Arabic version was not a literal translation of the French; although the analysis and arguments were the same, the tone was less cold and more engaging. I am now proud to present a version for the English reader. This English version is an updated and modified translation of the third Arabic edition published in 2006.[3] This preface is intended to give the English reader a note on the Egyptian context of the study and an idea of how it was received in its earlier versions.

One of the main takeaways of this book is that the authoritarian, bureaucratic, and narrow-based regime of Hosni Mubarak has been the main source of the state's weakening. This book's earlier version was published in the middle of increasing political dissatisfaction and opposition to the existing regime during 2004 and 2005. The number of political dissidents was increasing, and some public figures abandoned the circles of the regime and joined the opposition, including Dr. Ossam al-Ghazali Harb, the editor in chief of the monthly *al-Siyassa al-Dawliya* [Foreign Policy], published by the prestigious government-owned al-Ahram, who used to be a member of the Policies Committee of the National Democratic Party headed by the president's son. The harsh critiques of the regime, previously limited to the government and not aimed at the president, finally reached home, directly attacking Mubarak and his family. The demonstrations in Cairo in 2005 were the first to target Mubarak and his son Gamal, the potential successor to his father. Bloggers and Internet activists were engaged in denouncing torture and oppression and were unrestrained by the traditional media restrictions. The Kefaya movement and other unofficial political groups calling for an end to Mubarak's rule were formed.

The messages of the book were welcomed by some circles of Egyptian opposition and independent media, which found in it a scientific grounding for their critique of the regime. I believe that the main service this book has offered the rising democratic movement in Egypt is its analytical distinction between the state and the political regime. The study clearly intended to send this message: the opposition to Mubarak and his regime is not necessarily a rejection of the Egyptian state or a challenge to its authority. On the contrary, the book argues that the weakening of the state, manifested in the deterioration of public services and the low level of law enforcement, is a result of the inflation of the security machine and logic needed to reproduce political authoritarianism. I have never adopted the simplistic neoliberal wisdom that the problem in Egypt is the strength of its state and the weakness of its society. The crisis rather, as explained in this book, is the weakness of both the state and civil society. The way out of the crisis is to equally strengthen both.

This distinction and suggested opposition between the state and the Mubarak regime was most challenging to the security apparatus. The Reuters review of the book stated that "Soliman dealt with one of the Ministry of Interior's branches, namely the State Security Department, saying that its name is not providing a precise definition of its mission which is to secure the regime, not the State. For when that department refrains from following the corrupt public officials because they are politically loyal to the authoritarian regime, it is therefore contributing to the deterioration of the efficiency of the State apparatus."[4] This citation earned the Arabic publisher an "invitation" to visit the State Security Department, where the officer was keen to stress that he and his colleagues are the servants of the state, not the regime.

The fiscal crisis of the Egyptian state is exerting increasing pressure on the political regime, while the capacity of the ruling bureaucracy to use money and public services to buy the consent of some segments of the population has dramatically shrunk, resulting in a metamorphosis of the social constituency of the regime. The social origin of the ruling coalition is no longer limited to the bureaucracy, specifically the military and security, but increasingly comprises some of the tycoons of the business community. The uprising that swept across Egypt at the beginning of 2011 is challenging the underpinnings of political authoritarianism. I am content that the English edition of this work will reach English readers interested in Egyptian and Middle Eastern politics at this critical time in the history of Egypt.

INTRODUCTION

> *The budget is the skeleton of the State stripped of all misleading*
> *ideologies.*
> **—Rudolf Goldshield[1]**

IN HIS 1989 BOOK *Mubarak's Egypt*, Robert Springborg, a well-known scholar of Egyptian politics, ventured some predictions about changes in the political orientation of the Egyptian regime, which was facing a stifling fiscal crisis toward the end of the 1980s.[2] Failing to continue the repayment of its foreign debts in 1989, the Egyptian state reached a situation of near-bankruptcy. Springborg believed that this crisis would cause the political regime to adapt to the deterioration of its resources and a reduction in its beneficiaries, and therefore would be more accommodating toward its increasingly numerous and influential opponents. Springborg presented a number of possible scenarios for political transformation in Egypt. The first was a dictatorship based on an alliance between the military and capitalism that would rule with an iron fist and implement ultraliberal economic policies. This is the scenario that prevailed in Latin America in the 1970s and 1980s, where countries were also exposed to acute indebtedness crises. The second scenario shares the first one's economic orientation and authoritarian tendency, with the difference being that the system would forge an alliance with the Islamists in order to give religious legitimacy to its monopoly of power, as did Ja'far al-Numayri in Sudan.

Springborg's third scenario eventually materialized, namely that the Egyptian regime would seek to entrench the de facto situation while once again awaiting an inflow of resources. This took place when Saddam Hussein's tanks rolled across the Kuwaiti border in August 1990. In the resulting war against Iraq, the international coalition led by the United States needed Egypt's participation and consequently agreed to write off about half of Egypt's foreign debts and pump aid into the empty public treasury. The state's fiscal crisis was mitigated, and the political regime was able to resume its authority and domination.

No one expected such a miracle to occur so quickly. For example, Reuters' analysis on the economic crisis in Egypt in 1990 quoted an Egyptian economist who said that every time analysts expected the Egyptian economy to reach an impasse, a miracle happened, but he predicted that there would be no miracles this time.[3] Only two weeks following this statement, Saddam Hussein occupied Kuwait, and foreign resources again flowed into the public treasury.

The momentum gained by the state in the early 1990s slowed down halfway through the decade, and the fiscal crisis resumed by the decade's end. As of 2010, there has not been another new miracle, other than a limited financial inflow from the United States in 2004 to compensate Egypt for losses incurred as a result of the U.S. invasion of Iraq.[4]

The relative improvement in the public treasury at the beginning of the 1990s was a brief hiatus in a long series of crises. Since the mid-1980s, the Egyptian state has been exposed to a structural fiscal crisis whose main symptoms are large budget deficits and chronic indebtedness, both external and internal. This is considered the most serious fiscal crisis faced by the state since the royal dynasty established by Muhammad Ali in 1805, with the exception of the debt crisis suffered during the reign of Khedive Ismail (1863–79), which culminated in foreign intervention and the British occupation of Egypt.

The Egyptian regime is achieving limited success in mobilizing and generating additional income to meet the increasing requirements of the state, but it has been unable to cut back its expenditures to match its declining public revenues. The deficit is the most fundamental challenge that has confronted the Egyptian political regime in the Mubarak era. Although the regime has failed to resolve the state's fiscal crisis, it has coped with it and has achieved relative political stability. The last phase of coping is managed by Minister of Finance Youssef Boutros Ghali, who has occupied this position since 2004.

This book explains how a political regime has succeeded in dealing with a rapid and steep decline of revenue. When Mubarak assumed power in 1981, the state's revenues stood at around 60 percent of GDP; now the state must make do with only half of what was available at the beginning of the 1980s.[5]

This success in achieving political stability, as we will later observe, is not due only to the regime's restriction of freedoms or to its resort to a higher level of repression.[6] Egypt since the mid-1970s is an instance of an authoritarian regime whose stability has depended on a quasi-rentier state that obtained large influxes of money from oil, Suez Canal revenues, and foreign aid. But how has the Mubarak regime managed to perpetuate its stability despite the sharp drop in rentier revenues since the mid-1980s, and how has Egyptian politics changed as a consequence of this decline? These were the central questions that prompted this study.

The stability of Mubarak's political regime should not obscure the political transformations taking place in Egypt as a result of the fiscal crisis, the attempts to overcome it, and the strategies to cope with it. In this book, we follow the causes of the fiscal crisis and analyze the regime's attempts to deal with it. We study its impact on the state and the state's relationship with society and analyze the increased share of public resources for some institutions and the drop in the share for other institutions. We also attempt to explain how the fiscal crisis led to a complex phenomenon: the accelerated tendency toward centralization of the state accompanied by an inclination to fragmentation into isolated islands. Moreover, we focus on the regime's attempts to boost state revenues and show how these attempts failed, one after another, and how the nature of the political regime is an obstacle to increasing revenues. The book monitors and analyzes the political consequences of the state's ailing finances, particularly the growth of independent economic centers of power that are moving into the political arena and seizing positions in the political regime. This seizure is facilitated by the increasing political role played by the president's son, Gamal Mubarak, who transmits demands and influence from the rising bourgeoisie to the old ruling bureaucracy, whose main representative has been his own father, Hosni Mubarak.

THE POLITICAL ECONOMY OF THE STATE

This study adopts the methods of political economy, the discipline that focuses on the dialectical relationships between the economic and political fields in order to explain the transformations in both. We believe that political economy is the most suitable perspective to study a subject such as state finance, in which economic and political variables must be taken into account to enable understanding. Since the inception of classical economic theory in the eighteenth century, mainstream economics has steered far away from politics, despite the close connection between the two. The discipline of economics was originally known as "political economy." This term was used by classic thinkers like Adam Smith and David Ricardo, and was later adopted by the radical Karl Marx to define the science that studies production and exchange.

Since the publication of Alfred Marshall's book *Principles of Economics*,[7] the term *political economy* has been supplanted by the term *economics* and has come to carry a leftist and radical connotation, sometimes being used in the sense of "radical economics," the tradition that focuses on issues like the theory of value, income inequality, and redistribution of wealth. Our approach in this book draws upon the radical and Marxist tradition of political economy, fully adopting the Marxist premise that political power has an important socioeconomic foundation. In other words, the question of who and how a group of people in a society hold political power cannot be answered without understanding who and how economic resources are owned and managed. The influence of the Marxist tradition on the study is most noticeable in Chapter 5, where the diminishing size of the state and the rise of Egyptian capitalism are shown to exert deep changes on the political front.

This study draws as well upon the political economy of the neo-Weberian tradition that has been expanding since late 1980s, with many scholars studying the impact of political variables on the economic field. This tradition was not confined to studying the impact of the economy on politics but also studied the impact of the state and its institutions on the evolution of economic systems and on their success or failure. The neo-Weberian tradition has revived the field of political economy since the 1980s, after its marginalization because of its Marxist and radical flavor.

The revival of political economy has been accompanied by increased interest in the state. This can be attributed to many factors, the most important being the success of capitalist development in Southeast Asian countries. This development did not occur without the participation and even the leadership of the state. The Asian success produced wide-ranging discussions on the nature of the state in Southeast Asia, comparing it to the state in Latin America, where capitalist development was less successful. Some researchers explained that the Asian state was strong, especially according to the neo-Weberian approach,[8] whereas the Latin American state was weak. State strength here does not mean the ability to suppress opponents, but rather the ability to penetrate and change society, while also efficiently formulating and strictly implementing rational development policies. Here, Michael Mann's typology of state power makes the point. According to Mann, there are two types of state power, despotic and infrastructural. Despotic power refers to the range of actions that state elites can undertake without routine negotiation with civil society groups. Infrastructural power, in contrast, is the institutional capacity of a central state, despotic or not, to penetrate its territories and implement decisions.[9]

This neo-Weberian approach tried to formulate quantitative and qualitative indicators to measure the strength of the state. The quantitative indicators included the ability of the state to mobilize economic resources, as demonstrated by indicators such as the ratio of taxes to GDP. It also included the state's ability to mobilize human resources by reading indicators such as the ratio of children and youth enrolled in education. Qualitative indicators included phenomena such as harmony and internal unity of the state (low level of internal conflict) and "the State's ability to reorganize society and reshape its daily life," according to Joel Migdal.[10]

This study draws upon the important concept of state strength proposed by the neo-Weberian tradition in the last two decades, but not without a critique. Writings concerned with state strength often suffer from a theoretical problem: The indicators they use to measure state strength are often the variables that explain this strength. Therefore, the harmony and internal unity of a state, for example, are not only indicators of the strength of this institution but also factors that explain it. However, if a state's strength can be attributed to the existence of a technocratic developmental elite within it, and therefore its weakness would be due to disunity and conflict therein as maintained by these writings, where does the developmental elite come from? What are the factors that determine harmony or internal conflict in a state? These writings are sometimes trapped in circular logic, for they explain the state by the state. Therefore, a state is strong because it is strong. The authors of the strong state thesis started with the idea that the success of economic development is not related to the nature of the state (democratic or otherwise), but is closely related to the degree of the state's strength. They noted that capitalist economic development had succeeded in countries governed by authoritarian regimes. That is why they did not give much importance to the nature of the political regime when explaining the success or failure of development. This was a significant error. It is true that the success of capitalist development has little to do with whether a ruling regime is democratic or authoritarian. There are successful development examples under democracy and others under authoritarianism. But the nature of a political regime is not only measured by the degree of democracy but also by its relationship with society—that is, the social alliance upon which the regime is based. Even the most repressive regimes require some social support to achieve economic or social objectives.

In other words, the strength of the state is derived from the ruling social coalition that is formulated and organized by the political regime. This alliance permits the regime to realize the institutional changes needed for capitalist development process. This hypothesis stems from the observation that successful capitalist experiments in the third world occurred in countries that witnessed strong social polarization that reached an explosive stage. Authoritarian regimes in Asian countries and in Chile came to power following social conflict that was ended by force of arms. Most of these countries had leftist (Chile) or communist (Indonesia) movements that managed to assume power or came close to doing so. That is why social conflict reached its zenith, dividing society into two large camps. This problem was resolved militarily, and one party suffered a crushing defeat. The road was thus opened to implement capitalist development by force. The Asian dictatorships, however repressive, had a social constituency composed of a solid societal alliance between capitalist groups and sections of the middle class founded on fear of the communist or leftist alternative. This strengthened the efforts of regimes in applying radical institutional changes. A solid social alliance is the prerequisite for carrying out institutional reform that will have adverse effects on certain groups in society, a matter that will foment hostility against the regime by those who will lose positions or benefits. In this case, the regime will not be able to impose change unless it can rely on a societal alliance as it daily encroaches on the state's institutions in a bid to redefine them. Hence, countries that have succeeded in capitalist economic development have in the past had strong anticapitalist movements, either leftist or communist. Countries where socialism or communism had a certain measure of success are those where capitalism eventually succeeded. Those countries that failed, failed in both socialism and capitalism. That is to say, polarization is very important in the formation of a strong state.

Thus while this study benefits from the neo-Weberian concept of the strong state and uses it to understand the crisis of economic development and of public policies, it does not share the neo-Weberian disregard of the nature of the political regime and the class foundation of that regime. How can one study a state without understanding the nature of the organized ruling group managing that state? We hold that the state is the sum total of public institutions ruling a certain territory. The state is a structure, and it is transformed into an agent only by the management and leadership of an organized ruling coalition. The regime. This book, therefore, tries to correct the simplistic duality of state and society by a triangle of state, society, and political regime.

THE IMPORTANCE OF STATE FINANCE

While reading literature related to the state, I noted references that indicated that public finance was among the main gateways to studying the state. In the forefront is a 1918 article by Joseph Schumpter, the well-known economist, calling for establishment of a new discipline called fiscal sociology to study the interrelationships between society and state finance.[11] Schumpter noticed that state expenditures had a great impact on societal culture and structures. This article did not receive due attention, and Schumpter's name continued to be associated with his theory on the entrepreneur.

To study public finance from a political economy perspective, one should look to the main three traditions of political economy that have dealt with the question: Marxism, rational choice, and neo-historical institutionalism. In the following sections, we point to these traditions' most important contributions to the question of state finance. The objective is to show how they influenced the research and how it responds to their contribution.

The Marxist Approach

Although Marx did not develop an elaborate theory of the state, he had a distinct view of this institution. To him, the state is not a neutral arbiter between antagonistic classes prevailing in a society, but instead an instrument used by the dominant class to repress the dominated classes. In a capitalist mode of production, the state is the "executive committee of the bourgeoisie," as *The Communist Manifesto* suggests.[12] Under certain circumstances—that is, a weakness of the antagonistic classes—the state can elevate itself and dominate all classes in society, even the bourgeoisie. This was the case of the Bonapartist state proposed by Marx in his *Eighteenth Brumaire of Louis Bonaparte*.[13] It appears then that the main question that preoccupies the Marxist approach to the state has been the relationship between it and social classes. The main Marxist debate on the state dealt with the question of the relative autonomy of the capitalist state vis-à-vis the bourgeoisie.[14]

The concept of relative autonomy has been a step forward in the Marxist conception of the state. Without it, how could one account for the fact that the state in capitalist societies has imposed some regulations against the will of the bourgeoisie? The sole solution is Poulantzas's distinction between the short- and long-run interests of the bourgeoisie on the one hand, and the individual and collective interests of this class, on the other.[15] A good example involves wages. The short-run individual interest of a capitalist is to minimize, as far as possible, wages paid to his workers. But the long-run collective interest of the capitalist class as a whole is to accord the working classes some increase in real wages. This increase means a widening of the market for capitalist production, and it functions as a moderation mechanism for the working class, with social peace as the final outcome, in the interest of the dominant class. The state is the institution that can perceive and defend this collective interest of the bourgeoisie. Left to their own will, capitalists may destroy the system in which they are the dominant class. This conception of the state as the defender of the collective interests of the bourgeoisie and as the savior of the capitalists from their enemies, and even from themselves, later inspired James O'Connor, who produced the elaborate Marxist theory of state finance in his book *The Fiscal Crisis of the State*. His main research problem was the fiscal crisis of the state: Why does the state in modern times suffer from a chronic budget deficit? O'Connor answers this question with the following reasoning:

> Our first premise is that the capitalist State must try to fulfill two basic and often mutually contradictory functions—accumulation and legitimization. This means that the State must try to maintain or create the conditions in which profitable capital accumulation is possible. However, the State also must try to maintain or create the conditions for social harmony. A capitalist State that openly uses its coercive forces to help one class accumulate capital at the expense of other classes loses its legitimacy. But a State that ignores the necessity of assisting the process of capital accumulation risks drying up the source of its own power, the economy's surplus production capacity and the taxes drawn from this surplus.[16]

State expenditures thus have a twofold character corresponding to the capitalist state's two basic functions: social capital and social expenses. Social capital involves expenditures required for profitable private accumulation, such as infrastructure projects and state-financed industrial-development parks. Social expenses are projects and services required to maintain social harmony to fulfill the state's legitimization function, such as the welfare system.[17]

To this point, O'Connor's reasoning is correct: The capitalist state has two functions: accumulation and legitimization. I draw upon O'Connor's categorization of state expenditures in the discussion of the Egyptian regime's attempts to reorganize public expenditures in order to adapt to the contraction of public revenues in Chapter 2. However, the rest of his reasoning is based on incorrect assumptions. O'Connor thinks that state expenditures are characterized by the iron tendency to increase. First, the state should increasingly intervene in the economic sphere and raise expenditures on social capital (such as infrastructure and education) in order to make private capital profitable. Why? "The general reason," according to O'Connor, "is that the increase in the social character of production (specialization, division of labor, interdependency, the growth of new social forms of capital such as education, etc.) either prohibits or renders unprofitable the private accumulation of constant and variable capital."[18] In other words, he argues, contrary to conventional wisdom, that the growth of the state sector is indispensable for the expansion of private industry: The greater the growth of social capital provided by the state, the greater the growth of the monopolist capitalist sector; the greater the growth of the monopolist capitalist sector, the greater the state's expenditures on social expenses of production. According to O'Connor, capitalist production has become more interdependent, more dependent on science and technology, with labor functions more specialized and the division of labor more extensive. Consequently, capitalist production requires increasing numbers of technical and administrative workers. It also requires growing amounts of infrastructural transportation, communication, R & D, education, and other facilities.

Although the state has supported capitalists by assuming rising capital costs, profits continue to be appropriated privately. The socialization of costs and the private appropriation of profits create a fiscal crisis, or structural gap, between state expenditures and state revenues. The result, according to O'Connor, is a tendency for state expenditures to increase more rapidly than the means of financing them.[19] This formulation is very close to the Marxist contention that the basic contradiction in a capitalist society is between the social character of production and the private appropriation of the means of the production. In addition, the state should also increase its expenditure on social expenditures (the legitimization function) because "the growth of the monopoly sector is irrational in the sense that it is accompanied by unemployment, poverty, economic stagnation, and so on."[20] The fiscal crisis of the state then, according to O'Connor, is not something situational, but rather structural. In other words, the deficit of the state budget is due to the structural tendency of state expenditures to increase more rapidly than revenues. The only solution, according to him, is socialism; for there is no solution under capitalism.

O'Connor's theory has been defeated by the facts: The fiscal crisis of the state was lessened during the 1980s and 1990s. The Mastricht treaty has imposed a maximum fiscal deficit of 3 percent. Except some cases like Greece, European countries managed, more or less, to keep their deficits close to this limit. The empirical fallacy of O'Connor's predictions is a result of a deep epistemological problem in O'Connor's theory: the functional nature of his explanations. Because state expenditures are somehow functional or beneficial to capital, he concluded that the state increased its expenditures in order to maximize capitalists' profits. In other words, he considers the result of an action as its cause. So everything the state does should be in the interest of capital. Nicos Poulantzas's relative autonomy of the state does not solve the problem. His proposition that the state can act against the short-term interests of the bourgeoisie in order to save its long-term interests dooms the state to always serve capital. Indeed, the state knows capitalists' interests more than do the capitalists themselves. We find here the same functionalism: The function of something explains its existence, and the result of something is automatically transformed into its cause. Wage increases, for instance, according to functional explanations, are caused by the need of capital to expand its market. More wages mean more consumers for goods. So because wage increases are beneficial for capital, we should consider that they came into being because capital needed them.

This reasoning neglects the role of politics and class struggle. Wage increases, for instance, were imposed on capitalists via syndicalist resistance and by the process of democratization, which permitted the working classes to acquire more leverage on social and economic policy. The same applies to the rise of the interventionist and the welfare state since the 1930s. Moreover, ideas (such as Keynesianism) were central to the rise of the welfare state by providing the theoretical tools to formulate new economic policies. The main error of this kind of Marxist functional explanations, as elaborated by Anthony Giddens, is its supposition that social systems have needs, or functional exigencies. The best example is Marx's discussion of the reserve army in a capitalist economy. Capitalism has its own needs, which the system functions to fulfill. Since capitalism needs a reserve army, one comes into being. This argument, according to Giddens, does not explain anything about why a reserve army of unemployed workers exists: "not even the most deeply sedimented institutional features of societies come about, persist, or disappear because those societies need them to do so. They come about, historically, as a result of concrete conditions that have in every case to be analyzed."[21]

The second epistemological mistake in O'Connor's theory is its structuralism. The theory accords no role to agents, to institutions, or to ideas. Actors are naked social classes acting according to their structural positions and promoting their "objective" interests. O'Connor did not write about objective interests in this book, but it is the underlying concept of his reasoning. When he writes about interests, he never bothers to search for interests as defined by the actors themselves—by parties, by trade unions, or by business associations. He takes classes as actors, when classes are not actors. They can become actors via institutions that structure their interests. In this case, institutions of representation do not only reflect the interest of the classes they represent, but they often structure and shape their very interests.

The limitation of O'Connor's structuralism can be shown in his analysis of legitimacy. He thinks that state legitimacy is preserved by social expenditures that promote the well-being of the working classes. The state, therefore, cannot lessen its social expenditures without creating a legitimacy crisis that can threaten the whole social order. In reality, states did lessen their social expenditures in the 1980s and 1990s without creating a threatening legitimacy crisis. The process of liberalization was not undertaken without harsh resistance from social groups losing some gains accorded to them by the welfare state. But O'Connor underestimated the capacity of states to decrease social expenditures because he undervalued the role of institutions and ideas. He thinks in terms of objective material interests. Hence, the objective interest of the working class should be to increase its share in national wealth in the short term, and to destroy the capitalist state and create its own state in order to get control of the means of the production in the long term. The objective interest of the capitalist class should be to make profits in the short run and to preserve the social order in which it is the dominant class in the long run.

The problem with objective interest is its very objectivity: It is discovered by an outside observer. Actors do not define their interests as the outside observer does. Actors define their interests within a socioeconomic and political context, by institutions of representation and within the framework of the dominant paradigm. When the economic boom was at its peak in the 1960s and when the dominant paradigm was that of the welfare state, the working class's short-term interest was perceived by many of its organizations to be an increase in wages and the nationalization of big enterprises. When stagflation has become the norm and the dominant paradigm has shifted to so-called neoliberalism, the short-term interest of the working class is defined by many working-class organizations as the defense of real wages and more jobs. "More jobs" could mean the success of the state in creating favorable conditions for the functioning of capitalism. There have been states, such as the Asian tigers, enjoying some legitimacy thanks to their success in stimulating capitalist development, despite the fact that they were highly repressive, and despite the fact that capitalist development was achieved by the harsh exploitation of the working classes. In other words, state legitimacy is not static, but acquires new definitions and new meanings by institutions and by theoretical paradigms. Sometimes the legitimacy of the state is partly fulfilled not through social expenditures, but through the accumulation process itself, that is, by successfully stimulating capitalist development.

O'Connor's theory is deterministic. In his introduction to a new edition of *The Fiscal Crisis of the State*, he points out that he could not expect the lessening of the fiscal crisis because he did not take into account the question of globalization and imperialism, which gave the state in advanced countries the capacity to control its fiscal deficit.[22] We believe the problem lies at the heart of O'Connor methodology. Ian Gough is correct when he calls these kinds of models "theories of the State premised on 'break down' theories of the economy."[23] According to these theories, the growth of state expenditure represents part of the attempt to solve the crisis of profitability, brought about by the "law of the falling tendency of the rate of profit" under late capitalism—a law that has been subjected to harsh criticism following advances in Marxist political economy.[24] In brief, the expansion of state intervention in the economic field cannot be explained as a functional response to the profitability crisis of late capitalism. Otherwise, how can we account for the fact that capitalists think that the rapid growth of state spending has squeezed profits and has thus discouraged new investment? The sole explanation would be the concept of false consciousness—that capitalists are so stupid that they attack policies formulated to solve their crisis of profitability; an explanation that cannot be qualified as anything but vulgar functionalism. O'Connor's theory is a derivation of the law of the falling tendency of the rate of profit.

In dealing with the Marxist approach to the fiscal crisis of the state, we have emphasized O'Connor's theory because, as noted earlier, he formulated the most elaborate Marxist contribution to the subject and because his structuralist and functionalist reasoning is widely shared by many Marxists. However, this emphasis is not just to other Marxists who reject functionalism in dealing with this subject. Gough, for instance, criticizes O'Connor because he gives insufficient weight to the role of class struggle in shaping state expenditures.

The interaction of long-term socioeconomic trends, the political strategy of the capitalist state, and the ongoing class struggle rule out any simple, single-factor explanation of social policies. Above all, it is essential to distinguish their concrete historical origins from the ongoing function they play within that particular social formation. Social policies, originally the product of class struggle, will, in the absence of further struggle, be absorbed and adapted to benefit the interests of the dominant classes.[25]

Gough rejects the over-determination of the political by the economic in favor of according a sufficient weight to class struggle, that is, to the political level. The problem, however, is that he does not elaborate on this class struggle. His argument leaves us unsatisfied: If state expenditures are determined by class struggle, what determines class struggle? Why does class struggle increase in some periods and decrease in others? And most important, why does class struggle produce different state expenditure outcomes in different countries? These questions cannot be answered without integrating political institutions and ideas at the heart of the models of analysis, which most Marxists tend not to do.

Rational Choice

In "The Theory of Predatory Rule," Margaret Levi provided one of the most renowned conceptualizations of state finance from a rational choice perspective.[26] The history of state revenue production, according to Levi, is the history of the evolution of the state. How should one account for this state revenue production? Levi's conceptualization starts with rulers and uses rulers as the unit of analysis. By rulers she means "actors or sets of actors who perform as the chief executives of State institutions."[27] Contrary to the Marxist approach, Levi believes that the institution of the state is the wrong starting point for a theory of state policy in general and of revenue production policy in particular. Starting with rulers emphasizes the fact that actors make choices between alternatives; they are not simply the agents of a certain social structure. As we saw earlier, O'Connor's structuralism does not give any role to rulers: State revenues are determined by their functions in the structure, by the twofold functions of the state: accumulation and legitimization. By contrast, Levi's rational choice approach to state revenue is supposed to give a large margin of freedom to human action. We shall come back to this issue. Let us start now by giving a brief presentation of Levi's theory.

Rulers are predatory in that they try to extract as much revenue as they can from the population. They may use the funds to line their own pockets or to promote their personal power. They may use the funds to support social or personal ends. They may want to promote ideological ends. They may be altruistic. But whatever the rulers' ends, revenue is necessary to attain them. It is by means of the state and its revenues that rulers achieve their personal and social ends.[28]

Note that the state here is an instrument for rulers to achieve their ends. In fact, Levi shares the instrumentalist approach of orthodox Marxism, in which the state is an instrument of the dominant class. Yet Levi does not accord an independent role to the state, a role emphasized by the state-centered approach of Skocpol and others.[29]

What about rulers who do not maximize state revenues? Levi raises this objection: "What about those few pious kings of history, or the nineteenth-century liberals, or the twentieth-century monetarists, social reformers, and other rulers whose concern is revenue reduction?" She admits from the outset that "there are rulers who cannot be characterized as revenue maximizers," but she suspects that they constitute the exception and that they refrain from extracting the greatest amount of revenue possible from the population not because they are refraining from maximizing behavior, but because of the constraints to which they are subject. The question now is, why should revenue-maximizer rulers maximize their revenues? To that Levi replies: "My hypothesis follows from two paired assumptions. The first is that all the actors who compose the polity, including the policy makers, are rational and self-interested. The second is that actors who compose the state have interests of their own."[30] The assumption of self-interested rulers can explain why despots maximize their revenues—to build more palaces, or to have more wives, or to have more power—because there is no distinction between state revenues and ruler revenues. But what about rulers of democratic states who are agents for certain social groups?[31] What is the interest, for instance, of rulers who increased the revenues available to their states in order to finance their welfare programs? If we limit ourselves to interest as the explanatory variable, the answer is that their interest is to maximize the interests of social groups that form their electoral constituencies. Here Levi's methodology ceases to be useful because the interests that she highlights are individual, not collective, interests.

Levi tries to show that the greed of rulers to extract revenues is not unlimited. The main argument of her theory is that rulers maximize revenue to the state, but not as they please. Their maximization drive is subject to the constraints of their relative bargaining power vis-à-vis agents and constituents, their transaction costs, and their discount rates. The relative bargaining power of rulers is determined by the extent to which others control resources on which rulers depend and the extent to which rulers control resources on which others depend. Rulers will have more bargaining power the more they monopolize coercive, economic, and political resources. Transaction costs are the positive costs of bargaining a policy and of implementing a policy once it has been bargained. The most important transaction costs are those of negotiating agreements, measuring revenue sources, monitoring compliance, using agents and other middlemen, punishing the noncompliant, and creating quasi-voluntary compliance. A policy is not viable if the transaction costs are too high. Rulers' discount rates—how much present value future returns have for them—are another major factor in the calculation of the costs and benefits of a policy choice. Rulers with high discount rates care little for the future. They are less concerned with promoting the conditions of economic growth and increased revenue over time than with extracting available revenue, even at the risk of discounting output. Rulers with low discount rates do have an interest in securing future revenues. Rulers' discount rates are always something of a function of personal psychology, of whether they have a short- or a long-time horizon. However, the principal determinant is security of office.[32]

We thus have to expect that the amount of revenue available to a ruler is a function of these three factors. We may say that rulers today can extract double the revenue they extracted at the beginning of this century (relative to GDP) because they have more bargaining power vis-à-vis constituents. But this explanation needs another explanation: What has given rulers more bargaining power? Here Levi's rational choice ends, and she has recourse to structural variables, which are:

1. Productive and economic structures: What is produced, how, and by whom delimits the revenue rulers can extract from producers. An affluent economic structure gives rulers more chance to extract revenues.

2. International context: International trade, overseas colonies, and other aspects of the international political economy are also important in determining rulers' available sources of revenue and their relative bargaining power. The existence of rival powers to whom constituents can flee or with whom they can bargain delimits rulers' extraction power.

3. Form of government: Whether the government is a monarchy, military dictatorship, oligarchy, or representative democracy has consequences for the decisions and actions of rulers or heads of state. Forms of government affect the bargaining strategies and resources available to citizens; they affect also the ability of rulers to use the public coffers as their own. Each major change in government has predictable consequences for transaction costs, discount rates, and relative bargaining power.[33]

According to Levi, these structural variables are drawn from the Marxist tradition. However, Marxist logic is turned on its head by Levi. Marxists start with a social formation in order to see the prevailing modes of production and class structure, and then they proceed to study the state. For them, the state cannot be understood except by locating it in its social context. The logic is the opposite for Levi. She starts from rulers, with the assumption that they want to extract the maximum revenues they can, and then proceeds to analyze their constraints, which are determined by the structural factors mentioned above. The question here is, what does this rational choice reasoning and assumptions—about the self-interested rulers—add to the analysis if we will always end up with the structural variables that explain the difference in the extraction capacities of rulers?

The limitation of Levi's approach lies in her neglect of the relationship between rulers' revenues and rulers' expenditures: Rulers usually extract revenues in order to finance their expenditures. Without seeing the expenditure side of the budget, we cannot account for the evolution of state revenues. For example, in dealing with the income tax in eighteenth-century Britain, she maintains that "the Napoleonic Wars provided the justification for the tax."[34] For her, war was simply a justification to impose new taxes. We believe, on the contrary, that ends are important in explaining the evolution of revenues. If Cheops extracted enormous resources from Egyptian peasants, this was for the purpose of building his huge pyramid. Without taking this pyramid into account, one fails to understand why Cheops had to maximize his revenues. By the same token, if Churchill increased his revenue from the British people in the late 1930s and early 1940s, it was to finance the war against Hitler. But Levi is unable to see the other side of the equation, that is, state expenditures, because she starts with the idea of self-interested and predatory rulers, a concept that should explain the policies of all rulers. Unsurprisingly, Levi arrives at the conclusion that her theory applies to all societies, from ancient China to modern Western societies. The rational choice perspective claims to give actors (in this case, rulers) more margin of liberty than actors in structural Marxist models, who are the agents of a social structure, as in the case of O'Connor's analysis. Yet one cannot but conclude that if Levi's actors are not the prisoners of their structures, they are the prisoners of their self-interest.

Levi tries to distinguish herself from public choice theorists like James Buchanan who assume that taxation is theft.[35] But the political implications of Levi's model are equally conservative. If Levi starts from self-interested predatory rulers to explain the amount of resources they extract from society, states become parasitic entities trying to rob the people. True, that is often the case. But one cannot put a ruler who extracts revenues to build an arsenal for external aggression in the same category as a ruler who extracts resources to pay for health care programs. By the same token, one cannot put a ruler who extracts revenues from poor, starving peasants in the same category as a ruler who extracts revenues from big business. All these issues are ignored in Levi's analysis because she limits herself to the study of the revenue column of state budget without linking it to the expenditures column. One cannot but assert the conservative political agenda of this kind of rational choice reasoning. Levi's book was published in 1988, during the paroxysm of state retreat from the economy after more than a decade of the advance of neoliberal policies all over the world. Surprisingly, she chose this time to research the extension of the state under revenue maximizer rulers.

In conclusion, we think that Levi's model for understanding the historical evolution of state finance cannot tell us why the state extracts more resources today than it did a century ago and less than three decades ago. But her focus on the constraints facing predatory rulers can help us understand why rulers who want to maximize their revenues sometimes fail to do so. We draw upon the idea of the constraints on revenue maximization in Chapter 5 when we analyze the efforts of the regime to increase its revenues from the population and the resistance encountered in that effort.

Neo-Historical Institutionalism

In dealing with the formulation of economic policy, the starting point of neo-institutionalists is not Levi's self-interested rational rulers or O'Connor's state functions, but institutions. The neo-institutionalists define institutions as "the formal or informal procedures, routines, norms and conventions embedded in the organizational structure of the polity or political economy."[36] Thus, the definition includes such features of the institutional context as the rules of constitutional order, the rules of electoral competition, the structure of the party system, the relations among various branches of government, the standard operating procedures of bureaucracy, and the structure and organization of economic actors like trade unions.[37] Their starting point—institutions—does not share the visibility or the simplicity of Levi's rulers. We can see rulers, but not institutions. Institutions—particularly informal ones—have to be discovered. Yet institutional analysis, which emphasizes how political struggles are mediated by the institutional setting in which they take place, has many advantages over Levi's rational choice.

As indicated earlier, Levi's model is built on the assumption that rulers are rational and self-interested actors who want to maximize their revenues. Institutionalism, on the other hand, takes the formation of goals and preferences more seriously; it is not considered to be exogenous. While rational choice deals with preferences at the level of assumptions, historical institutionalists take the question of how individuals and groups define their self-interest as something to be studied and explained.[38] According to Steinmo, rational choice perspective deduces the preferences of actors from a meta-historical assumption of self-interest. Institutionalists think that "unless something is known about the context, broad assumptions about 'self-interested behavior' are empty," as Steinmo maintains. For "not only the strategies, but also the goals actors pursue are shaped by the institutional context."[39]

This is, in brief, the first advantage that institutionalism claims over rational choice: The goals of the rulers are discovered not only by deduction, but also by induction.

The second advantage of their methodology is the claim that, by focusing on institutions, institutionalists work at the level of mid-range theory. They do not produce grand theories that explain things by universal laws, applicable over time and across countries. The institutionalist perspective would not produce models like the Levi's, which pretends to explain all rulers' actions at all times. By focusing not on the structural-macro level but on the middle level, they can explain differences among countries. For instance, the welfare state swept most countries in the world. It was induced by many structural forces, one of which was the economic boom of the 1950s and 1960s. The structural forces were universal, but they took different forms and had different outcomes in different countries. Some welfare states were stronger than others. The institutionalist analysis can explain the differences between welfare states not by the structural forces, since these forces were applicable everywhere, but by the institutional settings in which these they took existed.

Steinmo's *Taxation and Democracy* is a good example of the study of taxation from a neo-institutionalist perspective.[40] Steinmo was puzzled to find the tax system of socialist-minded Sweden less progressive than that of the capitalist United States. The explanation, according to his book, is not to be found in established models of comparative political theory based on interest groups, value differences, or varying perceptions of the state's role in society. He does not believe that the interests of bureaucrats and politicians explain this puzzle. The explanation, he argues, lies in the different institutional arrangements by which fiscal decisions are made in the countries.

The institutionalists think that their middle-range focus is an answer to the structure-agency problem. Institutionalists try to transcend structure-agency dualism in their own way. According to Rothstein, by focusing on these intermediate institutional features of political life, institutionalism provides the theoretical "bridge between men who make history and the circumstances under which they are able to do so."[41] According to this perspective, institutions are the locus of human action and are created by human beings. By focusing on institutions not as a dependent variable determined by macro-socioeconomic structures, but as an independent variable that shapes policies, one can give a role to human action.

This focus on institutions has been criticized on two grounds. First Richard Musgrave, one of the most famous economists of public finance, thinks that institutions explain too little. Commenting on Steinmo's *Taxation and Democracy*, he objects to the book's contention that tax systems differ along with the institutions by which they are installed: "The common forces of rising revenue requirements, war finance, changing social trends, and opening economies, along with the economic limitations of rising taxation, sooner or later came to impose common patterns. Differences in institutional arrangements, it appears, did not keep overall developments and eventual outcomes from being rather similar."[42]

Jonas Pontusson provides the second objection to the focus on institutions in explaining variations between countries, claiming that it is due to the incorrect assumption of institutionalists that "Socioeconomic institutions or structures of advanced capitalist countries are essentially the same, but their institutional settings are different." There is in fact a great deal of variation among advanced capitalist economies. Raw material endowments vary; so do the relative sizes of the primary, secondary, and tertiary sectors; the degree of concentration and centralization of capital; the degree of export dependence; the structure of ownership (for example, the degree of public ownership), corporate organization, and management practices; and so on. According to Pontusson, institutionalists tend to explain the commonalities of advanced capitalist states by economic-structural variables, and explain their differences by political-institutional variables. The question for him is theoretical: Why should some causal variables operate only over time and others only across cases?[43]

This focus on institutions as the locus of interactions between variables raises another question: If institutions, in the institutionalist model, are the independent variable, how can we account for institutional change? Institutionalism is capable of explaining stability—how institutional traditions impose their will on the actors—but it is not suited to accounting for change. The focus on institutions therefore gives a bias in the analysis to stability over change.

The critiques of institutionalism lessen the claims of the centrality of institution in political economy analysis. Yet the current study, in its analysis of Egyptian public finance, is inspired by the focus neo-institutionalists give to the middle level—to the level of state institutions. The study of state institutions is not new; Marxists, for instance, have focused on the state institution.

Yet, their focus on the institution of the state—often described as bourgeois state, rather than on state institutions in the plural—has produced much abstract speculation on state actions. In addition, we value the interest neo-institutionalism gives to the study of informal institutions and informal rules. This interest in the informal level of politics is of much benefit in many third world countries when the rule of law is weak and where the informal sometimes has advantage over the formal.

THE ABSENT VARIABLE: RENTIER REVENUES

Levi claims that her model is applicable over time and across countries, that rulers' capacity to extract resources is determined by their bargaining power, their discount rate, and the transaction costs of their policies. Yet there are rulers who can afford not to pay attention to these constraints. They do so for the simple reason that most of their resources come from outside. Following Beblawi and Luciani, we call this kind of state a rentier state.[44] A rentier state is a state whose revenue derives predominantly from oil or other foreign sources, and whose expenditure is a substantial share of GDP. The definition applies to many Middle Eastern and North African states, and also to some African and Latin American states. These states are not confronted by Levi's constraints or O'Connor's dilemma of incurable fiscal deficits.

In such oil-rentier countries, the state becomes the main intermediary between the oil sector and the rest of the economy.[45] It consequently has a high leverage on society. The government not only distributes benefits and favors to its population, but is also the major employer in the economy.[46] The rentier state concept assumes that the specific characteristics of oil production and trade will have an impact on the configuration of state formation and on its relationship to the society in which it is embedded. Here, the rentier state's main function is to guarantee and distribute rents, in contrast to other states whose income is based on tapping the domestic economy. In the latter case, the state can grow and perform its functions only to the extent that the domestic economy provides the income needed to do so.[47]

The rentier state concept proposes an explanation of the lack of democracy in rentier societies. According to Luciani:

Although the immediate link between taxation and representative democracy may well not exist, as countless examples demonstrate, it is a fact that whenever the State essentially relies on taxation the question of democracy becomes an unavoidable issue, and a strong current in favor of democracy inevitably arises. This is the result of the fact that people will naturally be induced to coalesce according to their economic interest, and those groups that find no way to influence the decision-making process in their favor claim appropriate institutional change.[48]

If rentier revenues induce authoritarianism, the meltdown of this kind of revenue and the turn to taxation should enhance a democratization process. This proposition needs further discussion because one has the impression that the drying up of rentier resources and the increasing reliance on taxes in Egypt has not produced the expected outcome proposed by the rentier state theory. We resume discussion of the rentier state thesis in Chapter 5, which deals with the question of the political economy of democratization in Egypt. It is sufficient to note here that the rentier state theory has heavily influenced this book and has provided a very interesting hypothesis.

EGYPT: A MODEL OF A RENTIER STATE

Certain Egyptian economists have not refrained from interacting with the rent question. They studied the phenomenon of rentier revenues or external revenues. The Egyptian economy since the 1970s had experienced the flow of considerable external or rentier resources such as foreign aid and workers' remittances from abroad. The prominent economist Galal Amin viewed rentier revenues as the fundamental motor of the Egyptian economy since the mid-1970s.[49] The Egyptian economy grows due to rentier revenues such as petroleum, Suez Canal income, and workers' remittances from abroad. Declining growth rates are caused by a drop in such resources. The rentier issue continues to draw the attention of economists who study the Egyptian economy. This can be seen in a recent French doctoral dissertation by Hélène Cottonet on the negative impact of rentier resources on Egyptian industry and by her compatriot Marie-France Vernier on applying "the Dutch disease" theory to the case of Egypt.[50]

Unlike studies by economists, our study deals with the phenomenon of rentier resources from a political economy perspective. We study the effect of decreasing rentier revenues not on the Egyptian economy, but on the state and on politics. We also analyze the strategies of the political regime and the tactics applied by state institutions to boost revenues and to accommodate to declining rates. To reiterate, this study focuses on the state's resources, not on those of society. Therefore, it distinguishes between rentier revenues received by the state and those that go to society. Some of the rentier revenues mentioned by Egyptian economists are remittances transferred by Egyptian workers abroad. These were considered rentier because they were not derived from a productive activity inside the country and they do not contribute to establishing any productive activity. Yet, they do not enter the state treasury and thus are outside the framework of the revenues of the rentier state. The rentier revenues acquired by the Egyptian state are composed of revenues derived from petroleum, the Suez Canal, and foreign aid. In other words, we are addressing public non-tax revenues, not deducted from society but rather descending as a gift from heaven.

That these resources are a gift from heaven does not exclude the fact that certain people play a role so that they produce revenues. Petroleum requires extraction and transformation into the form received by the consumer. The Suez Canal necessitates thousands of workers to dig and to manage the circulation of transport. Even foreign aid that flows into Egypt is partly the result of efforts; whether direct, such as the political regime's involvement in regional politics and activity to convince foreign countries of Egypt's strategic importance, or indirect, such as activities carried out by generations of Egyptian intellectuals and artists who largely influenced the Arab world, thus allowing their country to gain cultural importance in the region. This in turn gives the political regime that is firmly in control in Cairo grounds for requesting a significant share of foreign aid from international powers. Yet, though the sources mentioned above require work in order to bear fruit, they are characterized by the limited number of personnel in comparison with the volume of revenue. Moreover, these revenues are garnered quite easily, unlike taxes, which require a modern mechanism of collection, coercion, and persuasion so that citizens pay up. Later, we discuss how the decline in rentier revenues and the growing reliance of the Egyptian state on taxation will lead to the reformulation of the state's relationship with society. This study is an attempt to monitor and analyze the decline of the rentier state in Egypt, a process that continues, which we believe to be one of the major structural variables that will formulate the political transformation taking place in Egypt today and that will become more apparent in the coming years.

DEFINING THE CONCEPT OF POLITICAL POWER: THE STATE OR POLITICAL REGIME

There is discord in the social and political sciences on the best concept for analyzing political power. Who rules society? Is it the state, the government, or the rulers? This is not a terminological disagreement but one that reflects a difference in approaching political power and its relationship with its society. The structural school speaks about the state and gives the rulers no mentionable importance, for the whims and orientations of rulers are assumed to have no meaningful importance in deciding matters. For example, according to Nicos Poulantzas's radical structural formulation, the function of the state is basically to achieve stability in society to the benefit of the owning capitalist class.[51] Hence, the state formulates policies to serve the long-term interests of this class. The relationship between capitalists and the state is an objective one. Capitalists do not need to forge direct relations with civil servants, and they do not need to place their sons at the top of the executive authority to ensure the elaboration of beneficial policies by this authority. The state is obliged to protect capitalist interests because its basic task is to ensure the stability of a social structure in which the capitalist class is dominant.

By contrast, rational choice proponents argue that the political regime embodies the ruler or rulers who are driven by their own interests, and who should be the focus of the analyst. To them, the ruler is a rational person who tries to maximize his self-interest, and he is thought to be the real starting point for studying the political regime. Therefore, while the structural school focuses on the objective impersonal nature of the regime, the rational choice school focuses on its personal and individualistic nature.

While refuting any reification of the state, in this book the state is the sum total of public institutions that rule over a specific territory, with their organizational structures, laws and regulations, and formal and informal rules. It is an entity with continuity that surpasses individuals and political regimes. The use of the term *state* rather than *government* or *ruler* is not just a difference of vocabulary. This concept, as Stephen Krasner maintains, makes us see a different political universe, ask different questions, investigate different empirical phenomena, and offer different kinds of answers.[52] The use of the concept of the state, according to Colin Hay, Michael Lister, and David Marsh provides an institutional contextualization of political actors, that is, it offers a context within which political actors are embedded and with respect to which they must be situated analytically.[53] The concept should correct the behavioralist inclination to emphasize an actor's preferences. It attracts attention to the opportunities and constraints offered to the regime or to the ruling group by the institutional framework in which it is embedded. The concept also provides a historical contextualization; it corrects the bias of political science with its analytical focus on the present.[54] In other words, it invites us to integrate the influence of history that is registered in the institutional configuration of the state into our analysis of the present.

The specificity of this study lies in the fact that while it exploits the concept of the state, it also makes use of the concept of the political regime or the ruling group. The regime is the organization of individuals who lead the state. The concept of the state is wider than the concept of the political regime. The regime means the president of the republic, the top security officials, the council of ministers, and the high public officials who lead and direct diverse state institutions and organs—individuals, human beings with flesh and blood. Therefore, we can speak of the regime as an actor who thinks, plans, and executes. The state, on the other hand, is not an actor and is not a unified entity. The state is the sum total of public institutions that provides a framework for the regime and other political actors.

Using the two concepts simultaneously is of great analytical utility. The concept of the state alone will probably lead to speaking of a fictitious entity whose presence and continuity are outside history. This is quite apparent in certain analyses of the Egyptian state that give it an eternal nature (such as centralization) going back to the era of Mohamed Ali, even sometimes to Merner, head of the first unified state that ruled over Egypt around 3200 B.C. In addition, using the term *regime* alone could lead to ignoring a reality; any ruling group that gains power finds public institutions that have traditions, laws, and norms awaiting it. This heritage interacts with the new political regime. It may allow for the achievement of some objectives and block others. Hence, one of the most important tasks to be undertaken by any new political regime is to bring about changes in the state that will allow it to succeed in responding to the regime's projects. This distinction between the state and the political regime is a political analytical distinction that is not identical to the legal concept of the state and the political authority. The same distinction does not rule out a gray space between the regime and the state because the borders between both are in a permanent movement.

EGYPT: AN AUTHORITARIAN REGIME AND A RENTIER STATE

It is useful to present the conceptualization we have adopted about the Egyptian political regime during the Mubarak era. The major feature that distinguishes this regime, and that is relevant to our study, is that it is authoritarian.

We concur with the definition of democracy expounded by Evelyne Huber and Dietrich Rueschemeyer that democracy contains three elements: (1) regular and fair elections by which the people choose their representatives; (2) state machinery that is subjected to control by elected representatives; and (3) freedom of expression and association.[55] By applying this definition to Egypt, it becomes evident that this regime is authoritarian. Although there are periodic elections, they are largely tainted by fraud or interference of state organs in support of candidates at the expense of their competitors. Freedom of expression has been extended during the last years of Mubarak's rule with the creation of new private television, the spread of satellite channels, the creation of many private newspapers, and the Internet revolution. Yet the limits to freedom of expression are manifested in the imprisonment of bloggers and the harassment of writers who tackle the two big taboos: religion (especially Islamic religion) and the army. Freedom of association is practically nonexistent. The pluralism of trade unions and syndicates is not allowed, and the creation of voluntary associations and political parties is subjected to veto by security organizations. Moreover, the state organs are not subjected to the elected representatives but rather to the president, who enjoys almost absolute power. In sum, as we see later in the study, the Egyptian authoritarian regime is based on violent instruments on the one hand and soft mechanisms on the other in its monopoly of power.

This authoritarian political system is the natural extension of the regime established by the Free Officers since 1952. President Nasser chose Sadat, and Sadat chose Mubarak. In both cases, the chosen successor continued to rule. In both cases, the successor did not take power by a coup d'état. The quiet and peaceful transition of power indicates that the regime did not change fundamentally, although it did experience certain alterations. Sadat regressed on many of Nasser's policies, and Mubarak curbed Sadatism and Sadatists after assuming power, but such changes do occur in all authoritarian regimes when power is transferred from one ruler to another. Differences between the policies of successive rulers at the head of authoritarian regimes are the result of several factors: the different nature and orientations of each president; the metamorphosis of the group in power; changes in the internal and external environment. Despite alterations of the regime's economic and foreign policies from Nasser to Sadat and from Sadat to Mubarak, certain immovable features of the Egyptian regime remain, particularly the authoritarian nature. This nature abated somewhat when a new president took over, but then it rapidly became prominent.

The other important feature that resisted change during the rule of the three presidents was the clientelist state founded by Nasser and continued under Sadat and Mubarak. A clientelist state controls most resources, which it uses to dispense grants to certain active sectors of the population. Thus it succeeds in containing and domesticating these groups. Grants range from subsidizing commodities or health care up to direct appointment in state organs, the latter being considered "the mother of all grants" because it allows the political regime to dominate individuals. The clientelist state in Egypt is the other side of the coin of the rentier state. What the state obtains from rentier revenues permits the caretaker state to distribute grants and thereby achieve political domination. This explains the Egyptian political regime's main characteristic of the fervent increase of rentier revenues, especially from foreign aid. This particularity prevailed under Nasser, Sadat, and Mubarak. During Nasser's years, Egypt ranked first in the world in terms of Soviet aid, while under Sadat and Mubarak it ranked second in terms of American aid.

Certain researchers in Egyptian policy believe that Nasser established an unwritten contract between the state and society stipulating the state's commitment to extend services to the population in return for acceptance of the political regime and abandonment of political rights and participation in politics.[56] That is, Nasser's regime bartered social rights in exchange for political rights. This explains why the regime that took power in a coup d'état on 23 July 1952 resorted to excessive force in quelling any action by the labor movement, executing two labor leaders, while at the same time granting workers many social rights. Nasser went beyond that in allowing the state itself to bestow such rights. If work was a right, the state had to provide it. If health care was a right, it was up to the state to supply it. This was conducive to an unprecedented growth in the state apparatus and the growing influence of bureaucracy. The caretaker state was the instrument Nasser utilized to entrench his political regime. Without it, the regime would have turned into a mere repressive and authoritarian system founded on terror and violence.

The clientelist state under Nasser proved capable of achieving political stability. But its problem was the need to feed itself continuously with financial resources in order to maintain its political grip. After the initial push achieved by the Nasserist political regime, relying on funds sequestrated from landowners and capitalists, including foreign elements, the regime had to find other resources—resources that the regime failed to generate from the state itself. This became apparent by the end of the first five-year plan in 1965, which failed to generate resources to launch another plan. Hence the tendency to mobilize external resources and demand foreign aid became inherent to the political system established by Nasser and repeated by Sadat and Mubarak. Therefore, it was no surprise that the first clash between Nasser and the developed countries revolved around financing the construction of the Aswan High Dam when the World Bank declined to contribute.

With an economic recession starting in 1966 and Israel's defeat of the army in Sinai in 1967, Nasser's need for funds to pump new investments into the ailing economy and to rebuild the damaged armed forces became a matter of life and death. He successfully reconciled with conservative petroleum regimes. He rebuilt the armed forces in a few years with the help of the Soviet Union, enabling his successor to launch a partially successful war against Israel in 1973. But by the end of the war, Sadat found himself at a critical impasse. Petroleum countries did not wish to extend the same support to the Egyptian regime. The Soviet Union, the staunch supporter of the Egyptian regime, had already entered a recession and had begun to follow a rapprochement and détente policy with the United States, eventually losing both the capability and the will to provide the same level of support to third world countries such as Egypt.

The great reversal undertaken by Sadat from East to West, from alliance with the Soviet Union to alliance with the United States, partly represents an attempt to escape from the fiscal crisis that threatened the stability of the regime. Sadat did not tire of explaining the momentous transformations he had carried out in the regime's orientations, saying that by the end of the October 1973 War the balance in the Egyptian public treasury was zero. Such a statement did not draw much attention in Egypt because it was considered to be justification for Sadat's political choices and his strong admiration of the West. Nonetheless, attributing political and social changes undertaken by the Egyptian regime in the 1970s to Sadat's personality alone is an oversimplification. The dire need for resources placed the regime before two equally difficult choices: closer alliance with the Soviet Union at the external level and more socialist policy internally, or movement westward (especially toward the United States) at the external level and toward private capitalist development at the internal level. Facing such choices, the ruling group was divided. The first was led by Ali Sabri, the second by Sadat. The second direction won out, although it was the choice of the minority that controlled the presidency (constitutional legitimacy). The intelligence of its proponents—who included two shrewd politicians, Anwar Sadat and Hassanein Heikal, the prominent journalist and Nasser's top adviser—also played a role. This notwithstanding, the conflict between the two orientations in the Egyptian political regime in the 1970s should not conceal the fact that they are both wings of the same authority, with different answers to the same question.

Sadat and his group succeeded in mobilizing external resources, which enabled him to achieve stability for ten years. What Nasserists and Sadatists avoid saying is that the Egyptian state under Sadat, whose slogan was economic opening, had reached levels of inflation unprecedented under Nasser, whose slogan was socialism. (Our evidence is the rate of government employment to general employment in the economy and the rate of public expenditures to GDP, which is discussed in Chapter 1.) This growth relied on the petroleum and Suez Canal sectors in addition to foreign aid. The political regime opened the door to private capital and sometimes tried to cut down social expenditures such as subsidies (January 1977). Yet it is undeniable that Sadat took over an inflated state from Nasser and handed it to Mubarak with even more inflation, and the latter had no alternative but to let inflation continue to increase, as if an invisible but overwhelming power was driving the state to inflate even if the political regime was convinced of the need to curtail. This is one of the main characteristics of the Egyptian political regime since the late 1970s. It said one thing and acted a different way. When the state announced a relative withdrawal from the economy, bureaucracy continued its growth. What is uncontroversial is the impact on the regime's capability of political control. Undoubtedly, the growth of the state during the regimes of Nasser, Sadat, and Mubarak was a factor in the stability of the ruling regimes.

For other reasons discussed later in this book, the state's revenues quickly declined starting in the mid-1980s, and its ability to grow was limited, if not almost nonexistent. In time, the regime discovered that the drop in revenue was not accidental, but instead endemic. Thus the Egyptian regime entered its most difficult crisis since 1967. It was unable to produce jobs for the unemployed as well as stimulate economic development based on a private capitalism that could absorb job seekers. Despite this, it managed to retain power. The stability was not a coincidence. The regional situation was propitious (in particular, Saddam Hussein's invasion of Kuwait). However, the regime's ability to survive the sharp fall in revenue was the result of strategies it had implemented, sometimes with success and other times with failure. Today the crisis is deepening, and the ability of these strategies to withstand it has diminished.

As the rentier state wanes and the welfare state erodes, the Egyptian political regime is losing one of its most important instruments of control. Undoubtedly, Egypt is entering a new phase in its economic and political history. This study attempts to monitor and analyze this transitional period.

CREDIBILITY OF THE STATISTICS

Before concluding this introduction, we should point to the degree of credibility of the statistics we have studied, which differs among subject areas. In this part we focus on the credibility of the state's financial statistics, given the sensitivity and difficulty of obtaining them. Because those figures are the backbone of this study, our results will not be trusted unless statements are accurately and credibly analyzed.

Egyptian statistics on state finance can be found in two basic documents: the general budget of the state and the balance sheet of the general budget. The general budget is prepared at the beginning of the fiscal year and comprises forecasts of public revenues as well as allocations of public expenditures. During the fiscal year, revenues may fall below the expected level or rise above it. The same applies to expenditures, which often go beyond the planned figures. That is why the balance sheet, which is calculated after the end of the fiscal year and contains the real revenues and expenditures, is considered the most accurate source on the state's public finance. We basically rely on these statistics.

Public finance statistics are also available in bulletins published by the World Bank and International Monetary Fund, especially its *Government Finance Statistics Year Book*. These statistics are an adaptation of the aforementioned Egyptian sources; these international institutions have no private sources of information. Therefore, we prefer to resort to the balance sheet statistics, especially the balance sheet is very detailed and its contents are not always available in international bulletins. We refer to international institutions' statistics in some cases when making comparisons with other countries. Our sources also include statistics by the Ministry of Planning that are available in the annual and five-year plans for economic and social development, as well as reports such as "The Regional Dimension of the Plan."

To what extent is it possible to have confidence in the Egyptian state's finance statistics? There is a high level of corruption in Egypt. In 2008, Transparency International ranked Egypt very low, giving it a score of 2.8 out of 10 in the corruption index (a state is considered corrupt if it receives a score lower than 5). Egypt ranked 115 out of 180 countries for that same year.[57] Corruption affects statistics related to public finance because the figures do not include all the financial transactions that involve state revenues and expenditures. When a public official takes a bribe in return for exempting a citizen from paying his dues to the state, the official is decreasing the revenues that should flow into the public treasury. On the other hand, if official statistics indicate that the state has collected one billion pounds in taxes, for example, there is no doubt that the state has obtained this amount. Of course, the state would have acquired more if its officials had not gone astray, but that does not change the amount it did obtain.

The same applies to public expenditures. If the balance sheet of the public budget register an expenditure of 100 million pounds, for example, to build a hospital, there is no doubt that the state spent this amount. Perhaps some of it percolated down to officials in the form of bonuses and allowances for attending presumed meetings, or maybe an official took a bribe to authorize construction work by a particular contracting company. This official may also have been bribed to ignore the fact that the hospital did not comply with the agreed-upon technical specifications or that part of the investment allocated for the hospital was wasted on furnishing a grand office for the hospital's director. But it remains true that the state spent 100 million pounds to build the hospital. Although this study does not underestimate the importance of the corruption phenomenon in the Egyptian state's finance, it does not systematically address this phenomenon; our approach to the question of state finance aims, as mentioned before, is to study the evolution of revenues and expenditures as well as the strategies of the political regime in dealing with the decline in its revenues.

The main problem facing students of Egyptian public finance statistics cannot be attributed to corruption as much as to the violation of the principle of comprehensiveness of the state's public budget, a principle that is considered sacrosanct by experts in public finance. Presumably a public budget is a statement of account of all the state's revenues and expenditures. It should therefore comprise all revenues and expenditures in order to give a clear picture of the balance between incoming revenue and outgoing expenditure. When the state is more inclined toward extra-budgetary revenue and spending, its financial integrity is in danger because it will be difficult to get a clear and precise picture of the balance between revenues and expenditures. Such is the situation in Egypt today. The public budget does not include numerous revenues from areas such as the public sector and economic institutions. Still worse, the last two decades have witnessed unrestricted expansion in the state's creation of special funds that are outside the scope of the general budget.[58] The Egyptian political regime has not explained why it did not include these revenues and expenditures in the budget. Probably the regime wanted to keep the actual figures of public expenditures far from the eyes of the international financial institutions that had exerted pressure on the regime to curb spending. Probably it is also a result of the state's granting its institutions a margin of independence and flexibility in mobilizing and managing some of these revenues, making these funds subject to lesser restrictions than the normal revenues of the public budget. It is also likely that the regime wanted to keep certain revenues and expenditures out of sight. The special funds are subject to accounting and security supervision by the Central Accounting Authority, but they are not subject to supervision by the People's Assembly or public opinion, as is the regular budget.

The second major problem hindering students of Egyptian public finance is the absence of transparency. Although the Ministry of Finance publishes an annual finance statement and a statistical statement on the budget, these contain only general and sketchy figures of revenues and expenditures. Moreover, the figures concern the public budget, which as previously mentioned reflect estimates and planning figures for public revenues and expenditures, not actual figures. The Ministry of Finance never publishes the balance sheet, which continues to be held as confidential. Researchers are permitted to enter the library of the Ministry of Finance and can look at any accounts except the balance sheet, which is kept in one of the library's cabinets and can be viewed by only someone who obtains permission from the first undersecretary of state.

According to the constitution, the Ministry of Finance must annually submit the balance sheet to the Peoples Assembly. Article 118 of the constitution stipulates that "The final account of the State budget shall be submitted to the Peoples Assembly within a period not exceeding one year from the date of the expiration of the fiscal year. It shall be voted upon title by title and issued by law."[59] Through this loophole, some figures from the balance sheet filter through to circles wider than that of high finance officials. Thus, while the Ministry of Finance fails to keep the balance sheet in total secrecy, it has succeeded in making it very difficult to obtain. Furthermore, the balance sheet is a technically complicated document that can be comprehended by experts only, so obtaining in most cases does not mean dissemination of knowledge of its contents.

Financial officials claim that maintaining secrecy of the balance sheet is necessary for reasons of national security, but do not explain why other countries are able to protect their national security without suppressing public finance data. It also does not explain why these data are available to international financial institutions and not to Egyptian researchers. Although some people believe that the lack of transparency regarding these statistics is aimed at covering up corruption, that is not the case. Corruption by definition is the flow of finances outside the law and thus is not recorded in any official document. Concealing the balance sheet actually aims at hiding the real distribution of revenue in the Egyptian state. According to Rudolf Goldshied, "the budget is the skeleton of the State stripped of all misleading ideologies."[60] In other words, political regimes say that they do many things, but the actions of the state are facts that are registered and monitored in its account books. Some years after the completion of the fieldwork for this study, with the arrival of a new Minister of Finance, Youssef Boutros Ghali, in 2006, the government relaxed its control over the secrecy of public finance figures. Students of Egyptian public finance today are lucky enough to find some figures from the balance sheet on the official website of the Ministry of Finance.

ORGANIZATION OF THE BOOK

This book has five chapters. Chapter 1 presents the main parameters of the semi-rentier Egyptian state. It shows how the Egyptian budget, like those of rentier states, is mainly driven by the fluctuation of revenues. When they rise, expenditures follow, and vice versa. In a non-rentier state, on the contrary, expenditures often act as the driving force of the budget: when the regime needs more resources, it tends to increase the amount of tax revenues.

Chapter 2 looks at the way the regime adapted to the decline of public revenues by raising the share for some state institutions at the expense of others and of some social expenditures.

Chapter 3 deals with the impact of the financial crisis on the relationship between central and local government. It explains how the fiscal crisis led to the accelerated tendency toward centralization of the state accompanied by an inclination to fragmentation into isolated islands. With the contraction of public revenues, the regime tended to concentrate its resources on the central level while permitting or even inciting local units to mobilize their own resources by semi-official means.

Chapter 4 focuses on the regime's attempts to boost state revenues, most of which failed, and how the nature of the political regime is an obstacle to increasing revenues. This chapter records the shift of the Egyptian state from a semi-rentier one to a predatory one.

The final chapter turns to the political level in order to analyze the political consequences of the state's ailing finances. An important consequence is the growth of independent economic centers of power that are moving into the political arena and seizing positions in the political regime.

The conclusion summarizes the main findings of the study and draws the most important implications for the transformation of Egypt's public finance. An epilogue offers thoughts on the Egyptian uprising of 2011.

1 GROWTH OF THE STATE UNDER MUBARAK
Follow the Revenue Trail

THIS CHAPTER AIMS to define the main parameters of the semi-rentier state in Egypt and to trace and analyze the course of revenues and expenditures in Egypt since the outset of the 1980s. The purpose is to answer two questions.

First, what factors account for the fluctuations in revenues and expenditures? The theory we propose here is that the level of state revenues sets the pace of public spending. When revenues increase, so do state expenditures, and vice versa. Official economic policy, be it interventionist or laissez-faire, has little effect on the volume of public spending. Its rise or fall is not the result of a decision.

Second, what factors determine the volume of state revenues? The Egyptian state derives much of its income from petroleum sales, Suez Canal fees, and foreign aid. These are essentially rentier revenues, and they have driven national fiscal policy since the 1970s. Without understanding the fluctuations in these revenues, it is impossible to explain the transformations in economic policy.

MUBARAK ANNOUNCES A NEW ECONOMIC POLICY
"Prosperity is at hand," Egyptians were told during the 1970s. Toward the end of that decade, President Anwar Sadat promised that 1980 would be the "year of prosperity," and in September 1980, the minister of the economy proclaimed that the era of prosperity had begun. The upbeat tones faded quickly following the assassination of Sadat on 6 October 1981.

On 6 November 1981, several weeks after President Hosni Mubarak came to power, the editor-in-chief of *Al-Ahram* confirmed that the economic crisis was severe. His editorial ushered in a new official rhetoric on the economy that would contrast strikingly with the rhetoric that prevailed throughout the 1970s. The new official discourse was inaugurated in an economic conference that Mubarak convened in February 1982. In his opening address to the conference, cited in *Al-Ahram Al-Iqtisadi* on 22 February 1982, the president explained that the purpose of the conference was not to make general recommendations, but rather to assess the state of the economy with an eye to formulating an action plan. The conference's general conclusion, as laid out in the closing statement, was that the government would revert to central economic and social planning and steer the Open Door policy[1] toward production. As the secretary-general of the conference said in this statement, the process of liberalization had to continue, but there also had to be a drive to reduce consumption and increase production. He added that the government was keen to propel the private sector toward the productive sectors and would take all necessary measures to achieve this.

The new economic orientation triggered heated debate in the government and in the opposition press over the value of the Open Door policy. A major forum was the state-owned magazine *Al-Ahram Al-Iqtisadi*, which opened its pages to such left-wing economists as Fouad Mursi and Ramzi Zaki. In their opinion, the policy was a failure. Among the many reasons they cited, the most significant was that the policy generated consumerist tendencies and favored increased importation over strengthening the productive sectors, especially industrial production. Economic growth in the 1970s, they maintained, had been purely a consequence of the influx of rentier revenues, primarily from the Suez Canal, petroleum, and foreign aid. Egyptian capitalists, meanwhile, focused their energies on speculation and investment in quick-profit fields such as consumer imports and real estate construction. This entrepreneurial class made up the "parasitic sector" of Egyptian capitalism. In Mursi's and Zaki's opinion, the solution was to encourage nationalist capitalism by reducing imports (by increasing protective customs taxes) and, of course, by revitalizing the role of the state in production.

The opposing camp of right-wing economists took up the defense. However, even as they continued to advocate the Open Door policy out of principle, they had to acknowledge that it had promoted growth in the trade and financial sectors over industrial growth. They further admitted that it had encouraged a flourishing opportunistic entrepreneurial class that had come to form "actual power centers," as former Prime Minister Abdel Aziz Higazi was cited as saying, according to *Al-Ahram Al-Iqtisadi* on 26 April 1982. Higazi had been selected by President Sadat to head the government during the transition to a market economy.

The Egyptian intelligentsia concerned with economic affairs was thus unanimous in the opinion that the Open Door policy had to be reassessed and rectified. The difference between the right and left was over how to rectify it and to what degree.

It was not long before left-wing economists came to feel that all the work they had put into studies and preparations for the economic conference hosted by the new president had gone to waste. The president heeded none of the recommendations of the conference or, at best, adopted only the easy parts. But as partial as the regime's implementation of these recommendations was, the difference between its economic rhetoric and that of the previous regime was total. Under Mubarak, criticism of the Open Door policy was not only officially condoned but also actively encouraged. In addition, the government sought to boost both private and public sector industry. Toward this end it raised protective import barriers, lowered the interest rate on industrial investment loans, and, significantly, reduced taxes on industrial profits to 32 percent at a time when the capital gains tax in other commercial sectors was 40 percent.[2]

These measures did, in fact, help stimulate growth in the industrial sector. The government boosted spending on industrial expansion in the private sector, and a greater share of private sector investment went into industrial activities, increasing from 15.9 percent in 1981 to 34.7 percent in 1990 and 45.9 percent in 1995.[3] The share of industry (excluding the petroleum sector) in the GDP increased from 13.5 percent in 1980–81 to 18.1 percent in 1990–91.[4] The new emphasis tangibly manifested itself in the rise of such industrial cities as The Tenth of Ramadan and Six October. It was also reflected in the decision on the part of a number of import magnates of the 1970s to turn to joint production enterprises with foreign investors. For example, Mahmoud Al-Arabi shifted from importing Toshiba appliances to assembling them and manufacturing some of their parts, and the Abaza family turned from importing Peugeots to assembling them and manufacturing 40 percent of their components. These are two notable instances out of many.[5]

Most of the growth of private and public industry in the 1980s, especially in clothing and automobile assembly and manufacture, was heavily contingent upon customs protection, which is to say upon government intervention aimed at keeping prices of imported goods higher than prices of their Egyptian counterparts. This gave both state and private capitalism the opportunity to dominate the local market and set prices that often exceeded those that prevailed in other countries at Egypt's level of economic development.

EXPLAINING THE SHIFT IN ECONOMIC POLICY: FOLLOW THE REVENUE TRAIL

A common way for new presidents to establish their legitimacy is to point to the economic problems bequeathed by their predecessors and to disparage the policies that created them. It was only natural, therefore, that Mubarak would begin his reign with the refrain of severe economic crisis. Most analysts in Egypt have tended to dismiss that refrain as little more than propaganda. Yet, the new official rhetoric in the early 1980s reflected a change from the Sadat era, albeit not as radical as Sadat's about-face from the political orientation of the Gamal Abdel Nasser era (1956–70). Upon coming to power, Mubarak, like Sadat before him, applied himself to the task that any new regime has to undertake if it is not going to rely solely upon the instruments of violence and terror. That task was to build his own sociopolitical base. To do this, Mubarak had to clip the wings of powerful business magnates associated with the Sadat era, such as Rashad Osman and Esmat Al-Sadat, so as to clear the way for a new set of business magnates entirely loyal to him. The other social class that the Mubarak regime could easily court consisted of government employees. They were deeply resentful of Sadat's economic policies, which had cast them down from the elitist status they had enjoyed under Nasser to a much lower rung on the social ladder. The new official discourse about the return to central economic planning and the major economic role of the state was intended to reassure and win over this segment of the public.

Nevertheless, the shift in economic policy stemmed from more than the exigencies of building the legitimacy of the new president. Mubarak would not have partially reverted to economic planning had it not been for the growth in state revenues, a trend that began in the mid-1970s (see Figure 1.1).

The growth of the Egyptian state apparatus was the irony of the decade of the 1970s. While the official discourse emphasized the conversion to a market economy, the centrally steered economy burgeoned. Undoubtedly, the rise of a new and very conspicuous class of capitalist entrepreneurs and a very ostentatious nouveau riche gave the impression that the private sector was taking over an increasing share of the resources from the public sector. The fact

Figure 1.1. Public Revenues and Expenditures as a Percentage of GDP in Egypt, 1974–82

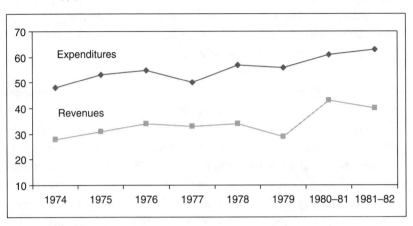

SOURCE: Sadiq Ahmed, *Public Finance in Egypt.* Washington, DC: World Bank, 1984.

is that this did not occur during the 1970s. As more money flowed into the pockets of the rising entrepreneurial class and a segment of the middle and professional classes, state-controlled revenue sources poured even more into the coffers of the national treasury. Consequently, government control over the nation's resources increased. According to a World Bank study, public spending soared from 48 percent of the GDP in 1974 to 62 percent in 1981.[6]

Despite the influx of revenues, the regime was still inclined to borrow and to demand more aid from abroad. One can not help but remark how similar this situation was to the era of the Khedive Ismail a century earlier. Then it was revenues from cotton that poured into the state's coffer as the extravagant khedive plunged headlong into debt. In the 1870s, the Egyptian debt crisis led to the system of Dual Control, whereby French and British commissioners took over the management of the Egyptian economy; in the 1970s, Egypt's creditors pressured the government into concluding an economic reform agreement with the International Monetary Fund (IMF). Signed in 1977, the agreement obliged Egypt to reduce the national deficit and reduce government spending. President Sadat complied; one of his first actions was to lift subsidies on essential foodstuffs such as bread, flour, oil, sugar, and rice. Egyptians awoke on the morning of 18 January 1977 to discover that the prices of the staples upon which millions of poor and low-income families depend had suddenly doubled. The popular reaction was instantaneous and powerful. Mass protests and violent rioting lasted two full days before finally being suppressed by the military and police. About a hundred people died, and several hundred more were wounded in the confrontation between security forces and demonstrators. The Bread Riots, as this uprising came to be known, marked the first time since the military coup in 1952 that the army was brought to the streets of the capital to maintain public order.

The Egyptian government was forced to rescind the new economic policies nearly as quickly as it had decreed them, delivering a debilitating blow to the economic liberalization program. The 1977 Bread Riots had a major impact on how the Egyptian regime would handle economic and fiscal policy. Their lesson was quickly grasped: Sudden and excessive reductions in public expenditures courted violent popular explosions. Henceforth, a slow and incremental approach to reductions became the economic scripture to which Sadat and then Mubarak would faithfully adhere. As it transpired, public expenditures did not decrease; they increased rapidly both in absolute terms and as a percentage of the GDP. What made this possible was the increase in government revenues from oil, the Suez Canal, and foreign aid, which had begun to flow into Egypt due to its much closer ties with the United States.

STATE REVENUES START TO PLUNGE

By the time Mubarak became president, the level of public spending as a ratio of GDP had risen to an unprecedented rate for a third world country. Figure 1.2 shows how Egypt compares with several other countries in this regard. The only Middle Eastern country to surpass Egypt in the ratio of public spending to GDP was Israel.

The powerful economic role of the Egyptian state in the 1980s rested on enormous rentier revenues. More than half the national income came from sources other than taxes. Figure 1.3 drives home how important non-tax revenues were in Egypt compared to selected third world and Middle Eastern countries.

Mubarak thus came to power at a time of a considerable surge in state revenues. Unfortunately, several years into his rule the revenue taps began to close. The collapse in oil prices played a principle role in this process. Although Egypt is by no means an oil-exporting nation of the stature of the Persian Gulf countries, oil is one of the most important determinants of financial fluctuations in Egypt. The prices of oil and energy in general do not

Figure 1.2. Public Spending as a Percentage of GDP in Selected Countries, 1982

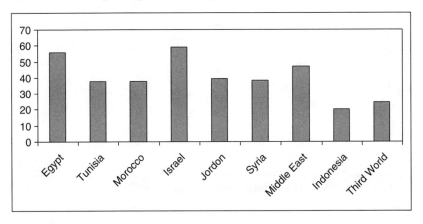

SOURCE: IMF, *Government Finance Statistics Yearbook*, 1991, pp. 88–89; and Sena Eken et al., *Fiscal Policy and Growth in the Middle East and North Africa Region*. IMF Working Paper No. 97/101, 1997.

Figure 1.3. Non-tax State Revenues as a Percentage of GDP in Selected Countries, 1981

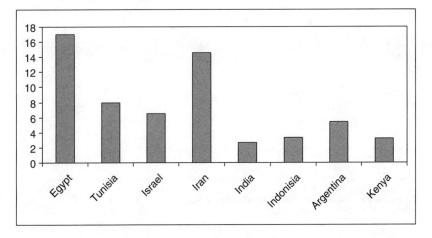

SOURCE: IMF, *Government Finance Statistics Yearbook*, 1991, p. 106.

only affect oil and natural gas exports; they also affect the yield from Suez Canal transit fees, which is heavily contingent on the oil trade.

As noted, Egypt was one of the largest recipients of foreign aid in the third world. These funds also began to decline in terms of their ratio to GDP, as illustrated in Figure 1.4, when the fiscal crisis in major industrial nations forced them to reduce levels of aid to third world countries. Simultaneously, the

Figure 1.4. Foreign Aid as a Percentage of GDP in Egypt, 1980–89

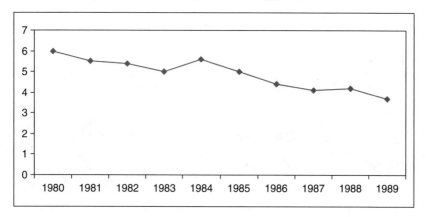

SOURCE: IMF, *Government Finance Statistics Yearbook*, 1991, p. 71.

Figure 1.5. Rentier Revenues as a Percentage of GDP in Egypt, 1981–89

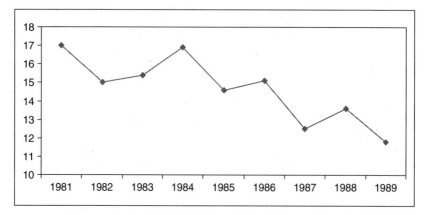

SOURCE: IMF, *Government Finance Statistics Yearbook*, 1991, p. 106.

population boom and the development of the Egyptian economy reduced the
effect of aid. Figure 1.5 depicts the declining trajectory of the rentier incomes
derived from petroleum, the Suez Canal, and foreign aid.

Tax revenues also declined. More than a third of the government's yield
from capital gains taxes comes from the General Petroleum Organization, the
Suez Canal Company, and the Central Bank. As rentier incomes dropped, so
did the taxes paid by these organizations. Figure 1.6 illustrates the downward
trajectory of tax revenues in the 1980s.

Figure 1.6. Taxes as a Percentage of GDP in Egypt, 1981–89

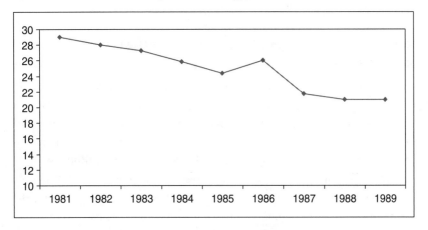

SOURCE: IMF, *Government Finance Statistics Yearbook*, 1991, p. 70.

Figure 1.7. Average Fiscal Deficit as a Percentage of GDP in Selected Countries, 1980s

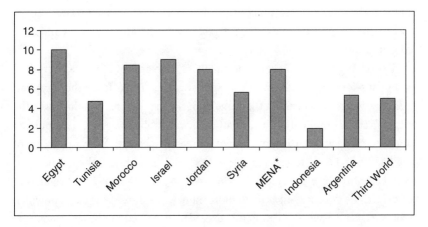

SOURCE: IMF, *Government Finance Statistics Yearbook*, 1991, pp. 53–55.
*Middle East and North Africa.

Lower income should lead to lower government spending. While such an adjustment makes fiscal sense, it is a political tinderbox. Reducing govern-ment expenditures means reducing or even cutting off the flow of funds to persons and groups that have come to expect them. An authoritarian regime such as Egypt's that depends on handouts to secure its control over society has very little flexibility when it comes to tightening the purse strings. As a consequence, the national deficit began to soar to the point that Egypt soon had one of the highest deficits in the world, as shown in Figure 1.7.

EGYPT SIGNS AN ECONOMIC REFORM AGREEMENT WITH IMF AND FAILS TO IMPLEMENT IT

The year 1986 marked a turning point for the Egyptian treasury. Petroleum prices dropped by nearly 50 percent, causing petroleum revenues to fall to $1.2 billion, down from $2.26 billion the year before, and Suez Canal revenues fell from $1 billion to $900 million. Egypt could no longer finance its imports. To make matters worse, Washington decided to hold back $265 million worth of aid until Cairo undertook the reforms prescribed by the IMF.[7] In May 1987, Egypt signed an economic reform agreement with the IMF, obliging the government to implement a package of measures. On the fiscal side, it had to reduce public spending, liquidate loss-making public sector companies, and liberalize the rest of the private sector. On the monetary side, it was expected to devalue the Egyptian pound with respect to the dollar. The purpose was to attract the billions of dollars that Egyptians held abroad, especially in the form of remittances from Egyptian workers in the Gulf. Egypt was further required to raise the interest rate to encourage savings and curb consumption.

In exchange for this agreement, the Paris Club approved the rescheduling of Egypt's foreign debt. A heavy weight was thus lifted from the Egyptian treasury, which had been on the verge of declaring bankruptcy. Such was the regime's sense of relief that instead of reducing public spending, as stipulated under the agreement, the government increased spending from 54 percent of the GDP in 1986–87 to 57.2 percent in 1987–88.[8] In addition, the net national deficit climbed from 5.3 percent in 1986–87 to 8.6 percent in 1987–88.[9] To finance its deficit, the government printed more money, the immediate effect of which was to trigger a wave of inflation that exceeded 20 percent in the late 1980s.

By the end of that decade, the Egyptian regime had become an international mendicant, so desperate was it for funding from any source. In 1990, the World Bank's International Development Association described the financial situation in Egypt as precarious.[10] When the Egyptian government stopped paying its debts, it was palpably evident that Egypt was on the verge of bankruptcy again. A 17 July 1990 Reuters' report quoted an Egyptian economic expert as saying, "For twenty years we've been saying that Egypt is on the brink of bankruptcy, but some miracle would always intervene to save the economy. This time I see no way out of the crisis." But, perhaps to the embarrassment of the economic expert, heaven stepped in again. Within less than two weeks after he issued the prognosis, Iraqi tanks rumbled into Kuwait. Soon, Washington began to mobilize an international coalition to free Kuwait. The war effort would depend heavily on the two most important regional powers—Egypt and Syria—and Washington would have to pay generously for their cooperation. The miracle was at hand.

THE ECONOMIC REFORM PROGRAM GOES INTO EFFECT, DUE TO A FRESH SPURT IN RENTIER INCOME

Creditor nations quickly agreed to cancel half of Egypt's foreign debt. But before they actually wrote off the debt, Egypt had to implement the economic reform program that had been jointly formulated with the IMF and World Bank. This time, the government showed a spirit of enthusiasm and dedication that it had lacked three years earlier.

Why did the Egyptian regime succeed in 1990 where it had failed in 1987? Some have suggested that the fall of the Eastern bloc and the wane of the interventionist state had boosted the liberal wing in the regime, which believed that there was no alternative but to hasten the process of capitalist development in Egypt. Some have also attributed Egypt's success in putting the economic reform program into effect in 1990 to effective coordination among creditor nations and between them and international financial institutions. In all events, Egypt pressed ahead with the reform program, and, accordingly, its debts were written off in several stages, each linked to the implementation of a set of reform measures.[11]

The focus of Egypt's economic reform program was on deficit reduction, and the deficit declined from 6 percent of the GDP in the year prior to the implementation of the program to 0.6 percent in 1993–94. International financial agencies could not praise this feat enough. To cite one of the many reports that extolled it, an IMF study of 1998 proclaimed that, in 1996–97, Egypt had achieved the highest level of fiscal balance in the Middle East and North Africa after Algeria.[12] Egypt's economic future seemed promising. The regime had brought inflation under control now that it had stopped turning to the mint to finance its deficit. The stock market, defunct since the nationalizations of the 1960s, had been resuscitated and was now showing some vitality. The slogan "Egypt: the tiger on the Nile" reflected the government's confidence that Egypt would soon surge to the fore of emerging nations.

The results of the economic reform program were a central subject of public debate in the 1990s. The government's claim that the program was an unmitigated success was corroborated by reports from international financial agencies. Critics, however, countered that this success was confined to fiscal performance (the shrinking budgetary deficit) and did not extend to the economy as a whole. Successful economic reform, they argued, would be manifested in many ways, most importantly in increased production and in higher per capita income levels.

While the debate homed in on such issues, little attempt was made to explain why fiscal reform had succeeded so well. Was the success in reducing the budget deficit the consequence of the reform measures themselves? Or did it have more to do with circumstances that coincided with the implementation of these measures? In the following section of this chapter, we attempt to demonstrate that the latter is the case, because apart from the sales tax that was introduced in 1991, fiscal policy underwent no other significant change.

In a letter to the World Bank in May 1991, Minister of International Cooperation Dr. Maurice Makramallah pledged that the Egyptian government would deregulate the economy.[13] The aim of the letter was to obtain a loan from the bank, and with this in mind Makramallah stressed, in particular, the Egyptian government's commitment to reducing public spending. The World Bank president presented this letter to the bank's board of directors along with his recommendation to accept the pledge and grant the loan. Among the other documents he presented was a schedule listing the maximum levels of public spending that the Egyptian government had vowed not to exceed. Table 1.1 reveals the huge gap between the promised and the actual levels of expenditures.

Table 1.1. Agreed-upon and Actual Public Expenditures, 1991–97

	1991–92	1992–93	1993–94	1994–95	1995–96	1996–97
Volume of Public Expenditure Agreed upon with IMF (billions of E£)	51,4	47,12	46,15	44,65	43,45	42,08
Actual Volume of Expenditure (billions of E£)	55,8	59,4	71,7	70,4	81,4	88
Actual Public Expenditure/ Agreed upon Maximum	108,5%	126%	155,3%	157,6%	187,3%	209%

SOURCE: For first and second lines, World Bank, *Report and Recommendation of the President of the World Bank to the Executive Directors*, 1991. For third line, Egyptian Ministry of Finance, *Balance Sheet of National Budget*, various years.

Figure 1.8. Public Expenditures as a Percentage of GDP, 1982–2002

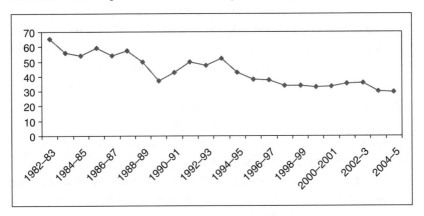

SOURCE: *Balance Sheet of the General Budget,* 1983–2002.

Not only did the government increase public spending in absolute terms; surprisingly it also increased spending in relation to the GDP from 37.3 percent in 1989–90 (before the economic reform program) to 49.9 percent in 1991–92 (see Figure 1.8).[14]

As Figure 1.8 illustrates, for many years public spending after the economic reform program was put into effect remained higher than earlier levels. Only in 1994–95 did it begin to decline. Clearly, then, it was not by fulfilling its pledges to the IMF that the Egyptian government managed to reduce the national deficit. What did produce this achievement?

The answer is higher revenues. Several factors contributed to the growth in revenues. In addition to taking part in the coalition to drive Iraq out of Kuwait, which brought many financial perks, the government reduced the value of the Egyptian pound (the official exchange rate for which was considerably higher than its worth on the black market). The effect was to raise the value of Egypt's oil exports and Suez Canal fees when calculated in Egyptian pounds. In addition, the government introduced a general sales tax, which also brought in several billions of pounds. These sources generated higher revenues and, hence, higher levels of public spending.

REVENUES DWINDLE ONCE AGAIN

The early 1990s was a grace period in the decline of state revenues. As of the middle of that decade, the downward trajectory of the 1980s resumed, primarily due to the fall in rentier incomes. Figure 1.9 shows the decreasing contribution of Suez Canal revenues to the economy during the later half of the 1990s.

As indicated in the introduction to this volume, the Egyptian state had been highly dependent on foreign assistance since the 1950s. Egypt was the first non–Soviet bloc recipient of aid from the Soviet Union. Starting in the 1970s, with around $2 billion every year, Egypt was the second-highest recipient of aid from the United States. This foreign assistance gave the Egyptian state the capacity to compensate for its weak power of mobilization of domestic resources. Yet, as can be seen in Figure 1.10, foreign aid consistently declined following the end of the Gulf War.

The rapid decline in aid was the product of several developments affecting creditor nations and the international order. Industrial nations had swung toward fiscal austerity in the 1990s. Keynesian theory was out, and neoclassical economic theory and its emphasis on budgetary balance was in, and with it the stress on deficit reduction. The new trend was epitomized by the Maastricht Treaty, which set a 3 percent deficit ceiling for European Union (EU) members. A second development was that many former communist countries and erstwhile creditors were now soliciting aid and loans. As a consequence, the 1990s ushered in an extended period in which the demand for aid exceeded the supply. To make matters worse, the strategic and political importance of the Middle East declined in the aftermath of the cold war. The upshot

Figure 1.9. Suez Canal Revenues as a Percentage of GDP, 1994–2010

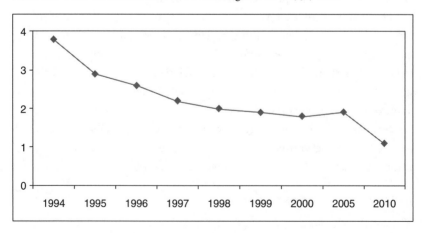

SOURCE: Ministry of Finance, *Closing Accounts of the Budget*, 1994–2010.

Figure 1.10. Foreign Aid as a Percentage of GDP, 1991–2010

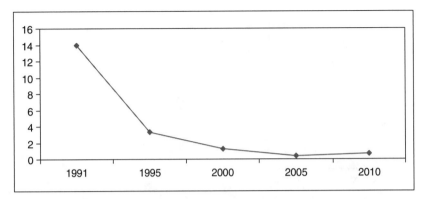

SOURCE: For 1990–2000, IMF, *Government Finance Statistics*, various years. For 2005–10, calculated by the author from Ministry of Finance, *The Financial Monthly*, March 2010.

was that Egypt found it increasingly difficult to secure foreign assistance, and its share of international aid plunged from an average of 14 percent in the 1980s to 7 percent in 2002.[15] The conventional wisdom for international aid providers, especially the United States, is that economic aid was not very successful in helping Egypt. In 1999, the United States and Egypt agreed on a ten-year plan to reduce assistance. Programs are now supposed to focus on increasing mutual trade and attracting more investment to Egypt. The slogan of USAID in the new millennium—"From aid to trade"—illustrates the trend.[16]

At the same time, the regime was unable to compensate for the loss in rentier income by developing domestic revenue sources. Figure 1.11 shows how the deficit in 2002–3 (expressed in relation to the GDP) surpassed that of 1989–90, which is to say before the implementation of the economic reform program.

The most significant achievement of the program was now history. But once again, extraordinary circumstances intervened to fish Egypt out of its financial troubles. This time serendipity took the form of the U.S. invasion of Iraq and the subsequent skyrocketing of petroleum prices, as well as the consequent rise in Suez Canal revenues. In addition, the efforts of the state to mobilize some domestic revenues, as is explained in detail in Chapter 4, yielded some results. Thus, the budgetary situation began to improve slightly starting in 2004.

Figure 1.11. Deficit as a Percentage of GDP, 1982–2010

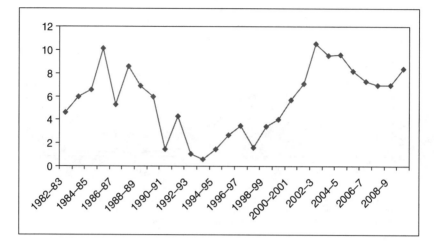

SOURCE: Ministry of Finance, *Closing Account of the Budget*, 1981–2002; *The Financial Monthly*, various issues, 2003–10.

Table 1.2. The National Debt in Egypt, 1999–2005*

	1999–2000	2000–2001	2002–3	2004–5
Total Debt	E£339.6	E£391.2	E£517.2	E£627.9
Domestic Debt	E£245.4	E£290.7	E£365.1	E£469
Foreign Debt	E£94.2	E£100.5	E£152.1	E£158.9
Total Debt in Relation to GDP	98.2%	109.1%	152.1%	116.0%
Total Domestic Debt/GDP	70.5%	74.3%	70.5%	101.0%
Total Foreign Debt/GDP	27.7%	28.0%	43.0%	31.1%

SOURCE: Ministry of Finance, *The Financial Monthly*, various issues.

*The reduction in foreign debt depicted in this table is less than the actual reduction because foreign debt here is measured in Egyptian pounds (E£), and the currency was subjected to several devaluations during the period covered by the table.

Finally, the government turned again to loans in order to finance the gap between income and expenditures. What distinguished the 1990s from the previous decade in this regard was that, with the sources of credit from abroad diminishing, the government needed to turn to sources at home. By the turn of the millennium, the government owed more than 70 percent of its debt to domestic creditors. Table 1.2 illustrates the trend.

The government thus found itself almost in the same predicament it had faced in the 1980s: Expenditures far outstripped available funds. Economic liberalization had failed to check the regime's proclivity for unrestrained spending, and economic reform had failed to secure additional revenue sources to finance the fundamental activities of the state. This leads us to the explanations that, since the 1990s, have been commonly propounded to account for the failure or, at least, the stalling of economic liberalization in Egypt. Alan Richards believes that the problem resides in the balance of power between the Egyptian state and interest groups: "a huge but relatively ineffective state confronts interest groups which are themselves too weak to impose their program (if indeed they have one) on the rest of society, yet are strong enough to block or subvert reforms which threaten their short-run interests."[17] Nazih Ayubi disagrees. He attributes the failure of liberalization and reform to contradictions within the ruling regime rather than to the resistance of interest groups. Third world regimes are inclined to expand their bureaucracies because doing so helps stabilize their rule. The larger the state bureaucracy, the more it can recruit and employ intellectuals and the educated classes, thereby containing these groups and their great aspirations.[18] Henry Moore Clement echoes this opinion, writing that economic liberalization policy in Egypt is no more than a strategy to perpetuate the rule of a despotic regime.[19]

Such explanations are not necessarily contradictory. In some instances, failure of economic liberalization arises from the resistance of interest groups, whether from groups within the state apparatus or within the business community. At other times, it may be due to the reluctance of the regime to implement policies that it fears might undermine its political control.

To the foregoing explanations, we would add that if resistance to economic liberalization succeeded, it did so in large measure because revenues poured in at some very crucial moments, thereby sabotaging a reform process that should have been grounded on austerity measures. Governments generally do not embark on fiscal and economic reform unless compelled by a crisis in state revenues. This occurred in Egypt in 1974 and in 1990. On both occasions, the government teetered on the brink of bankruptcy, forcing it to mobilize all its propaganda resources to rally the public behind liberalization. On both occasions, the government managed to introduce reforms. However, on both occasions, revenues miraculously shot up, triggering a growth in the volume and scope of government spending, thereby working against the reform program the government had chosen.

This increase in revenues at a time when a reform program is underway is no coincidence. The regime would never agree to an economic program unless its impact on state revenues was positive or, at least, neutral. Public revenues are of such vital importance because they enable the regime to perform its most essential functions. These entail spending in ways that create a general climate of public satisfaction that, in turn, enables the regime to reproduce itself.

CONCLUSION

An examination of the trajectories of government revenues in Egypt over the past quarter of a century reveals that the fluctuations in these revenues were primarily the product of developments affecting rentier sources of the national income. These fluctuations, rather than deliberate policy decisions, were the primary determinant of the levels of public spending. The transition from a state interventionist economy to a liberal one did not lead to a reduction in public spending; the reverse transpired. At a time when the official policy was to promote economic liberalization, public spending as measured against GDP increased. This phenomenon occurred most conspicuously over two periods, the first from 1974 to 1981, and the second from 1990 to 1994. The irony was that at these times, when opposition forces at home and critics abroad were lashing out at the government for abandoning its role in the national economy, the regime was at its most lavish. That the official policies of structural readjustment and economic liberalization should be accompanied by a rise in public expenditures was no coincidence. When the Egyptian regime proclaims a policy of economic deregulation, one can almost expect public spending to rise. The regime would not have ventured on such policies unless it could bank on an influx in foreign aid. In other words, the fluctuations in national revenues not only account for fluctuations in spending, but also for shifts in official economic policy.

From this perspective, one can also understand why the Egyptian regime always appears helpless. A significant portion of its revenues is derived from rentier income. Such income, as Alfred Marshall[20] put it, is a gift from heaven, and the Egyptian regime is strongly inclined to look up and pray for the skies to rain gold. Petroleum prices and income from the Suez Canal are controlled by outside factors over which the regime has little control. The only type of rentier income over which it has some influence is foreign aid, which is why soliciting foreign aid has been one of the regime's most prominent activities. It is also why the rhetoric it pitches to its audience abroad constantly reiterates the refrain that Egypt sets the beat in the Middle East. Only Egypt has the power to lead the Arabs to war against Israel, and only it has the power to steer the other Arab regimes toward making peace. It is little wonder that Mubarak has said that he devotes 70 percent of his time to the Palestinian cause. Nor is it surprising that Egypt's image abroad is one of the foremost obsessions of his regime and that the regime will give considerable free rein to opposition voices, apart from those whom it fears might threaten its sources of foreign aid. A well-known case in point is sociology professor Saad Eddin Ibrahim, who was sentenced to two years prison in 2008 on the charges of "tarnishing Egypt's reputation abroad" and asking the United States to link its aid to Egypt to the regime's performance on human rights.

Follow the revenue trail. This is the maxim we derive from our investigation of developments in Egyptian fiscal management and socioeconomic policy in general. If revenues are of such central importance to the regime, it is because these are the resources that fund the vital outlays that enable the regime to perpetuate itself. This is the subject of the following chapter on the distribution of public expenditures.

2 CHANGES IN THE DISTRIBUTION OF STATE EXPENDITURES
Security Prevails

IN CHAPTER 1 we attempted to explain the downward spiral in state revenues since the mid-1980s, which increasingly cramped the allocation of resources for the performance of various government services. Although there was no dramatic change in the way in which resources were distributed in the Mubarak era, some modifications were made in response to certain political and economic situations. Of particular note, while the shares of the Ministries of Interior, Culture, Religious Endowments, and Education increased, those of the Ministries of Defense and Supply were cut. Without entering into excessive detail, this chapter aims to identify what shaped the new contours of government expenditure.

CATEGORIES OF PUBLIC EXPENDITURE

In *The Fiscal Crisis of the State*, James O'Connor argues that in capitalist systems the state must efficiently manage the distribution of resources between expenditures on social capital (infrastructure, research, promoting exports, and so on), so as to help create the circumstances conducive to the growth of private capital, and social expenditures (health care, for example) so as to alleviate social discrepancies and, hence, secure the consent of the poorer segments of society.[1] These two forms of expenditure reflect what O'Connor holds are the two basic functions of the state: the promotion of capital accumulation (profits), and the promotion of legitimization (harmony).

The fact is that few public expenditures fall exclusively beneath either of these two headings. For example, educational allocations are generally categorized as social expenditures because they contribute to alleviating social discrepancies. They smooth the path to upward mobility: better education leads to better paying and more prestigious employment opportunities. However, educational allocations are also an investment in the development of social capital. A trained and skilled workforce is one of the prerequisites for increasing the productivity of labor and spurring the growth of private capital. In like manner, outlays toward the development of collective capital can be instrumental in promoting legitimization. The development of infrastructure, for instance, boosts investment, which creates job opportunities, which, in turn, promote economic and political stability.

In this chapter, however, we suggest a different categorization, one more helpful to acquiring a better understanding of how public resources are allocated in authoritarian regimes. Our point of departure is the political regime rather than the state. The fundamental aim of any regime is to perpetuate its rule. In the case of authoritarian regimes, this is accomplished by two means: controlling the minds and bodies of the people, and promoting economic development to bolster the regime's legitimacy (legitimization through achievement). Accordingly we can categorize public expenditures as follows: (1) political control expenditures, which include outlays for the security apparatus, for ideological control (the media, culture, religious affairs), and for social expenses that serve to promote legitimacy and political stability (food subsidies, for instance), and (2) economic development expenditures, which cover education, infrastructure, research, promoting exports, and so on.

As with O'Connor's system, these categories are not mutually exclusive. Public education, for example, serves a dual function. It furthers state control (by shaping the minds of children to accept the regime and social disparities), and it promotes economic development by imparting the skills and knowhow needed to create a labor force to serve as a pillar for industrial growth. It is therefore important to bear in mind that our categories are ideal types rather than empirically deduced discrete budgetary realities.

DEVELOPMENTS IN CONTROL SPENDING IN THE 1990S

As mentioned above, control spending includes allocations to the Ministries of Defense, Interior, Culture, Religious Endowments, and Supply. Asserting control over a country's land and people requires material power capable of enforcing demands where persuasion fails. Material power is essential to safeguard an authoritarian regime from its domestic competitors, these being all the forces, groups, and individuals who regard the existing regime as illegitimate and believe it should go. Under an authoritarian regime, therefore, a national police force not only performs the tasks of protecting private property and safeguarding public order (by regulating traffic, for example); it also protects the regime from its rivals. This is why the Egyptian police authority has a state security bureau. The name does not accurately reflect its function, which is to protect the regime, not just the state. The very creed of this agency is founded upon the obfuscation of the boundaries between the two, and not infrequently the police in Egypt end up protecting the regime to the detriment of the state. When the police turn a blind eye to acts of corruption committed by public officials loyal to the existing regime, they effectively contribute to the erosion of the efficacy of the machinery of state.

Agencies such as the Ministries of Culture, Information, and Religious Endowments undertake the persuasive side of social control activities. The latter ministry, for example, not only disseminates religious knowledge and supervises the spiritual affairs of the people, but it also propagates a religious vision intended to bolster the stability of the current regime. In like manner, the Ministry of Culture not only supervises artistic and cultural affairs and the practitioners of the arts and culture, but it also actively tames and co-opts the practitioners. Minister of Culture Farouk Hosni once boasted that he had succeeded in corralling the intelligentsia into the Ministry of Culture's pen. When a regime controls the taps that turn on and off all funding for the arts and cultural activities, artists and intellectuals are rendered dependent for their livelihood on the regime rather than on the market and the voluntary purchase of their products by members of society. Artists and intellectuals effectively become state employees, and their cultural output is consequently regulated by the state. The same applies to preachers who receive their salaries from the Ministry of Religious Endowments. They, too, are employees of the state.

Subsidies on food and other primary necessities are also a kind of control mechanism, especially in a country with a high poverty rate, such as Egypt. After all, it is difficult to control a populace whose bellies are empty.

SLASHING SUBSIDIES: A FIRST ATTEMPT

The purpose of subsidies is to make food and services available to limited-income sectors at rates below the market price. In the 1960s and 1970s, the Egyptian government greatly expanded the scope of subsidies. The lengthy list of subsidized goods and services included a variety of foodstuffs, gasoline, and public transportation. However, in 1977 the government was forced to cut subsidies after having signed an economic stabilization agreement with the IMF. The so-called bread riots of January 1977 quickly put an end to that plan. Just as quickly, Arab oil-exporting countries and the members of the OECD (Organization for Economic Cooperation and Development) rushed to aid the Egyptian regime with huge injections of money. Not only did the regime restore subsidies to their former level; it also expanded them. Whereas in 1977 subsidies accounted for only 15.5 percent of public expenditures, by 1980–81 they had climbed to 20.5 percent.[2] These figures refer solely to direct subsidies, not to indirect subsidies such as when the government sells goods, like petroleum, at prices lower than their international market value.

In Chapter 1, we noted that Mubarak inaugurated his regime with a reversion to the rhetoric of centralized economic planning, in contrast to the economic liberalization rhetoric that had prevailed under the Sadat era. We then demonstrated how this shift in rhetoric reflected the huge influx of money into the national treasury in the early 1980s. As illustrated in that chapter, the flow quickly began to trickle off. Reducing expenditures on subsidies was one of the solutions to which the Mubarak regime resorted in order to contend with dwindling revenues.

As Figure 2.1 illustrates, in spite of the 1977 uprising, the regime managed to reduce these expenditures with respect to public outlays over the long term. Moreover, it succeeded in doing so without triggering another major disturbance. The logical conclusion is that civil unrest is not solely the product of economic factors. In the 1970s, the domestic political climate was definitely conducive to protest activism. The student and labor movements were particularly keen to flex their muscles after their long, sometimes induced, at other times coerced, slumber under the Nasser regime.

The regime's success in forestalling disturbances was largely due to a carefully calibrated strategy of subtle and incremental cutbacks in subsidies. As this strategy has been examined in numerous studies, there is no need to discuss it further here.[3] However, success must also be attributed to another factor: a complementary strategy of ensuring a minimal level of content among the regime's social base, which was largely made up of the class of government functionaries.

Which sectors of society benefited from subsidies? In the 1970s and 1980s, every Egyptian family had the right to a monthly quota of subsidized foodstuffs,

Figure 2.1. Spending on Subsidies as a Percentage of Total Expenditure, 1982–90

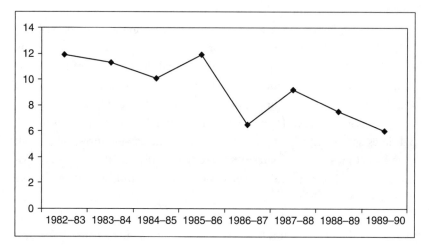

SOURCE: Ministry of Finance, *Closing Account of the Budget*, 1982–90.

which were made available through grocers authorized by the Ministry of Supply. However, due to the declining quality of subsidized goods and also because of the hassle involved in obtaining them (queuing for hours, for example), more prosperous families would either forego their allotments or would have servants queue for them and then distribute the goods among their domestic staff. Effectively, therefore, the beneficiaries of subsidized goods were the middle-income and poor sectors. As middle-income families would not be staring at catastrophe if they had to purchase unsubsidized goods, lifting subsidies has been regarded as a violation of the rights of the poor, in particular. However, the poor have never mounted a strong and systematic protest movement against subsidy cutbacks, in spite of the efforts of some political forces to mobilize them. A large and amorphous social sector such as the poor is extremely difficult to organize politically. The many divisions that pervade it (educated/illiterate, white-collar workers/manual labor, employed/unemployed, urbanites/villagers, and so on) impede efforts to unify behind a political dissent drive. This applies even more strongly under a regime in which the more disadvantaged segments of the populace have few if any avenues for representation of their interests.

　　If the poor are so hard to organize and spur into action, how did they stage the 1977 uprising, which has been ranked as one of the major landmarks in protest activism in twentieth-century Egypt? The fact is that they did not. Rather, it was produced by two influential segments of society: public sector workers and students. In *Egypt during 18 and 19 January*, Hussein Abdel Razeq relates how the uprising erupted with parallel demonstrations stimulated by members of these two social classes, the first already employed by the state, and the second expecting to join the former after graduation—let us not forget that the state was the chief employer at the time.[4] In other words, the uprising was primarily the work of current and prospective civil servants. While it is true that some of the more marginalized segments of urban society joined in, imparting a more violent and destructive flavor to the disturbances, their zealousness does not alter the fact that they boarded the train after it had set off.

The civil servant class at the time was seething with rancor. Its members grumbled against the rapid erosion of their incomes as the result of rampant inflation, and they resented their demotion in the social hierarchy as Open Door policy entrepreneurs and craftsmen leapfrogged over them. The erstwhile elite of the Nasser era had sunk to the limited-income class under Sadat.

It is important to note that the subsidy slashes that sparked the violent outburst in 1977 came to only about $28 million.[5] Clearly, then, they had a strong symbolic element, occurring as they did against a backdrop of the prevailing sense among public sector employees that the regime was abandoning them while smoothing the way to rapid profits and advancement for the private sector. The transition from the Sadat to the Mubarak era assuaged such sentiments. The president who had ushered in the Open Door policy was gone, and one of the first steps of the president who replaced him was to demonstrate his desire to rein in deregulation and revert to central planning. Mubarak's arrival to power thus alleviated a tense social climate in general, and soothed the civil service employees in particular.

That the Mubarak regime could taper off subsidies without igniting violent reactions stems from its very proficient management of public expenditures from the security perspective. Subsidized goods reached the cadres of the state bureaucracy, and they also reached the urban poor. The methods of distribution may have proved costly in terms of resources, but it was politically astute. The Mubarak regime knew it had to provide a minimum level of income security to the civil service sector, its primary base of support, even if that support was purely passive, as manifested in the willingness not to

Table 2.1. Total Wages as a Percentage of Total Public Expenditures, 1982–2001

	1982–83	1990–91	1996–97	2000–2001
Wages	17.0	19.0	20.6	23.4

SOURCE: Ministry of Finance, *Closing Account of the Budget*, various issues.

actively voice dissent. Table 2.1 lists the increase in public sector wages in the Mubarak era in terms of their share of public expenditures:

Table 2.1 confirms that rather than focusing on the poor, the regime concentrated its efforts on public sector employees. This emphasis is consistent with the image as the champion of the limited-income classes that Mubarak had carefully constructed for himself at the outset of his rule. Opposition forces attributed the term to the regime's fondness for euphemisms. After all, this was a regime that would refer to inflation as the "movement of prices." Yet, although the regime never actually indicated who fit the description of limited income, its use of the term suggested that it did not refer to the poor but rather to wage earners, the majority of whom were employees of the state. Of course, the term did not comprise senior civil servants. But neither could it have included the unemployed, for example, for the simple reason that they earn no income whatsoever.

Mubarak's image as defender of the limited-income sector was at its most vivid on Labor Day. It is on this annual occasion that he appears as the paterfamilias of the great Egyptian limited-income family. Like Nasser and Sadat before him, Mubarak delivers a Labor Day speech. As the event approaches, leaks appear in the official press about the "good news" that the president will reveal in that address. Not that the good news would come as a surprise to anyone; it was common knowledge that public sector employees would be awarded a bonus equivalent to ten days' wages. Still, the staging required that the president himself issue this proclamation at the end of his public address. As in some plays in which actors are planted in the audience with set lines to deliver at certain points in the plot in order to create the impression of an impromptu interaction between the actors on the stage and the audience, people would be planted in the president's audience to say, for example, "What about the bonus, Mr. President?" The president would smile and jest, "Not until the end of the speech. That way no one will fall asleep." One is reminded of the patient father who promises his children some candy if they behave themselves.

However, financial straits have compelled the Mubarak regime to gradually abolish the Labor Day bonus. As noted above, that bonus was equivalent to ten days' salary. Over the 1980s, basic salaries sloped off in relation to fluctuating incomes, such as allowances and perquisites. Consequently, the annual bonus gradually shrank until it was eliminated entirely at the outset of the 1990s, when the regime was forced to implement the economic reform program.

Mubarak simultaneously had to end subsidies for the limited-income sector, which naturally conflicted with the image he had painted for himself as their guardian. Nevertheless, he attempted to obviate the negative repercussions by creating the impression that the situation would be far worse if left to the cabinet without his personal intercession. The official media often portray Mubarak as the voice of the left wing of the regime and the obstacle to right-wing proposals that would be detrimental to the limited-income sector. He has also initiated social projects that target that sector of the populace and that are directly linked to him. The Mubarak Housing Project for Youth is a prime example.

MILITARY EXPENDITURES: UP IN THE 1980S, DOWN IN THE 1990S

One of the ironies of public expenditures in the 1980s was the sudden rise in military allocations (see Figure 2.2) in the wake of a decrease in these allocations in the 1970s. The irony resides in the fact that the Egyptian regime had recently signed a peace agreement with Israel, which led to the restoration of the Sinai (with the exception of Taba) to Egypt in 1982. The regime had declared that the 1973 war would be Egypt's last war, meaning that it would no longer resort to the military option in the Egyptian-Israeli conflict. Its commitment to this pledge was evidenced in its acceptance of international arbitration over the restoration of Taba, which Israel had refused to hand back.

One can only conclude that the level of military allocations in the 1980s was not determined, or at least was not exclusively determined, by the demands of the conflict with Israel, but by other factors. The nature of these factors is difficult to determine since military outlays in Egypt have always been shrouded in secrecy. Consequently, we can only propose a few hypotheses.

It could be that the rise in these outlays was connected to the requirements for safeguarding domestic stability. Perhaps, too, it was connected with the growing influence of the army in the early 1980s. According to some scholars,

Figure 2.2. Military Spending as a Percentage of Total Public Expenditure, 1980–96

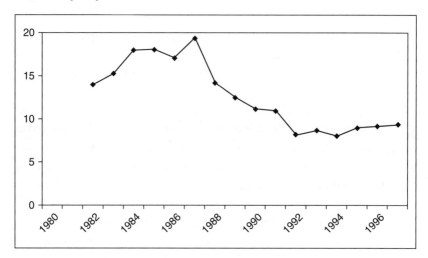

SOURCE: IMF, *Government Finance Statistics Yearbook*, various issues.

Sadat had curtailed the political influence of the armed forces.[6] One of the indicators that Robert Springborg cites to substantiate this is the reduction in the appointments of military officers to government positions.[7] It has been rumored that the military establishment grumbled about this. It has also been suggested that the armed forces disapproved of Sadat's strategy for reaching a peaceful settlement with Israel. Perhaps for such reasons Mubarak felt that he needed to secure the loyalty of the armed forces upon coming to power, and increasing military outlays was one way to do so.

What we can be sure of is that the increase in military expenditures in the 1980s coincided with rise to command of the armed forces of the military's strongman, Field Marshal Abdel Halim Abu Ghazala. It was well-known that Abu Ghazala had strong ties to the United States after having served as military attaché at the Egyptian embassy in Washington before being handed the defense portfolio back home. He was a vehement opponent of communism and believed that Egyptian military policy should lend itself to the American-led strategy to dismantle the Soviet camp.[8] There was also considerable talk behind the scenes of tensions "between the field marshal and the president," arising from the former's political ambitions.[9] The president eventually settled the conflict by kicking Abu Ghazala upstairs to the purely honorific post of Assistant to the President of the Republic, after which he removed Abu Ghazala from power entirely following the exposure of his relationship with a stunning socialite, Lucy Artin. The so-called Lucy-gate did little to diminish the field marshal's popularity among senior military staff, which continued until his death in September 2008, and which was largely due to his ability to secure larger budgetary allocations to the armed forces. With such allocations, he could expand the services provided to officers, such as subsidized housing, food products at reduced prices, and officers' clubs and banquet halls that could be rented for special occasions at purely token rates.

At the end of the 1980s, military outlays began another downward trajectory. This may be connected with the political fall and removal of Abu Ghazala, but it was definitely necessary in view of the grim state of the Egyptian economy, which was teetering precariously again. Several factors worked in Mubarak's favor when he moved to cut the military budget. The armed forces had recently begun to invest in certain civilian commercial sectors, which had earned the army considerable financial independence from the national budget. Although there are no available statistics on the activities of the armed forces in the production of goods and services for the civil sector, one could see the spread of retail outlets selling foodstuffs produced by the army to military personnel and the general public, as well as the proliferation of manufactured goods produced by the army such as electrical appliances.

THE MINISTRY OF INTERIOR RECEIVES A GREATER SHARE OF THE PIE: THE EFFECTS OF THE WAR AGAINST MILITANT ISLAMIST GROUPS

The Ministry of Interior topped the list of government agencies whose share of budgetary allocations went up in the 1990s (see Figure 2.3). The increase can be understood in light of the regime's war against militant Islamist groups, which required considerable resources for recruiting and arming the growing numbers of security troops. The increase must also be seen in the context of the weakness of the caretaker state, which secures political and social stability through handouts. In the 1990s, the regime had to resort more and more to the stick because the carrots were running out.

The Ministry of Interior's share of national resources is not restricted to its budgetary allocations. It also has access to free labor. The approximately 450,000 central security forces are conscripts serving their terms of obligatory military service, which can last up to three years. Imagine what it would cost

Figure 2.3. Expenditure on Security as a Percentage of GDP, 1987–97

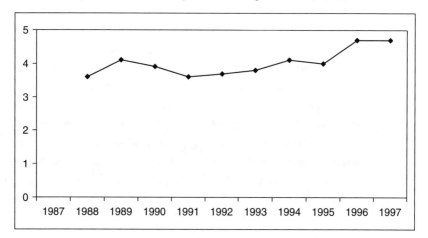

SOURCE: IMF, *Government Finance Statistics Yearbook*, various issues.

the ministry to recruit that many people if it had to resort to the labor market. At the very least, it would have to offer the minimum wage to attract its manpower needs. Therefore, the increase in allocations to the performance of the security function should take into account the corvée labor available through the draft, making the preservation of law and order relatively inexpensive.

These recruits' primary task is to suppress protest demonstrations. The central security force was created in the wake of the 1968 students' and workers' demonstrations that erupted in response to the lenient sentences pronounced against the army officers held chiefly responsible for the 1967 military defeat. This force was further extended after the Bread Riots in 1977, during which the police were unable to bring the wide-scale disturbances under control, and the army had to be brought in. We should also bear in mind the minister of defense's pledge in the early 1990s that the army would not take part in suppressing the militant Islamist movement as long as the police could take care of the job.

Nevertheless, police reliance on corvée labor is laden with risks and contradictions. Keeping armed "slaves" under control is not easy; money and favors do not ensure their submission but, rather, pure force and coercion. In 1986 the situation slipped out of control entirely when large numbers of central security troops rioted, wreaking widespread destruction and numerous casualties. Once again, the army had to be brought in to quell the rebellion.

The irony is that the central security force was created precisely so that that army would not have to put down unrest.

As we said above, the increase in allocations to the Interior Ministry in the 1990s was related to domestic challenges to the regime. At a time when a cold peace prevailed between Egypt and Israel, reducing the external threat, the militant Islamist movement was battling to overthrow the regime. In addition to the boost in material resources, the police also received some symbolic boosts. The regime had to express its appreciation to them as the country's shield against terrorism. The presidential speeches around this time made frequent references to the heroic sacrifices of police martyrs. Simultaneously, the regime turned a blind eye to mounting human rights abuses by the police. Perhaps what most epitomizes the growing influence of the police in the 1990s is the replacement of the motto "The police: in the service of the people" with the motto "The police and the people: in the service of the law." The significance of the change resides not so much in the (theoretical) recipient of the service, but rather in the fact that where there were once two parts to the equation (the police and the people) there are now three (the police, the people, and the law). As the new motto would have it, the police and the people are equal parties, presumed to be working side by side for the benefit of the law. One is strongly reminded of a similar situation in the Nasser period, when the army was elevated to the status of an entity separate from and equal to the people, as couched in the official rhetoric, "The army and the people."

In all events, the increase in budgetary allocations to the Ministry of Interior was a definitive factor in the police force's success in overcoming the violent militant Islamist campaign against the regime.

EXPENDITURES ON IDEOLOGICAL CONTROL: THE INDIRECT EFFECTS OF THE FIGHT AGAINST MILITANT ISLAMISM

Public expenditures in the 1990s were also characterized by increased allocations to the agencies that oversee cultural and religious activities. Such injections into the state's ideological machinery were vital to its war against the Islamist movement. The Ministry of Religious Endowments during this period essentially nationalized many privately endowed mosques that had served as pulpits and recruiting centers for the jihad against the state. One of the purposes of the extra money was to ensure the loyalty of the official preachers who buttressed the religious legitimacy of the regime—the legitimacy that the Islamists were seeking to undermine.

The regime also upped spending on various types of publications that championed the concept of the civil state in contrast to the theocratic state that the Islamists advocated.[10] One of the most salient projects in this regard was Maktabat Al-Usra (The Family Library), founded under the sponsorship of First Lady Suzanne Mubarak. More money was pumped into the cultural infrastructure in general (museums, libraries, theaters, and so on), which was essential to winning support from the intelligentsia. The investment paid off. Many intellectuals shifted from opposition to open or tacit support for the regime, a trend aided by the mounting anxiety in those circles over the Islamist peril.

We are only speaking of a rise in expenditures on culture in relative terms. This does not conflict with the commonly held notion among the intelligentsia that culture in Egypt remains underfunded.

SPENDING ON DEVELOPMENT: EDUCATION

Earlier in this chapter, we divided public expenditures into two categories: security and control spending, and spending on economic development. With regard to the latter category, we suggested that the primary area of change was in education. Until this point, outlays on education in Egypt were relatively low compared to those in other countries around its level of economic development (see Figure 2.4).

Table 2.2 illustrates the rise of the ratio of educational outlays to overall public expenditures from 3.3 percent in 1981–82 to 6 percent in 1996–97. This increase was curious. As a general rule in the economic reform programs applied under IMF and World Bank supervision, social expenditures are cut.

Several factors combined to call attention to the crisis in the Egyptian educational system in the early 1990s. When school buildings collapsed on students during the 1992 earthquake, the public homed in on the low levels of government outlays on the construction and maintenance of schools, and the consequent overcrowding of classrooms and poor quality of the facilities, such as lavatories, in existing buildings. Soon, however, the public began to ask why some third world countries, such as the Asian "tigers," had far outstripped Egypt in economic development. The conclusion was that Egypt did not spend nearly as much on education as those countries did.

At this point, the business community chimed in, complaining of the lack of appropriately skilled labor. In theory, at least, the development project of

Figure 2.4. Expenditure on Education as a Percentage of Total Expenditure in Selected Countries, 1984

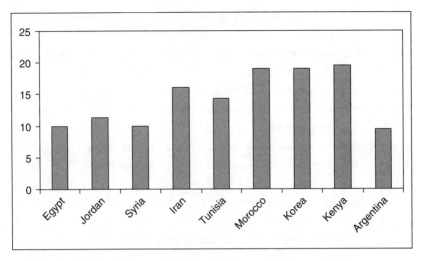

SOURCE: IMF, *Government Finance Statistics Yearbook*, 1991, pp. 60–61.

Table 2.2. Percentage Distribution of Public Allocations in Various Domains, 1981–82 and 1996–97

Field of Expenditure	1981–82	1996–97
Agriculture and Irrigation	2.6	2.5
Industry and Petroleum	22.4	16.7
Electricity and Energy	3.6	6.8
Transportation	9.7	13.4
Trade and Subsidies	13.5	3.6
Economy and Finance	0.6	0.4
Housing and Infrastructure	4.5	6.8
Health, Religious Affairs, and Labor	1.4	2.13
Education, Research, and Youth	3.3	6.0
Culture	0.6	1.2
Tourism	0.6	0.7
Security, Defense, and Justice	5.8	4.9
Presidency	0.58	0.7
Social Insurances and Welfare	11.0	19.0
Miscellaneous Expenses	17.6	12.9
Local Administration	1.8	1.5

SOURCE: Ministry of Finance, *Closing Account of the Budget*, 1981–82 and 1996–97.

the 1990s was founded on the goal of Egypt's assimilation into the global economy. It was felt that Egypt's greatest advantage resided in its relatively cheap labor. However, it was quickly realized that cheap labor alone was not sufficient to attract foreign investment and that more resources would have to be poured into education and training. Meanwhile, from another front (especially the left) came the charge of declining educational standards and, more ominously, the proclamation of the doom of free schooling now that private lessons had become the almost obligatory key for students to acquire the necessary knowledge to pass exams and gain admittance into university. In short, there was a virtual consensus across the political spectrum about the need to increase outlays on education. On numerous occasions, the president stressed how crucial education was to the cause of development. His statements were cited by the Ministry of Education when it asked for a higher budgetary allocation.

The lion's share of the rise in educational expenditures went toward physical infrastructure.[11] The General Organization for Educational Buildings was established to oversee the construction of many schools. At the same time, the First Lady sponsored a charity drive to collect donations from the business community to reconstruct or repair the schools ruined or damaged by the earthquake. The 1990s thus brought a boom in the construction of schools, whether paid for out of the national budget or from the contributions of donors.[12] However, as important as this was, it was not sufficient to reform the educational process. This required a focus on the pedagogic side.

A newly hired public school teacher these days makes about E£500 (less than $100) a month.[13] Clearly such a sum is far from sufficient to set up a conjugal home or support a family after marriage. As is common knowledge in Egypt, the teacher's solution is to impart scant information to his students in the classroom so as to compel them to take private lessons with him after school hours. In the mid-1990s, then Minister of Education Hussein Kamel Bahaa El-Din launched a vehement campaign against the institution of "private tuition." The campaign was based on a very logical premise: The only way to end the phenomenon is to eliminate the fertile ground that breeds it. That ground, of course, was paltry wages, and the minister promised to tend to teachers' material concerns. Unfortunately, the raises barely made a dent in alleviating these concerns. The minister pleaded insufficient funds, what with the limited resources in the treasury having to cover all other government staff and activities as well. So, teachers' salaries remained abysmally low, and the private tuition phenomena remained as firmly entrenched as ever.

If, as mentioned, there was a universal consensus over the need to increase expenditures on education, the government's educational reform program pleased no one. The economic liberals were pressing for the partial privatization of the educational system, which would be tantamount to revoking the right to free universal education. They believed that the state should pay only for primary education and the higher education of outstanding students from poor families, leaving ordinary families to pay the rest. The left was clamoring for a restoration of free universal education, which had effectively disappeared. The regime did neither this nor that. It refused to go with the economic liberals and abolish universal free education, but it also refused to go with the left and restore substance to the principle. Free education remained available to all, but the quality was so poor that, sometimes, whole generations would emerge from the system semiliterate. Parents who want their children to have a decent education have to pay for private tuition. As private tuition fees account for the bulk of public school teachers' income, society is effectively paying to support them and their families. Everyone knows this. So why does the regime insist on adhering to the principle of free education in theory while failing to apply it in practice?

The answer could well lie in the Mubarak regime's mode of operation: institutional torpor, or pronouncing the resolve to introduce sweeping changes and then letting them come into effect very, very slowly. Perhaps the one-tiny-step-at-a-time approach has helped the regime sustain its much vaunted stability, but the only service it has performed for society is to abandon the entire educational process to the process of decay. The approach avoids facing the facts, shrinks from calling things by their real names, and stems from a security mode, rather than a political mode, of managing the affairs of society. Were the regime to adopt a political mode in addressing the problem of education in Egypt, it would acknowledge how grave the problem is, then set into motion a search for solutions that would obtain the consensus of society, which in turn requires reaching compromise solutions. However, in the absence of such an approach and the concomitant absence of grassroots representation, such solutions are impossible. There is no opportunity for representatives of diverse interests to sit around the table, express their needs and concerns, and hammer out broadly acceptable solutions.

The regime pumped some money into the Ministry of Education's investment budget, which pays for the construction of schools. However, only a trickle of funds found their way into the ministry's current expenses budget, from which wages and salaries are disbursed. Obviously, the current budget is not as flexible as the investment budget. When resources run short, the government can cut back on investment allocations, but it cannot cut back on salaries and wages; if it did, tens of thousands of teachers would take to the streets. Yet the regime's hands are tied when it comes to raising teachers' salaries, which are governed by laws 47 and 48 of 1978, as amended under law 136 of 1980, regulating civil servant salaries.[14] True to form, the Mubarak regime altered nothing in the official institutional and legal framework governing the distribution of wages, making it virtually impossible to give public school teachers a meaningful raise, as conscious of its necessity as the regime might be.

Teachers form the largest single sector of civil servants. Numbering approximately 1 million, they make up about 16 percent of the employees on the government payroll. Giving them a tangible raise would require adding billions of pounds to their slot in the salary budget. This would be inconceivable without fundamentally revising the philosophy upon which the distribution of salaries is based, a philosophy that is certainly not broadcast in the official rhetoric and, indeed, mere mention of which is virtually taboo. Still, we can arrive at this philosophy through a process of reverse engineering; we can induce it from the actual government payroll. The Egyptian government employees who receive the highest salaries are those that staff the security and defense agencies, the judiciary, the foreign ministry, auditing agencies such as the Central Accounting Agency, the General Petroleum Authority, and the Suez Canal.

The obsession with security explains one set of these relatively high salaries. The allegiance of personnel in the security agencies, the courts, and foreign affairs is vital to the stability of the ruling regime. In Egyptian bureaucratese, they are referred to as the "special cadre," and their salaries are governed by special laws and regulations.[15] The security mentality also explains the higher levels of pay of the staff of the auditing agencies. With their storehouse of sensitive information on the state, their loyalty to the regime must be assured. Salaries in the General Petroleum and Suez Canal authorities are subject to a different logic: the logic of revenues. The employees in these agencies manage and perform the activities that yield the state's greatest sources of income, in reward for which they deserve a big chunk for themselves. Although the security mentality still predominates in the distribution of salaries, the revenue logic has been steadily gaining ground as a consequence of the government's financial straits. This development was succinctly captured by Medhat Hassanein who, when serving as finance minister from 2000 to 2004, categorized government agencies as "income-generating institutions" and "spending institutions."[16] Another example comes from a speech on the budget delivered by the chairman of the Foreign Relations Committee to the People's Assembly in 2003. During parliamentary deliberations over the national budget, the chairmen of special committees (such as the committee for defense or education) customarily present the financial requirements that they want incorporated in the forthcoming budget. On this occasion, the foreign affairs committee chairman not only rested his case for an increase in the allocation to the Foreign Ministry on the importance of supporting the Egypt's regional and international role but also on the notion that this ministry was an income-generating agency that brought in revenue in the form of foreign aid.[17]

Unfortunately for teachers, they do not figure in either the security or the revenue logic. Their support is not crucial to the survival of the regime, and they do not generate income for the state. Only when the regime reorders its priorities in a way that gives prevalence to the development function over the security and income-generating functions will it be able to readjust the government payroll in a way that makes a significant difference to teachers' pocketbooks. However, this requires an entire gestalt shift, which is difficult to envision in an authoritarian order, the perpetuation of which depends first and foremost on security logic.

The Egyptian regime is fully aware of how crucial education is to capitalist development in Egypt and to the assimilation of the Egyptian economy into the global order. It has designated educational reform as one of its highest priorities. The president himself has indicated this on numerous occasions, and his personal intervention in discussions on public policy means that his regime takes the matter seriously. Clearly, then, the regime definitely wanted to develop the educational system. Educational reform was urgently needed in order to stimulate economic development, create jobs, and promote political stability. The regime also grasped one of the central keys to the deterioration of the educational system: private tuition. Moreover, it saw a logical solution to the problem: Put an end to the private tuition business by improving teachers' material welfare through salary hikes. However, it failed to introduce the necessary reform, and the reason it failed was simple. The security mentality prevailed over the political approach to government and, together with the attendant institutional rigidity, impeded progress.

DEVELOPMENTS IN THE DISTRIBUTION OF INCOME
WITHIN GOVERNMENT AGENCIES

The preceding section examined how salaries were allocated across government agencies. Now we turn to wage distribution within the agencies themselves. While, as we observed, the philosophy governing salary allocations to different agencies remained essentially unchanged in the 1990s, the same does not apply internally within the agencies. Here, salary scales underwent a major change, creating an ever-widening gap between the higher and lower echelons of the hierarchy.

Income disparity within government agencies long precedes Mubarak's arrival to power. In the Nasser era, the disparity was founded on employees' level of education, position on the bureaucratic rungs, and years of service. The general formula continued into the Sadat era, when it was codified into the laws governing civil service employees, namely laws 47 and 48 of 1978, which were then amended with law 136 of 1980. The shift to a market economy under Sadat threw everything off kilter. First, the 1970s brought high rates of inflation, which eroded the real value of wages. Second, the conversion to a market economy gave rise to a capitalist class and an emerging private sector middle class. As general perceptions of poverty tend to be almost instinctively measured against the rich, the patterns of conspicuous consumption of the nouveau riche, combined with the sudden influx of previously unavailable consumer goods and products, compounded average wage earners' sense of economic hardship. Suddenly, government functionaries found themselves having to fight to retain the status they had under Nasser. In view of the relatively limited wage resources, one of the consequences was that the upper echelons of the civil service hierarchy secured the larger chunk of the salary pie for themselves.

In the Mubarak era, the disparity in income between the higher and lower rungs of the bureaucratic hierarchy was, more often than not, achieved through pseudo-official methods that soon became open secrets and that were dubious enough for the Central Accounting Agency to take note and caution against them.[18] We are not speaking here of outright corruption, such as bribery, but rather of officially documented flows of cash that wended their way around the regulations governing maximum wage levels. For instance, departments would form fictitious committees in which senior staff would participate and then harvest the legally stipulated stipend entitlements. Or, to take another example, ministers or other high-ranking officials would have themselves appointed to the boards of directors of companies that fell under their ministries and then receive fees for serving in this capacity.

The case of editors in chief of state-owned newspapers offers a vivid example. The journalist syndicate law prohibits syndicate members from receiving commissions on the advertisements that appear in their publications. But, today, editors in chief can also head their newspapers' boards of directors, in which capacity they are entitled to such commissions plus a percentage of the profits. Thus, editors in chief rake in hundreds of thousands and sometimes millions of Egyptian pounds a month, while the newly appointed reporter earns around E£500 a month.

The implementation of the economic reform program in the 1990s drove the income gap in the civil service to unprecedented proportions. New agencies cropped up, such as the Social Development Fund, which was meant to extend loans to the young and small entrepreneurs. Other institutions were resuscitated, such as the Cairo stock exchange, which had been laid to rest at the time of the nationalization process in 1961. In addition, many ministries and other government agencies created technical bureaus whose purpose was to supply skills and expertise that were unavailable among the existing civil service structures. These bureaus were generally staffed by young men and women who were proficient in foreign languages and were graduates of prestigious universities, such as the American University in Cairo. Their salaries were often more than ten times those of the employees of the ministries to which the bureaus were attached, and they had elegant, modern, air-conditioned, computerized offices to match.

The vast differences in incomes and working conditions between the technical bureau staffers and ordinary ministry employees generated no small amount of envy and resentment. The seething rancor sometimes erupted, as in 2002 when MP Kamal Ahmed took the floor of the People's Assembly to question then Minister of the Economy Youssef Butros Ghali about the extraordinary salaries received by some employees in the Cairo stock exchange, which could exceed E£15,000 a month. He angrily waved a printout of the salary list in front of his parliamentary colleagues. Obviously, that printout had been leaked to the parliamentary representative by one or more of the ordinary administrative employees in the stock exchange, who were understandably incensed at the interlopers' incredibly high paychecks as compared to their own, the purchasing power of which, to top things off, was steadily shrinking. Defending the high salaries paid to the newcomers, Ghali argued that the stock exchange needed skills and know-how that were not available among the older staff and that this expertise could only be obtained at those wages.

The case of the stock exchange not only casts into relief the problem of nepotism, whereby the children of the well-to-do and influential receive salaries far exceeding the standard pay scales. It also epitomizes the dilemma of a state bureaucracy and public sector in which the available skills and the performance levels have come to lag miles behind those in the private sector. The technical bureaus that began to proliferate among government departments were a quick and easy solution for the new department heads. Instead of overhauling the entire administrative system, they created a parallel stream. It may have been a practical response to the urgent need to repair a dilapidated state bureaucracy, but its chief side effect was to defer the task of comprehensive reform.

The natural by-product of the growing wage disparity was rampant corruption and, at a more mundane level, the proliferation of the *baksheesh* (gratuities) syndrome, which is now so endemic that it has become an unofficially accepted institution. Government employees not only receive baksheesh for breaking the law or bending the rules; they also expect it for performing their routine jobs. Such palm greasing is sometimes now required for one government agency to work with another. An example of this are the fictitious committees, mentioned above, that would have to include members of the Ministry of Planning to ensure the ministry's cooperation when it came to augmenting allocations.[19] (Until 2003 the Ministry of Planning controlled the distribution of allocations to the various ministries.) Currying favor with its senior officials was vital for the other government agencies in their competition for shares of the national budget.

CONCLUSION

In this chapter we examined how national budgetary allocations changed during the 1990s as a consequence of the fiscal crunch and political factors. We focused on such significant developments as the increase in allocations to the Ministries of Interior, Culture, Information, and Religious Endowments. We argued that this increase was related to the rise of the militant Islamist movement and the growing importance that the regime attached to these ministries' functions in safeguarding security and stability. The higher allocations proved crucial to the regime's success in bringing the security situation under control in the 1990s. However, security considerations alone do not explain all the changes in resource distribution in that decade. At other times, they were dictated by the needs of economic development, as was the case with the Ministry of Education. Yet, contrary to the situation with the security-related ministries, here the injection of money came too late (in the 1990s) and in insufficient quantities (little went to the current budget from which salaries are drawn). The regime was much quicker and firmer in its response to security needs than in its response to economic development needs. After all, the regime heads a caretaker state whose legitimacy is based more on its policies of bestowing the resources it has than on its development policies.

We have also seen that one of the most important developments in resource distribution in the 1990s was the broadening wage gap in the government hierarchy. The phenomenon reached such a magnitude that senior officials now earned hundreds of thousands more pounds than underlings on the lower rungs of the hierarchy. Whether such earnings were acquired through outright corruption, such as bribes, or through dubious schemes for circumventing official wage laws and regulations, the mounting income disparities in the civil service hierarchy, both between government agencies and within individual departments, can only exacerbate the trend toward the fragmentation of the state. The same trend, which is the product of the regime's approach to fiscal crisis management, also applies to the way central government departments distribute their financial resources to their subsidiary branches in the provinces. This is the subject of Chapter 3.

3 THE IMPACT OF THE FISCAL CRISIS ON THE RELATIONSHIP BETWEEN CENTRAL AND LOCAL GOVERNMENT

Decentralization or Fragmentation?

THIS CHAPTER TREATS the impact of the state's fiscal crisis on the relationship between the central government and the governorates. It examines how revenues are generated for local government, the central government's strategies for alleviating the financial burden of local government, and the latter's strategies for coping with the decline in fiscal support from Cairo. In the course of this analysis, we home in on two governorates, Alexandria and Qina, that serve as contrasting models of the relative success in generating revenues locally in order to compensate for the tightening purse strings of the central treasury. First we discuss the origins of the local government revenues problem, for the dilemma that the Mubarak regime faces today in this regard is an extension of dynamics of the post-1952 revolutionary order ushered in by Gamal Abdel Nasser.

NASSERISM AND THE ESTABLISHMENT OF THE CONTEMPORARY CENTRALIZED STATE

In his seminal work, *Oriental Despotism*, Karl Wittfogel ranked Egypt as a country that was geographically destined to political centralization because the dependency of its inhabitants on the Nile chained them to the authority that controlled this sole artery of life.[1] Societies that depended upon rainfall were not similarly vulnerable because no central authority could easily seize control over the life-sustaining waters emanating from the heavens. Wittfogel held, in brief, that where societies depended upon rivers, we would find heavily centralized and despotic forms of rule.

Although the theory has a certain logical appeal, it has come under heavy fire from sociologists. Without delving into their criticisms here, suffice it to say that even if the Nile had been instrumental to the rise of centralism and despotism in agrarian Egypt, since the nineteenth century agriculture has been steadily ceding way to industry, commerce, and services as the country's sources of wealth. Therefore, the search for the roots of contemporary Egyptian political centralism should begin not with geographical imperative but with politics.

The origins of the contemporary form of centralism in Egypt date to the rise to power of the Free Officers through the military coup of 1952. It is not difficult to see why the revolution's drive to reshape society was implemented in a centralized fashion. Change came from the top—from orders issued from the President of the Republic's office in Cairo—and radiated outward and downward through various executive agencies. The Nasserist model was straightforward: At the pinnacle of power sat a wise and patriotic authority with a vision for national reform inspired by the "genius of the people," as the rhetoric of the time put it. That authority would assume the burden of eliminating the social classes and political groups that stood in the way of the vision. Centralized control was a necessary corollary.

The Nasserist brand of centralism was not merely the product of the nationalization of a large portion of the wealth in the country and the drift toward a statist economy. It was also the product of the type of authoritarian regime that Nasser established. Parliamentary democracies generally permit and, indeed, require a degree of decentralization that may expand or contract over time depending upon the political history of the state. Authoritarianism is inherently incompatible with decentralization. To give the masses the leeway to launch grassroots initiatives is to open the gates to the coalescence of locally based autonomous political forces, and this is something no authoritarian regime can tolerate.

The centralization process set into motion by the Nasserist authoritarian populist regime ground to a halt with the death of its leader. His successor had to turn for support to forces outside the Nasserist establishment in order to eliminate opposition. This remained embedded in the state apparatus even after opposition leaders were rounded up and imprisoned as "centers of power" in 1971. The forces to which Anwar Sadat resorted consisted of social classes that had fallen out of favor under the Nasserist regime and political forces, such as the Muslim Brothers and the communists, that Nasser had actively suppressed. But what concerns us here is the attendant loosening of the authoritarian grip, permitting a degree of decentralization. Pushing in the same direction was the fact that the central government was severely strained financially, if not on the verge of bankruptcy, from years of bitter conflict with Israel. It could no longer afford to meet the needs of local government agencies.

The trend toward decentralization was soon translated into local government law 52 of 1975. Regarded by some scholars as the most pro-decentralization law in Egypt's modern history,[2] it provided for the creation of elected governorships and gave people in the governorates an unprecedented prerogative: the right to question their local officials. On financial matters, the law gave governorates the right to set up special bank accounts in which they would deposit locally levied revenues and from which they could disburse funds with considerable autonomy from Cairo.

But by the end of the 1970s, Sadat found himself under mounting pressures at home. The peace agreement with Israel had triggered vehement domestic opposition, and the Islamist movement, which the president increasingly played off against the left, turned against him. In addition, the Open Door policy led to the rise of new social classes and the simultaneous decline of older ones, whose resentments erupted violently in 1977. Sadat's response was to narrow the scope of civil liberties and to clamp down on his opponents. His regime's swing back to stricter authoritarianism manifested itself at the local level in law 48 of 1979, restricting local government rights, especially the right to call local officials to account. That particular right had become an enormous headache for the regime, for it had created a channel through which the public could voice its demands, the stream of which had quickly burgeoned into a flood. The regime was only too glad to shut the floodgates, thereby drawing to a close a brief and limited chapter of decentralized government.[3] It had lasted only three years, but that was enough for the authoritarian regime to recognize the advantage of centralization at all times, whether under a statist economy or a free economy.

MUBARAK: A TREND TOWARD DECENTRALIZATION

Upon coming to power in 1981, President Hosni Mubarak strove to dispel the climate of fury that had driven Sadat to imprison his opponents from across the political spectrum and that had brought his rule to an end. Mubarak's first actions were to release the political detainees and restore the scope of liberty that Sadat had eliminated during his final years in power. Conceivably, Mubarak could have reinstated the decentralization that Sadat had begun

with law 52 of 1975 and revoked with law 43 of 1979. However, given his regime's proclivity for institutional inertia, Mubarak was disinclined to introduce a new local government law and, instead, lightened the security grip over
the municipal elections of 1982.[4]

Yet, the development thinking abroad at the time was zealously pro-
decentralization. The sway that the notion of local development held over international development organizations extended well beyond the conceptual
level; many of these agencies poured material and technical support into the
promotion of decentralization in Egypt. Foremost among them was USAID,
which expressed the trend in the form of the dozens of research papers, reports, and conferences it sponsored and in the projects it financed.[5]

The trend also manifested itself in the national budget, which allocated
increasing resources to local government. The ratio of such allocations to the
overall current expenses of the state rose from 13.8 percent in 1980–81 to 20.5
percent in 1989–90.[6] In addition, the same decade brought a rapid increase in
the special funds that were supervised by governorate authorities. Unlike the
central government's outlays to local government units, decisions regarding
the disbursement of these funds were made at the local level. Although management of the funds was subjected to legal oversight by such supervisory
agencies as the Central Accounting Authority, governorates had considerably more leeway in how they spent the funds than they did with the money
coming from the central government. With the latter, for example, local authorities could not transfer the surplus from one year's to the next year's budget;
with the special funds they could.

Thus, following two decades of intensive centralization under Nasser
when local government had no margin of autonomy, the process reversed itself somewhat under Sadat, apart from the recoil during the last few years of
his rule. Then, in the opening years of Mubarak's rule, the center once again
loosened its grip on the peripheries. However, the results of the trend toward
decentralization in Egypt remained very modest in comparison to that in
other countries. At the outset of the 1990s, Egypt was still one of the most
centralized countries in the world. As Figure 3.1 illustrates, local government
in Egypt had the highest rate of dependency on central government outlays in
the world.

Figure 3.1. Central Government Transfers to Local Government Agencies as a Percentage of Total Expenditures for Selected Countries, 1984

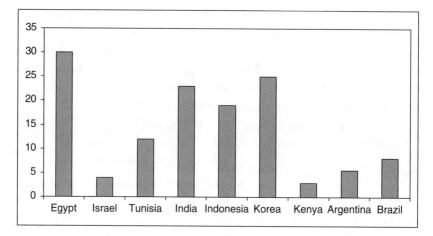

SOURCE: IMF, *Government Finance Statistics Yearbook*, 1991, pp. 74–75.

THE REVERSION TO CENTRALIZATION

In 1988, the government amended law 43 of 1979, changing the name "local government" to "local administration." The justification was not without logic: Egypt has a unitary system of government and, thus, gives no legislative authority to local government entities.[7] But the cogency of the logic aside, the amendment heralded a sharp swing back to centralization.

Several factors propelled the government in this direction. First, central government agencies were strongly resistant to any tendency toward decentralization, which would inevitably curtail their influence. The Ministry of Finance, in particular, was disturbed by the rapidly growing special governorate funds because they were beyond its control.[8] From the ministry's perspective, the funds ran against one of the pieties of public finance, budgetary unity, in accordance with which the national budget should embrace all public revenues and expenditures. Funds collected and allocated at the local level posed a direct challenge to this sacred principle.

Second, the government's revenue crisis, which had peaked at the end of the 1980s, was forcing the government to bring spending under control or, at least, to reassess how its money was being spent. An obvious area of scrutiny was outlays to local government, these having increased much more rapidly than government spending at other levels. Also, when cutbacks have to be made, the burden of belt-tightening is not shouldered evenly across the board. Some government institutions have to make more sacrifices than others, and local government agencies were undoubtedly in the weakest spot.

A third factor was the rise of the militant Islamist movement at the end of the 1980s. Centralization was regarded as essential to tightening political and security control. In the 1980s, local government agencies tended to be more open to the Islamist movement and, as some studies have observed, frequently struck accommodations with it.[9] Diaa' Rashwan cited the governorate of Sohag as an example.[10] Rashwan attributed the low rate of violent confrontation with Islamists in that governorate to an unpublicized agreement between the governor and Islamist leaders, in accordance with which the former pledged not to hunt down Islamist activists if the latter refrained from violence. The policy of centralizing decision-making powers as a means for containing the Islamist movement was made explicit when the law regulating the mayoral selection process was amended to replace mayoral elections by government appointments.[11]

In short, the combined need for austerity measures and tighter security led to a reduction in allocations to local government. Table 3.1 sums up the decline in local government's share of budgetary outlays in the 1990s.

Cutbacks were not the sole cause of the drop in local government budgets. Another was dwindling revenues at the local level. Local taxes and municipal charges plummeted from 1 percent of GDP in 1991–92 to 0.7 percent in 1999–2000.[12] The decline in local revenues stemmed from various factors. But first let us take a look at Table 3.2, which indicates where these revenues come from.

As we can see from the table, local tax revenues dropped in relation to total governorate revenues during the 1990s. Real estate tax (the most important local tax) fell to only 1.8 percent, although it should be added that Egypt

Table 3.1. Governorate Shares as a Percentage of Total Public Expenditures, 1989–90 and 1996–97

	1989–90	1996–97
Governorate Current Expenditures / Total Current Expenditures	20.5	18.3
Governorate Employee Wages / Total Government Wages	51.1	47.9
Governorate Current Deficit / Total Current Deficit	43.2	40.2
Investment Outlays to Governorates / Total Development Outlays	22.0	9.3
Deficit in Development Outlays to Governorates / Overall Deficit in Development Outlays	22.7	8.7
Financial Support to Governorates / Overall Budget	10.3	10.1

SOURCE: Ministry of Finance, *Closing Account of the Budget*, 1989–90 and 1996–97.

Table 3.2. Local Revenue Sources as a Percentage of Total Local Revenues, 1989–90 and 1997–98

Source of Local Revenue	1989–90	1997–98
Real Estate Taxes	2.3	1.8
Entertainment Taxes	0.5	0.4
Automobile Fees	2.0	0.8
Joint Revenues	1.6	1.0
Mutual Funds	1.8	1.1
Taxes on Suez Canal Profits	0.7	0.1
Municipal Services	0.8	0.6
Revenues from Local Properties	0.7	0.02
Municipal Taxes	1.1	0.8
Revenues from Local Projects	2.3	1.0
Miscellaneous Income	1.5	1.6
Special Funds	7.9	9.0
Other	0.3	0.8
Total Autonomous Resources	**23.2**	**18.6**
Support from Central Government	**76.8**	**81.4**
Total Local Revenues	**100.0**	**100.0**

SOURCE: Ministry of Finance, *Closing Account of the Budget*, 1989–90 and 1997–98.

is not alone in having low real estate tax revenues. The problem is common to all developing countries due to the lack of a sophisticated real estate market that periodically reassesses property values.

The decline in local government tax revenues can be explained by the fact that the central government retains a monopoly on the type of taxes whose yield increases with greater economic activity, such as income and sales taxes. The taxes that have been left to the governorates are rigid and hard to stimulate. If the regime has resolved to reform the national income tax structure (a subject to which we return in Chapter 4), it has shown little interest in reforming the local government tax structure.

As we can see in Table 3.2, revenues derived from governorate properties also fell off during the 1990s. The privatization of some governorate-owned enterprises largely accounts for this decline. Figure 3.2 depicts how central government allocations to the governorate climbed from under 50 percent of revenues in 1980 to 68 percent by 1996–97.

Figure 3.2. Percentage of Allocations from the Central Government to Total
Governorate Income, 1980–97

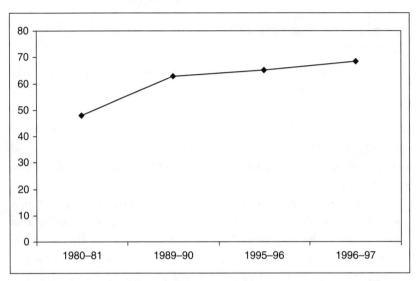

SOURCE: Ministry of Finance, *Closing Account of the Budget*, various issues.

The mounting dependence of the governorates on central government resources is a recurrent theme in the rhetoric of central government authorities
when they are keen to shed some of the burden of local government from the
national budget. In fact, the claim is untrue. Outlays to the governorates in
relation to overall national allocations did not rise at a rate sufficient to substantiate the official complaint. The ratio rose from 9.3 percent in 1980–81, to
9.5 percent in 1989–90, to 10.5 percent in 1995–96, but it dropped to 10.1 percent
in 1996–97.[13] Thus, while local government agencies grew more dependent on
allocations from the central government, the latter did not significantly increase its financial support for the agencies. The governorates' share of investment allocations fell from 30.8 percent in 1980–81 to 22 percent in 1989–90
and to 9.3 percent in 1996–97.[14] Meanwhile, current expenditures for local
government took a longer time to decline, as these outlays (which cover wages)
are far less flexible than are development allocations. They ultimately did
drop from 20.5 percent in 1989–90 to 18.3 percent in 1996–97.[15]

In sum, in the 1990s revenues from local taxes, properties, and enterprises
were plunging, and local government agencies were growing more and more

dependent upon central government funds, but the central government was not responding because of its own dwindling resources.

CENTRALIZATION AND PRIVATIZATION ARE THE SOLUTION

The central government's neglect of local government agencies was reflected in the severe deterioration in their performance during the 1980s and 1990s. It helped little that employees in these agencies were the lowest paid in the entire government bureaucracy. Table 3.3 shows the wage disparities between the different levels of government. Local government employees receive only 48 percent of total government wages, whereas they make up 61.5 percent of government employees.

The natural consequence of this wage policy is that local government agencies attracted the least skilled and least competent job seekers in the labor market. You get what you pay for. When insufficient resources are allocated to poorly qualified staff, one can expect poor results. The services that the government supplies at the local level are the worst of all government services.

One can also expect to find that corruption is not an incidental phenomenon, but rather the very motor of local government. The expectation is borne out by the reports of the Central Accounting Authority.[16] The ruling clique uses these reports to criticize local government, thereby painting themselves as opposed to corruption. An intervention by Chief of the President's Bureau Zakariya Azmi in the People's Assembly illustrates this. Angrily waving a Central Accounting Authority report before the assembled MPs, he proclaimed, "Local government is a swamp corruption!"[17] To put his outcry into perspective, it is important to understand that his function in the parliamentary context is part of the assigning of roles. As an official close to the president,

Table 3.3. Distribution of Wages Among Sectors of Government Employees, 1996–97

Sector	Proportion of Total Government Employees	Proportion of Wages Received
Central Government Employees	28.3	37.1
Local Government Employees	61.5	48.0
Service Organizations	10.2	14.9
Totals	**100.0**	**100.0**

SOURCE: Abdel Khaleq Farouq, *The National Budget and Human Rights* (Cairo: Center for Legal Help and Human Rights, 2002).

his criticism of the government is meant to establish distance between the president and the ills of government, thereby projecting an image of a president untainted by those ills. As local government agencies are the most corrupt and inefficient, the distance between them and the president must be perceived as great. But there is another reason that central authorities can be so openly harsh in their criticism of local government: As the weakest link in the bureaucracy, it is the easiest target.

In addition to leaving local government prey to vehement criticism, the regime further curtailed its functions by means of more centralization and privatization. The greater the deterioration in local government agencies, the more appealing and justifiable the notion of centralization appears. The opposition to decentralization, which is widespread in central government institutions, gains impetus from the exposure of corruption and incompetence in local government, and central agencies end up assuming functions that presumably should be performed by local ones. Under the local government law, services such as health care, education, and social affairs should be handled at the local level. The logic is that the inhabitants and their local authorities are more aware of their own needs than are the central authorities in Cairo. However, the law simultaneously gave the president the power to designate services that should not be relegated to the local level. President Mubarak kept control not only over such strategic functions as security, defense, and foreign affairs in Cairo, but also over most other functions of government as well. The trend toward greater centralization can be seen in the creation of new institutions, such as the General Organization for Educational Buildings, established in the early 1990s. It was also evidenced in such centrally administered projects as the Mubarak Housing Project for Youth and the Suzanne Mubarak Housing Project, as well as in the growing influence of such national bodies as the General Waste Water Organization.

Local functions and services that were not taken over by central government were often handed to the private sector. In many governorates, garbage collection and street cleaning were privatized. This did not pass without some strong resistance by the inhabitants or by the garbage collectors formerly charged with these tasks. The privatization of garbage collection and recycling in Cairo and Giza is revealing. Both governorates signed contracts with foreign or jointly owned companies to replace the old garbage collectors. The latter rioted, staged attacks on the employees and vehicles of the new companies, or plundered the bins that the companies had placed in the street. The conflict between the old garbage collectors, the new companies, and the governorate authorities has not yet been resolved. Also, inhabitants of these governorates objected to the higher cost of the service. Some refused to pay the street-cleaning charge that suddenly appeared on their electricity bills. Others appealed to the courts, which eventually ruled against this method of collecting the fee.

As much as the central government curtailed the responsibilities of local government, there remained some tasks that local authorities still had to undertake. Here the central government's strategy was to give the governorates a certain amount of leeway to "do what they see fit" in order to obtain some revenues for themselves.

LOCAL GOVERNMENT STRATEGIES TO ACCOMMODATE DWINDLING ALLOCATIONS FROM CAIRO

To this point we have looked at the problem from the perspective of central government. It is now time to turn to the governorates. How did they manage to adjust to the decline in financial support from Cairo? For the most part, they relied on the special funds that the central government allowed them to create and operate. Unfortunately, we have no accurate information on these funds, and to my knowledge there is no agency in the country that possesses such information. However, according to an official in the Ministry of Finance, by 2003 there were some five thousand such funds; he did not reveal how much money they contained.[18]

The special funds are fed by several sources: profits from governorate-run enterprises, various local fees and taxes, and private donations. We have no data on the profits of governorate-run enterprises, but it is probable that the yield from this source of revenue must have declined due to privatization. Nevertheless, municipal fees and charges have been and remain the most important source of local revenue, judging by popular dissatisfaction surrounding their collection as manifested in the People's Assembly, where representatives have presented angry pleas on behalf of their constituents, and in the courts to which some citizens resorted in order to have the fees abolished.

In 1998 the Supreme Constitutional Court ruled that taxes levied by the governorates were unconstitutional.[19] It based its ruling on constitutional article 119, which states, "Taxes can only be introduced, modified and abolished through law."[20] The central authorities had to act quickly to contain the situation, because abolishing the special funds would paralyze local government. It decided that governorates could levy "fees" on the condition that they obtain the prior assent of the prime minister.[21]

The third source of revenue for the special funds—gifts—increased considerably in the 1990s. Many governorates turned to the business community to fund their projects, a tactic that flowed naturally from the central government's appeal to "the social role of businessmen." We return to this point in more detail in the discussion of the governorate of Alexandria.

The main advantage of the special funds from the point of view of local authorities is the flexibility they offer, contrary to the allocations from the national budget, which are heavily encumbered by rules and red tape. Unfortunately, the funds created more problems than they solved. From a legal standpoint, they are tainted by an unacceptably high level of corruption due to poor central government oversight. That shortcoming could have been avoided by means of mechanisms for supervision by the local community through its elected representatives. However, the lack of democracy obviates such a solution. Financially, the special funds constituted a flagrant breach of the principle of an all-embracing national budget covering all public revenues and outlays. It is not surprising, therefore, that the bastion of opposition to these funds would be the two ministries responsible for drawing up the national budget: the Ministry of Finance and the Ministry of Planning. We mentioned the former ministry's reservation above. The Ministry of Planning did more than grumble; it included its objections in its annual social and economic development plans. For example, its plan for 1997–98 specifically states that the national budget must cover all public revenues and expenditures, including the special funds.[22]

ALEXANDRIA AND QINA: TWO MODELS OF LOCAL DEVELOPMENT

All the stratagems and tactics the governorates tried could not protect them from fiscal debacle and deteriorating performance. However, some governorates managed to weather the crisis better than others. Alexandria and Qina have been billed as models of successful local development independent of the national budget. But the two models could not be more different.

Alexandria: The Partnership Between Government and the Business Community

Both the official press and the private press have hailed Alexandria as a paragon of success. In the space of a few years, its governor, General Abdel Salam Mahgoub, made the city gleam again after gradual decay that began in the 1950s. Before the 1952 revolution, Alexandria was Egypt's second capital. The government took up residence there in the summer in order to escape the heat of Cairo. Because of the diversity and vibrancy of its Egyptian and foreign communities, the "Pearl of the Mediterranean" was a cosmopolitan economic and cultural center. Naturally, it could not attain the full status of the capital, but it came in a close second. However, for various reasons, among which are the departure of most foreigners and Egyptian Jews following the tripartite invasion of 1956 and the heavy centralization of the Nasserist regime, Alexandria was reduced to an ordinary provincial city.

It is little wonder, therefore, that Mahgoub's modernization and beautification project was so warmly welcomed by the people of Alexandria. There is a story about this project that the media like to relate. Briefly, it goes that, upon assuming the governorship, Mahgoub was shocked to discover how little money was in the governorate coffers for fulfilling his great ambition to clean up and modernize the city. As he did not want to overburden the already strained national treasury, he decided to see what he could come up with on his own. His flash of inspiration was to form a partnership between the governorate and the business community whereby the latter would finance the development of the former.

So runs the official version. The part that the press leaves out, though it is common lore in Alexandria, is that when Mahgoub came to power, he was shocked to discover how much corruption there was in the governorate. Accordingly, his real flash of inspiration was that the business community, instead of handing its money to a bunch of corrupt bureaucrats, should deposit it directly into the Alexandrian treasury. In other words, rather than bribing governorate functionaries, businessmen could make gifts to the governorate.

Both versions of the story accord a major role to the business community. Unfortunately, we have no way to verify this, because the actual donations from that quarter remain a secret closely guarded by the governor and the governorate secretary-general. Some independent sources believe that the official version of the "Mahgoub miracle" grossly exaggerates the amount of contributions from businessmen.[23] However, it is highly likely that the governor managed to come up with a considerable amount of development funding from sources outside the governorate budget. As Figure 3.3 illustrates, Alexandria's share of the total outlays to the governorates for development in the national budget did not increase in the late 1990s, when Mahgoub took over the governorship.

As he set out on an ambitious project to reorganize and beautify Alexandria, Mahgoub signed a partnership protocol with the Alexandrian Chamber of Commerce. Under this agreement, the chamber's members would be given priority in carrying out the city's beautification projections. In exchange for depositing a portion of their profits into a special account for the development of the city of Alexandria, they would be rewarded with free land for the construction of commercial premises. In addition, the governor would use his good offices to intercede on their behalf with the central authorities in order to facilitate their business and commercial interests. Mahgoub, as a former chief intelligence officer, had the qualifications and connections to perform this role effectively. For example, he succeeded in persuading the Ministry of Finance to exempt the Alexandrian businessmen from certain taxes on the grounds that, through their contributions to the development of the city of Alexandria, they were easing the load on the national budget.[24] One could thus say that, with such tax exemptions, they were taking back with one hand what they were giving with the other. But the real winner was the governorate because the taxes that would have ordinarily gone to the national treasury in Cairo remained in Alexandria. The loser, of course, was the national treasury. It was a form of decentralization, albeit proceeding from the bottom up instead of from the top down.

Figure 3.3. Percentage of Alexandria's Share of Development Outlays to the Governorates, 1987–2008

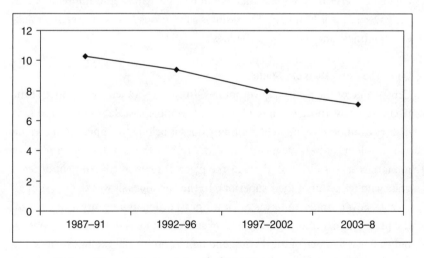

SOURCE: Ministry of Planning, *Five-Year Economic and Social Development Plan*, various issues.

Mahgoub's strategy of collaborating with the Alexandrian business community is consistent with his free market economic outlook. He also made his governorate a model of privatization. Alexandria was the first governorate to hand garbage collection and street cleaning to a private firm, the French-owned Onex Company. Cairo, Giza, and other governorates soon followed suit. The governorate also privatized the management of the majority of Alexandria's beaches.

In addition to material rewards, the governorate's partners in the business community were also rewarded morally through official recognition of their role. Recognition also was more direct—blatant, in fact. A businessman's or company's name would be etched onto a plaque affixed to the edifice he sponsored, for which reason Alexandria today features a plethora of fountains and bus stops sporting the names of merchants and entrepreneurs. It is a form of privatization of the public space, or shrinking of the symbolic space of public ownership: Where one would expect to see names that betoken the community or the communal bond, one now finds names of individuals. On top of this, there was the not-infrequent aesthetic problem; leaving urban beautification to the judgment of businessmen offers no guarantee of the highest artistic standards.

Perhaps one of the harshest criticisms leveled against Alexandria's beautification experience falls under the heading of social justice. A great deal of attention homed in on "mirrors," which in bureaucratese refer to the facelifts applied to certain focal areas that would best give an overall impression that the governorate is beautiful. The result is a luxurious façade concealing thickets of ugliness and pits of wretchedness.

Qina: The "Just Despot" Model

Qina is one of the poorest governorates. In 1998 it ranked twenty-first of the twenty-six governorates on the human development scale.[25] Qina has a long history of underdevelopment. Not only does it belong to Upper Egypt, which as a whole has always lagged behind the rest of the country, but under the monarchy it was also notorious as the place of exile of government bureaucrats who fell afoul of their superiors. In the late 1990s, it was the worst of all Egypt's governorates in terms of cleanliness, order, and beauty. But by 2001, the press was extolling it as a model of successful local development. Within only a few years, one of the dirtiest and ugliest provincial capitals turned into the cleanest, prettiest, and most orderly city in the country. It would be no exaggeration to say that the city of Qina rivals the cleanest cities in Europe, although naturally it pales next to them in wealth and beauty. The transformation clearly merits closer inspection.

The miracle of Qina was the work of Adel Labib, who took over the governorship in 1999. Originally a general in the police force, Labib had served as security director in Alexandria in the mid-1990s and had thus observed first-hand the "miracle" performed there by Governor Mahgoub. This encouraged him to repeat the performance in Qina; according to the official version of the story, his success was the product of his ability to mobilize resources locally without having to tap the coffers of the central government. According to the government-owned daily *Al-Akhbar* on 2 June 2002, he "transformed Qina into a European city without asking for a single extra piaster from the national budget." The official version relates that, upon taking office, General Labib managed to secure the prime minister's approval for levying various local fees. He also introduced high penalties for traffic violations and other such offences, raising some fines to as much as E£500. With such revenues, the governor modernized the city of Qina.

When I arrived in the office of General Adel Labib to interview him on the successful experience of Qina, his assistants immediately handed me a long list of the local fees charged by the governorate. This in itself took me by surprise. Normally, authorities in Egypt are secretive about the charges they levy for fear of incurring the wrath of the press and the people. At least my expectations were not shaken when I asked how much those fees yielded. The governorate secretary refused to disclose any figures on the revenues in the special funds, which remain heavily shrouded in mystery. I later learned that detailed information on these funds is available to no one other than the governor and the governorate secretary; they are so highly confidential that even the governorate's finance department knows almost nothing about them. So, as was the case with the donations from the business community in Alexandria, one can only guess at the extent to which local fees and taxes contributed to the Qina urban development project. However, one certain indicator raises some questions around the official line that the progress was achieved without "a single extra piaster from the national budget."

Development outlays from the central government reach the governorates through two different routes. The first is directly from the national treasury to the governorate treasury, which is overseen by the governor. The second is from central agencies in Cairo to their branches in the governorate. For example, the

Qina judiciary receives its funds from the Ministry of Justice in Cairo. Table 3.4 lists the transfers to Qina via the first route over a period of six years. In order to give a clearer idea of the rate of the flow, we compared them to the allocations to Assiout, a governorate with a similar population size (Assiout is home to 4.7 percent of the population of Egypt, compared to 4.1 percent in Qina). As can be seen, the flow of money into Qina from the national budget increased slightly at the end of the 1990s with the arrival of General Adel Labib.

We find the same trend in the allocations to the governorate departments of education, health, and social service, known collectively as the service directorates. In Table 3.5, we have also given the corresponding figures for Assiout. It is useful to bear in mind that Assiout, as the capital of Upper Egypt, has traditionally claimed a larger share of budgetary resources.

Still, these allocations to Qina, even through they increased somewhat, could not have made much of an impact. They do not exceed a few dozen millions at best. However, the most important funds come through the second route, the central government agencies to their branches in the governorates. These account for about 90 percent of the development outlays that reach a governorate. Table 3.6 shows that whereas Assiout received a greater share of such outlays until the end of the 1990s, from 1999 onwards Qina surpassed Assiout.

One must conclude that, even if Qina managed to augment its resources autonomously from its own inhabitants in the Labib era, it definitely saw a rise in outlays from Cairo. So why this emphasis on the part played by locally

Table 3.4. Development Outlays to Qina and Assiout, 1997–2004, in E£ Million

Year	Qina	Assiout
1997–98	62.6	n/a
1998–99	58.1	n/a
1999–2000	69.4	43.7
2000–2001	90	91.2
2001–2	72.2	68
2003–4	51.7	117

SOURCE: Governorate of Qina, *Closing Account of the Qina Governorate Budget*, various issues; Governorate of Assiout, *Closing Account of the Assiout Governorate Budget*, various issues.

Table 3.5. Outlays to the Service Directorates of Qina and Assiout, 1997–2004, in E£ Million

Year	Qina	Assiout
1997–98	12.8	n/a
1998–99	13.9	n/a
1999–2000	15.7	13.4
2000–2001	18.2	11
2001–2	17.8	12.6
2003–4	13.2	6

SOURCE: Governorate of Qina, *Closing Account of the Qina Governorate Budget*, various issues; Governorate of Assiout, *Closing Account of the Assiout Governorate Budget*, various issues.

levied fees in Qina's development to the exclusion of financing coming from the central authorities? To understand, we must set it in the context of the official rhetoric of the time, which stressed the role of autonomous efforts in local development. The government was actively encouraging governorates to develop their own sources of revenue in order to compensate for the shortage in the outlays from the national budget. For example, the 1997–98 development plan speaks of the need to promote the participation of local communities in the development process.[26] In profiling the role of autonomous efforts in the transformation of Qina, the governor was effectively advertising this experience as a practical embodiment of the wisdom of government policy. This is a common practice in the Egyptian regime. Another example is to be found in former Minister of Education Hussein Kamel Bahaa el-Din's statements that tirelessly cited the emphasis that President Mubarak placed on the importance of education to economic development. One major objective of such statements is to obtain a higher allocation in the national budget. When Labib markets the Qina model as consistent with government policy, he is signaling that it merits the support of the central government. The tactic paid off. The president instructed the ministries to meet the needs of the governor of Qina.[27] In addition, Mubarak visited the governorate in 2003 in a demonstration of the highest moral and symbolic support he could give the governor.

There is another no less important reason that Labib played up local revenues as the source of development financing. He wanted to divert attention from the influx of money from the central authorities, thereby protecting

Table 3.6. Total Public Outlays to Qina and
Assiout, 1992–2003, in E£ Billion

Year	Qina	Assiout
1992–97	0.92	2.09
1998–99	0.27	0.34
1999–2000	2.50	2.23
2000–2001	3.19	1.70
2001–2	2.90	2.00
2002–3	1.20	1.17

SOURCE: Ministry of Planning, *Economic and Social Development Plan*, various issues.

himself and Qina from the envy of other governorates that were fighting over
the limited resources of the national treasury.

Alexandria and Qina: Two Different Models of Revenue Generation

Because the Alexandria "miracle" came first and General Labib had served as
the governorate's chief of security at the time and was a close associate of
Mahgoub, it is generally thought that the Qina "miracle" was only a repeat of
the Alexandrian one. But Labib has repeatedly stressed that his governorate
has never accepted donations from businessmen because that would have restricted his independence. The governor was correct. The Qina experience
was totally different than Alexandria's. It was founded on a completely different means of generating revenues, which stems not only from the difference
between the personalities of Labib and Mahgoub, but also from the different
socioeconomic makeup of the two governorates.

Alexandria is the second most populous and second wealthiest city in
Egypt, after Cairo. It is the largest producer of petrochemicals, the most important modern industry in Egypt since the wane of the textile industry.
Qina, by contrast, is one of the poorest governorates, as noted above. Apart
from the sugar refineries in Nagaa Hamadi, Qina has no major industries.
The two governorates also differ demographically. Whereas Alexandria has a
relatively sophisticated entrepreneurial class, no such class exists in Qina,
which only has some wealthy families here and there. Naturally, a partnership
between the governorate and the business community could not have existed
in Qina.

On the other hand, the absence of an entrepreneurial class alters the relationship between the local authorities and the people in a governorate. The governor of Qina could be sterner and tougher with the inhabitants without encountering considerable risks. He could do what a governor of Alexandria could not: He could use the stick. While I was in the governor's office conducting my interview, General Labib took time to have words with a building contractor engaged to perform public works for the governorate. The governor angrily rebuked the contractor and accused him of cheating. According to sources in Qina, the governor is notorious for saying "I'm going to have you arrested" to people he regards as lazy or otherwise not up to scratch in their jobs.

Perhaps the best term for the Qina experience is the "just despot" model. The governor uses tough autocratic means to get what he wants, but what he wants is a form of justice and public order. The governor of Alexandria could never have attempted to achieve his objectives in the same manner. It is inconceivable that he would be so highhanded and imperious toward the sophisticated business community and powerful elites of Alexandria. Were Mahgoub to have imposed municipal fees on the people of Alexandria the way that Labib did in Qina, he would have encountered formidable resistance. Both governors suited their resourcefulness to their environment. Mahgoub had to use a more diplomatic approach, and his was to solicit donations beneath the sobriquet of a partnership. Labib did not have such wealth to draw on, but he did have the luxury of decreeing and enforcing local taxation.

Just as the models differed in method, so too they differed in results. Alexandria today bears the stamp of the business community. Squares and public fountains carry the names of prominent businessmen, and the beaches have been privatized. In Qina, the Nile Corniche is still public property in substance and in name.

CONCLUSION

The central government's fiscal straits and its declining ability to finance local government agencies coincided with a growing emphasis on decentralization as a means of improving the performance of the functions of the state by enabling local agencies to be more responsive to the needs of the local populace. However, decentralization requires a restructuring of the relationship between the central government and local government agencies so as to permit greater autonomy of the latter. No such restructuring took place in Egypt. The constitutional and legal framework regulating the relationships between the various levels of government remains largely unchanged. One of the characteristic traits of the Mubarak era is institutional inertia. Therefore, decentralization fell short of giving governorates the right to levy local taxes, instead conferring upon them the right to create special funds fed by certain municipal charges or private donations from businessmen.

There is a virtually unanimous consensus in the political science literature that decentralization has a major role to play in improving public services. To do the Egyptian ruling elite justice, they are aware of this, as testified by the relative autonomy given to local authorities at the outset of the Sadat and Mubarak eras. But in both cases, the regime quickly repented and recentralized. Authoritarian regimes find it very difficult to release their grip. In Egypt's case, where financial straits propelled the government strongly toward decentralization, but where the regime could not tolerate the consequences of true decentralization, the solution was the special funds. The autonomy thus granted was quasi-official, certainly not constitutionally or legally codified, and therefore easily retractable. In addition, this autonomy is exorbitantly costly, first because it flies in the face of one of the most important fiscal principles of the state, the all-embracing unified budget, and second because it is necessarily associated with a high level of corruption. If anything, recent developments in the relationship between the central authorities and the local government speak not of decentralization but of fragmentation.

4 FROM THE RENTIER TO THE PREDATORY STATE
Transformations in the Mechanisms for Generating Public Revenues and Their Political Consequences

PREVIOUS CHAPTERS HAVE DISCUSSED ways in which the regime tried to adjust to the decline in rentier revenues. But there is another side to the coin: the regime's attempts to develop other sources of revenue. To this end, it turned its sights to the Egyptian people and slowly made the transition from a rentier state to a predatory one.[1] A predatory state is a state that sets income generation above all other considerations, one that will do anything to rake in more money from society regardless of whether that necessitates unconstitutional means and even if it wreaks havoc on the economy.

This chapter focuses on the mechanisms the Egyptian regime used to augment its revenues. These mechanisms were the inflation tax, foreign and domestic loans, the remittances tax, the general sales tax, appeals to capitalist "donations" and business community's "social responsibility," the masked export tax, regulation of the unregulated sectors, income tax reform, and real estate tax reform. The order in which the regime resorted to these methods reveals two chief factors that have governed its decisions on how to augment its revenues: first the prospective political costs, and second the administrative or transaction costs.

The regime has always been inclined to exhaust the least politically costly routes first. Political costs are the degree of resistance the regime would risk encountering from society in general, and in particular from those sectors of society it would like to target as a source for increasing its income. As this chapter shows, the regime's ability to persuade society of the need to accept taxation has been limited. This stems not only from the regime's lack of legitimacy but also from the absence of political institutions that are truly representative of society. When, for example, an authoritarian regime so tightens its grip on trade federations that are supposedly meant to represent the interests of the business community and converts them into instruments for controlling that community, the federations lose their mediating capacity, thereby precluding opportunities to effectively negotiate solutions to trade concerns.

The regime has also always preferred to exhaust the least administratively costly routes first, which is to say that it has shirked creating and running a sufficiently strong and effective bureaucracy to deal with the generation and management of financial resources from the public. Most indicative of this tendency is its readiness to coin money, which does not require a sophisticated administration. The inclination is further betrayed by its long procrastination of the task of income tax reform, which does require a sophisticated bureaucracy with the administrative know-how and expertise needed to gather and process information on the economic activities of various sectors of society, not to mention a minimal level of integrity in the application and enforcement of the law.

THE INFLATION TAX: EASY MONEY WITH DIRE ECONOMIC REPERCUSSIONS

In general, taxes are a way to make money flow from the public into the national treasury. In this sense, inflation can be regarded as a tax. When a government prints money in order to make up for its limited cash resources, it reduces the purchasing power of the national currency. Thereby, it effectively takes money out of people's pockets. From the perspective of any regime, the inflation tax has two great advantages, the first being the relative secrecy that surrounds it. Unlike other taxes that are imposed by the Ministry of Finance and that have to be made public knowledge, this tax is levied by the central bank without informing the public. Also, whereas other taxes require a parliamentary bill, all it takes to print new currency is a decision by the central bank's board of directors. Of course, sudden price spikes betray the issuance of new banknotes, but here the government has room for deniability: It can always blame inflation on the rising prices of imported goods, or it can lash out at greedy merchants. The latter is one of the regime's favorite ploys, as shown by the 2003 campaign against merchants in the official press cited by *Al-Ahram* newspaper on 30 September 2003, which culminated in the declaration by the heads of the various chambers of commerce (which are presumed to represent business interests, but are effectively controlled by the regime) of their intent to publish a blacklist of merchants who raise their prices.

The second advantage of the inflation tax is its random nondiscriminatory nature. It hits everyone—it "spreads the blood among the tribes," as the Arabic proverb has it. True, it hits some sectors of society harder than others. Wage workers feel the crunch more than businessmen and practitioners of the liberal professions. Also, some sectors are better poised to pass the strains on to other parts of society. Merchants, for example, can raise their prices to compensate for the shrinking purchasing power of their money. In theory, however, minting new money does not single out a particular group, which diffuses the possibility of resistance. Thus, with the inflation tax, the government can extract money from society and then let the various sectors of society sort out the consequences of inflation among themselves. Generally, the popular anger will home in on merchants who raised their prices to reflect the lower value of the currency rather than on the regime that actually lowered the value.

In the second half of the 1980s, the Egyptian regime adopted an energetic policy of turning to the mint. According to a World Bank study, Egypt was one of the third world governments that most frequently did so.[2] Table 4.1 shows that the revenues the Egyptian government obtained by this means exceeded those of all other countries studied in 1987.

Table 4.1. Inflation Tax Revenues as a Percentage of GDP in Selected Countries, 1987

Country	Inflation Tax as Percentage of GDP
Argentina	4.0
Côte d'Ivoire	0.5
Egypt	11.7
Ghana	2.0
Mexico	3.7
Nigeria	0.9
Peru	4.8
Philippines	0.6
Turkey	2.8
Zaire	4.2

SOURCE: Hinh Dinh and Giugale Marcelo, *Inflation Tax and Deficit Financing in Egypt*. Working Paper No. 668 (Washington, DC: World Bank, 1991), p. 13.

Because the inflation tax is a surreptitious sleight of hand, its political costs are low in the short term, when compared to the costs of officially introducing taxes. However, overuse of this method can wreak havoc on the economic system. Vladimir Lenin, leader of the communist revolution in Russia, is reported to have said that the most effective way to destroy the capitalist order is to destroy the currency on which it is based.[3] John Maynard Keynes expressed the same idea more fully:

> By a continuing process of inflation, governments can confiscate, secretly and unobserved, an important part of the wealth of their citizens. By this method they not only confiscate, but they confiscate arbitrarily; and, while the process impoverishes many, it actually enriches some. . . . As the inflation proceeds and the real value of the currency fluctuates wildly from month to month, all permanent relations between debtors and creditors, which form the ultimate foundation of capitalism, become so utterly disordered as to be almost meaningless; and the process of wealth-getting degenerates into a gamble and a lottery.[4]

The situation in Egypt has not yet reached the gambling phase that Keynes warns of. Egypt did not experience hyperinflation in the 1980s. However, an inflation rate of over 20 percent distorted the fundamental variables of the economy. The interest rate (about 10 percent) became a negative rate, which encouraged consumption and discouraged saving. The collapse of their currency also drove Egyptians to real estate speculation, precipitating an expanding bubble in real estate prices. Meanwhile, many who had the means changed their savings into hard currency, a sensible choice for the individual, but one that generated an unprecedented wave of dollarization.

Although, as noted above, the political costs of the inflation tax were low in the short run, the effects ultimately hit the civil servants themselves. In other words, the measure that was instituted to finance government bureaucracy ricocheted against that bureaucracy. As inflation ate away at civil servants' salaries, the mid- and long-range political costs of the inflation tax grew increasingly serious. Fortunately, the need for the government to commit itself to a program for economic reform in 1990 put an end to the spiral. Now the government had to stop financing its budgetary deficit by minting new currency and turn to more solid sources, such as government bonds and certificates. The shift is reflected in decreasing inflation rates in the 1990s, as illustrated in Figure 4.1.

Figure 4.1. Inflation Rate After Economic Reform, 1990–2007

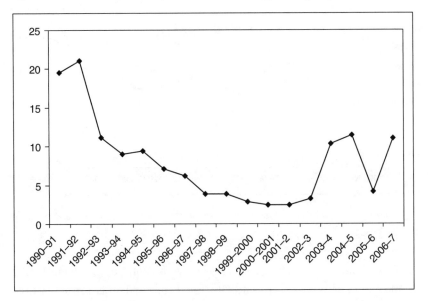

SOURCE: Ministry of Finance, *The Financial Monthly*, various issues.

The reduction in inflation rates in the 1990s gave wage earners a much needed respite. However, with the turn of the millennium, the rates started to climb again, as shown in Figure 4.1, and independent sources suggest that the increase was larger than that supplied by the Ministry of Economy.[5] Explanations of the causes of inflation in Egypt in recent years vary, but the inflation tax is likely to have played a major role. The trend toward budgetary deficit ratios nearly as high as they were in the 1980s would have made recourse to the mint too difficult to resist. Figure 4.2 depicts the increase in the issuing of new currency in recent years with respect to GDP.

THE DWINDLING ROLE OF FOREIGN LOANS
IN FINANCING THE STATE

Like the inflation tax, foreign loans also have a low short-term political cost because they spare the regime the tensions that arise from attempts to levy revenues at home. The ruling clique in Egypt relied heavily on this mechanism in the 1980s, but in the following decade it increasingly began to turn to domestic loans.

Figure 4.2. Money Supply as a Percentage of GDP, 1995–2003

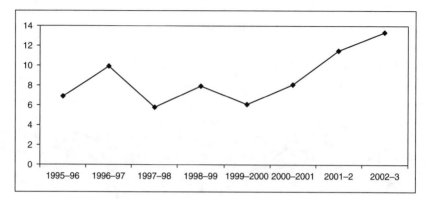

SOURCE: Computed by the author from Ministry of Finance, *The Financial Monthly*, various issues.

Egypt's foreign loans have been largely governmental, unlike in most third world countries, which borrow heavily from banks and other private institutions. As a result, Egypt has had considerably lower debt charges than other third world countries. When governments loan money to other governments, they do so primarily for political or indirect economic considerations, not in order to profit on the interest. It is largely due to Egypt's strategic importance that this option was more available to it than to many other countries. Tangible evidence of this can be seen in the fact that foreign government loans to Egypt only began to taper off in 1985, whereas the reduction began to hit other countries with the outbreak of the debt crisis in the international banking system in 1982.[6] Throughout the 1980s, many industrialized countries kept their coffers open for Egypt, as indicated by Egypt's rapidly growing foreign debt during that period (see Figure 4.3).

Despite its strategic importance and the preferential treatment it received, Egypt was not spared by the deteriorating loan conditions for third world countries. The crisis that struck the international banking system when several developing countries defaulted on their loans forced banks to take extra precautions. The average interest rate on loans to third world governments climbed from 0.97 percent between 1974 and 1979 and to 5.85 percent between 1980 and 1989.[7]

With increasingly disadvantageous lending conditions in the latter half of the 1980s came higher debt servicing costs, which nearly doubled, increasing

Figure 4.3. Egypt's External Debt in Billion $US, 1982–90

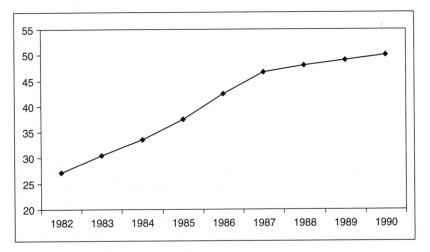

SOURCE: IMP, *International Financial Statistics*, various issues.

from 24 percent of exports in goods and services in 1980–81 to 46 percent in 1989–90. By 1986, Egypt's outstanding installment and interest payments on its loans had reached $9 billion. That year, Egypt defaulted. In May of the following year, it was forced to sign a debt rescheduling agreement with the Paris Club, in accordance with which debt service payments were halved, from $4.7 billion in 1986 to $2.2 billion in 1987. The relief was temporary. Before long, budgetary strains returned, and in 1990 Egypt defaulted again. That year, its outstanding payments totaled $11.4 billion.[8]

As mentioned in Chapter 1, the Iraqi invasion of Kuwait came to Egypt's rescue, and creditor countries wrote off half of Egypt's debt. In this Egypt fared much better than all other third world countries, which have had no choice but to pay off most of their debts. Egypt has been surpassed in this regard only by the Iraqi regime that the United States created following its invasion of that country, which in November 2004 was exempted from debts to the tune of $100 billion.

Nevertheless, the Egyptian regime did not weather its debt crisis without some political costs. Since the mid 1980s, Egypt's fiscal policy has not been a purely domestic issue. Foreign governments and international financial institutions began to have a growing say in shaping this policy, a development that culminated in 1990 when the Egyptian government was forced to sign

Figure 4.4. Egypt's External Debt in Billion $US, 1999–2007

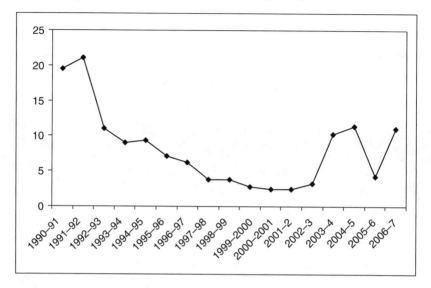

SOURCE: Ministry of Economy, *Monthly Economic Review*, various issues; Ministry of Finance, *The Financial Monthly*, various issues.

economic reform agreements with international agencies like the World Bank and the IMF. This explains why Egypt in the 1990s stopped accumulating the volume of foreign debts it had racked up in the previous decade. The president had had to issue strict instructions to all government institutions to keep their borrowing from abroad to an absolute minimum and not to take out a loan unless they had the resources to pay it back. As it transpired, Egypt would ultimately have little choice but to cease its heavy dependence on foreign loans. Egypt's strategic importance declined due to major changes in the international order following the end of the cold war. This, together with the extra precautions on granting loans taken by governments and financial institutions in the wake of the 1982 banking crisis and Egypt's agreement with the IMF in 1990, explains why Egypt's level of foreign debt has remained constant since the outset of the 1990s, as Figure 4.4 illustrates.

INCREASING DOMESTIC DEBT AND THE GOVERNMENT'S GROWING ACCOUNTABILITY TO SOCIETY

During the 1990s, the government's expenditures continued to exceed its income, and it still had to borrow. What is unique about this period, though, is that the government turned to local instead of foreign sources to finance its

Figure 4.5. Egypt's Domestic Debt in Billion E£, 1993–2009

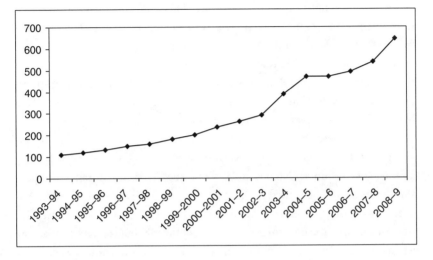

SOURCE: Ministry of Economy, *Monthly Economic Review*, various issues; Ministry of Finance, *The Financial Monthly*, various issues.

deficit. Figure 4.5 depicts the rapid and considerable rise in the domestic public debt since the early 1990s.

The absolute value of the domestic debt does not fully convey the nature of the problem, which becomes more apparent when we take two factors into account. The first is the ratio of the debt to the GDP, which climbed to approximately 67.4 percent by 2009.[9] The government says that this ratio is still within the safety range, but this claim may be resting on thin ice. The Maastricht Agreement, for example, states that the ratio of debt to GDP of European Union members should not exceed 60 percent. EU economists clearly felt that a ratio over this figure was worrisome. There is no clear reason why Egypt should be able to exceed the 60 percent threshold without courting danger.

To what institutions did the regime turn for loans? The government's largest creditor is the National Investment Bank, which furnished more than half the loans. The primary purpose of the National Investment Bank, founded in accordance with law 119 of 1980, is to finance government-sponsored projects. It simultaneously functions as a bank for public sector companies, to which it also furnishes loans according to the criteria of economic soundness. The bank controls vast resources. Its assets chiefly come from insurance and pension funds, which accounted for two-thirds of the bank's assets at the end of the 1990s.[10] Why should insurance and pension funds lend money to the state? The answer is simple: They have no choice. They are controlled and administered by the Ministry for Social Affairs, which is required by law to deposit the money for these funds in the National Investment Bank.[11]

It would appear, then, that the people are lending money to the state via the National Investment Bank. Insurance and pension funds are private property; they are deductions from people's income that will presumably be paid back to them in the event of retirement or disability. In fact, it would be more appropriate to describe the state's access to their retirement and pension funds as a partial tax rather than as a loan, because it lacks the free and voluntary approval of the donors. No one asked them whether their insurance and pension funds should be loaned to the state. They have no say in the matter. Another reason that these loans have more in common with a tax is the negative interest rate that the government was paying throughout the 1980s. At a time when the inflation rate was more than 20 percent, the government was paying 6 percent interest.[12] In other words, the government was appropriating a portion of the funds. This situation changed in the 1990s, when the decline of the inflation rate to below 10 percent as of 1993–94, in conjunction with the rise in the interest rate on the insurance and pension funds to about 11 percent, meant that the funds were receiving real interest.[13]

The government had little choice but to stop forcing the funds to grant subsidized loans. In the 1990s, the funds were showing a disturbingly growing deficit that the government had to cover in the form of allocations from the national budget. Figure 4.6 illustrates the steadily rising trajectory of these allocations.

What a deficit in the insurance and pension funds means in practical terms is that less money is coming into the funds from people's salaries than is being paid out to pensioners. This imbalance was in large measure due to the privilege that the government had enjoyed for so many years of using the money in the funds at a negative interest rate and then a very low interest rate.

Another problem is that the administration of the funds is governed by political logic. The idea of insurance and pension funds is based on the principle that the payments people make into them are a form of savings that they draw upon at retirement or incapacitation. Yet, many people who have paid nothing into the funds draw pensions. The reason is that the regime uses the funds to diffuse the social and political tensions arising from widespread poverty. In fact, some rulers have used them to build their popularity. Sadat led

Figure 4.6. Allocation of the Budget to the Insurance and Pension Funds as a Percentage of Public Expenditures, 1995–2004

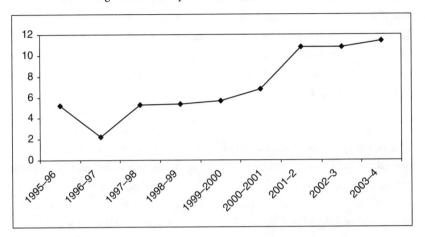

SOURCE: Computed by the author from Ministry of Finance, *Closing Account of the Budget*, 1995–96– 2001–2, and the National Budget, 2003–4.

the way when he decided to grant a number of poor families the so-called Sadat Pension Fund. A couple of decades later, Mubarak followed suit, allocating E£500 million to the Mubarak Pension Fund in 2000.[14] There is nothing wrong, in principle, with granting pensions to the poor, disabled, and unemployed who have never paid into social insurance funds, and the Ministry of Social Solidarity continues to do just that. The problem is that these disbursals are coming not from the government's own resources but from the payments of wage earners, which is to say from private pockets. In general, wage earners' incomes decrease drastically after retirement. That is when all bonuses, allowances, tips, and other variable income that, in Egypt today, are much more important than the basic wage come to an end. In other words, pensioners tend to join the ranks of the poor, which means that the government's pensions to the poor who have never contributed to social insurance funds is coming from the pockets of another segment of the poor.

Clearly, the regime had to find a solution to the potentially explosive problem of the deficit in insurance and pension funds. In November 2003, former Prime Minister Atef Ebeid told *Al-Ahram*, as cited in the 4 March 2004 issue, that the Council of Ministers was studying a proposal from the Ministry of Finance to give shares in public sector companies to the funds in exchange for the government's debt to the funds. The idea, which had been voiced several times prior to the prime minister's statement, aroused considerable anxiety, which prompted the People's Assembly to ask the prime minister for clarification. Ebeid allayed the mounting concerns, assuring his audience, as cited in *Al-Ahram* on 15 March 2004, that the funds were perfectly safe and the government was still the chief guarantor of pensions. That is, even if the funds went bankrupt, the government would issue payments to pensioners out of the national budget.

The unspoken message was that the government was still looking for a way to disengage itself from the pension funds and thereby achieve its basic goal of reducing the domestic public debt. But disengagement would be dangerous for the funds if it meant converting funds into shares in unprofitable public companies. Turning pension funds into stockholders is also problematic in another way. The funds are administered by the Ministry of Social Solidarity, which not only lacks experience in the private investment domain but also, as a public institution by definition, would not be able to refuse a government directive to invest in areas of questionable profitability. Indeed, this occurred in the 1990s, when the government believed that having the investment funds play the stock market would stimulate the market. The investment funds bought a billion and a half Egyptian pounds worth of shares and suffered drastic losses when the stock market collapsed. In May 2010, the former minister of social affairs revealed that she had been pressured by Kamal al-Ganzouri, then prime minister, and Youssef Botros Ghali, then the minister of economy, to invest some of the insurance fund money in the stock market in 1998.[15]

The insurance and pension funds are still controlled and administered by the Ministry of Social Solidarity, which is to say by a government agency. Increasingly, however, the management of these funds must presumably respond to the laws of the market. The government began to wash its hands of the funds after having drained them of their value and turned them into a burden. However, the process of freeing the funds from the government grip could lead to a form of contractual relationship between the government and the funds whereby the government could continue to borrow from them but would now have to pay a positive interest rate and, additionally, obtain approval from representatives of the funds' recipients.

Treasury bonds and certificates are the government's second source of domestic loans. Most of the bonds and certificates that the government issues are purchased by the national banks. The government still controls a significant share of the banking system in Egypt. In 2003, public sector banks (including the National Investment Bank) held approximately 77.8 percent of all bank deposits in the country.[16] When public sector banks decide to buy treasury bonds and certificates, their decision emanates in part from the fact that they are state-owned enterprises. We thus have another situation in which the state is borrowing money from private parties via another public agency (the national banks). Here, however, the loans have more of a contractual nature than is the case for the insurance and pension funds, because public banks retain a margin of freedom in deciding whether to purchase treasury bonds and certificates, whereas the insurance and pension funds had no choice but to hand over their assets to the National Investment Bank.

Theoretically, the government's growing indebtedness to the public should transform the nature of the relationship between the two. If private agencies are to grant loans to the government, they will inevitably want guarantees that they will get their money back at the highest possible interest rate. The government, in turn, should be able to convince the public that it is financially sound and capable of paying back the loans. Such a transformation would naturally heighten public interest (concern) in fiscal policy. Some political economists regard the extent to which private agencies are willing to lend money to the government a barometer of confidence in the fiscal performance of the government as well as in the regime and its stability.[17] That is, the greater the government's debt to the public, the more the public presses for government accountability. As things stand in Egypt, this type of transformation has yet to take hold. The state, as noted, still controls the banking sector. Still, the decreasing role of compulsory loans from the insurance and pension funds and the increasing role of bank loans to the government may constitute a step forward in the evolution of contractual relations between the state and society.

THE GENERAL SALES TAX: A MAJOR SOURCE OF REVENUE SINCE 1991

As explained in Chapter 1, fiscal reform formed the backbone of the economic reform protocol that the Egyptian government signed with the World Bank in 1990. One of the major aims of the program was to rein in the budget deficit by reducing expenditures and increasing revenues. The primary means to accomplish the latter was the general sales tax. Egypt was the seventy-sixth nation to implement this type of tax, which many countries of the industrialized and developing worlds had begun to introduce in the 1970s and 1980s.[18] The sweeping spread of this tax reflected the rapidly growing hold of neoclassical economic thought on the fiscal and economic policies of governments and international financial institutions. Indirect taxation on goods and services is not welcomed by Keynesian and leftist economists because it hits both the poor and the rich indiscriminately.

In July 1990, *Al-Ahram* announced that the prime minister was studying the possibility of introducing a general sales tax. The tax was to be introduced in two stages, the first comprising manufacturers and importers and to be put into effect immediately, the second covering retailers and to be implemented later. The prime minister's announcement did not create much of an immediate stir apart from a few apprehensive newspaper reports and commentaries. But by the end of the summer holidays, more powerful reactions began to emerge from both corporatist and independent business organizations. The 12 April 1991 edition of *Al-Ahram* reported that the chairman of the Federation of Egyptian Chambers of Commerce declared his opposition to the sales tax on the grounds that it would hamper economic activity. The importers' opposition was voiced by the head of their branch in the General Federation of Chambers of Commerce. Then the 3 May 1991 issue of *Al-Mussawir* magazine cited an objection by the chairman of the Association of Egyptian Businessmen that imposing such a tax so rapidly without phasing it in would trigger inflation and a decline in sales. Even the economic committee of the ruling National Democratic Party (NDP) asked the government to reconsider the tax, according to *Al-Ahram* on 12 April 1991.

The opposition did not succeed in putting a halt to the tax. In April 1991, it was approved by the People's Assembly—not surprising, dominated as the assembly is by the governing elite via the ruling NDP, whose parliamentary deputies have to vote the government line whatever their personal opinions are. The general sales tax was signed by the president and put into effect for the 1991–92 fiscal year. Since then, this tax has been one of the chief sources of national income. Its share of the total government revenues increased from 13.1 percent in the year it went into effect to 14.4 percent in 1996–96, to 16.7 percent in 2000–2001,[19] and to 23 percent in 2007–8.[20]

The government had originally planned to implement the next phase, covering retailers, in 1993, but postponed doing so several times. That the government was aware of how difficult it would be to put phase two into effect was evidenced by the more than the seven-year interval between the time it announced its intention and the actual implementation. It was also apparent in the resources the government had to mobilize. A host of Ministry of Finance officials, including the minister himself, toured the length and breadth of the country in order to persuade merchants of the necessity of the tax.

From the perspective of political officials, indirect taxes on goods and services are easier to impose than are direct taxes on income. Indirect taxes, such as the sales tax, are indiscriminate. They do not target a specific group, unlike income taxes. In fact, it is not businessmen or merchants who ultimately bear the brunt of the sales tax. The consumer pays this tax, and businessmen and merchants simply serve as the government's tax collectors.

Phase two of the general sales tax finally went into effect in April 2001 and encountered stiffer resistance from retailers than it had from businessmen prior to the implementation of the first phase. Protest took many forms, but the most curious and most powerful was the "Moski Uprising." Merchants in that famous popular market area in Old Cairo simply decided one day to shut their stores and sit outside them or, in some cases, to join protest marches against the tax. The riot police were brought in to disperse the demonstrators and to intimidate the merchants into reopening their shops. Although the strike was aborted with relative ease, this by no means diminishes its significance. To my knowledge, it was the first organized protest demonstration against a tax in modern Egyptian history. There were other forms of resistance to taxes, but they were primarily negative and indirect, such as tax fraud, falsifying information, and paying bribes.

One can not help but to be struck by how much more difficult it was for the regime to implement the second phase of the sales tax than to implement the first phase. The first essentially targeted manufacturers and importers, who are inherently more powerful and have more clout with the regime than the retailers. So why did the resistance of the weaker sector cause the regime a greater headache than that of the stronger one? Numerous factors come into play. First, the target group of phase two was far larger. Merchants number in the millions, whereas importers and manufacturers only number in the thousands. Second, the state has more information and retains a tighter grip on the activities of importers and manufacturers than it does on the retailers. Then there was the difference between the economic and political context in 1991, when phase one was applied, and the economic and political context in 2001 at the time of implementation of phase two. In 1991, the Egyptian government had just signed an agreement with international agencies to implement an economic reform program. The first phase of the sales tax was one of the main pillars of that program, the aim of which was to increase state revenues and reduce the budget deficit. Also, the tax was presented as part of a bundle of reforms that ultimately sought to establish free market mechanisms in the Egyptian economy, which was presumably in the interests of businessmen. Such factors would have facilitated the acceptance of the sales tax in the business community.

Ten years later, the political and economic climate was very hazy. In 1996, the five-year economic reform program had come to an end without the government's having decided where to go from there. There was no alternative program, and there were no clear goals for political and economic policies to accomplish. Moreover, toward the end of the 1990s, the Egyptian economy fell into a long period of recession, and merchants were one of the foremost segments of the population to feel it. The recession was reflected in increased bankruptcy declaration rates, which are regularly recorded by the General Federation of Chambers of Commerce.[21] The end of the 1990s also saw the arrival of several major foreign retail firms, such as Sainsburys, Metro, and Carrefour, which quickly seized a large share of the market due to their competitive prices. The trend towards concentration, whereby a group of larger firms acquire a greater share of the market at the expense of small merchants, is a natural development in any society undergoing the growth of capitalist relationships. In Egypt, it aggravated merchants' already considerable anxieties.

There is another important factor behind the merchants' anger. The Egyptian government is very poorly informed on the volume of commercial activity in the country, which greatly hampers the job of collecting income taxes from merchants. These taxes eat directly into merchant's profits. Many merchants strongly suspected that the government's real motive for implementing the second phase of the sales tax was to familiarize itself with their activities and incomes so as to be able to tighten the screws on their income tax returns. In 1995 the director of the General Authority for the Sales Tax had personally assured merchants that no information from his authority would wend its way to the income tax department.[22] His assurances failed to convince merchants, and in view of their continued and strong opposition, the chairman of the Cairo Chamber of Commerce Mahmoud Al-Arabi had asked the government to hold off on the second phase until it reformed the income tax system. Thus, before the decade was out and before bringing in the second phase of the sales tax, the government had started to move on its income tax reform program.

Phase two of the general sales tax exposed the state's utter incompetence in the realm of generating revenue resources. The campaign to market the new tax was vague and misleading. In response to the angry outbursts from merchants, the government almost instinctively adopted a contradictory two-pronged rhetoric. To the merchants it effectively winked and said, "Why are you upset? Isn't it the consumer that's going to pay in the end?" Meanwhile, to the rest of society it said, "There's nothing to worry about. This isn't really a new tax. It's only a way to collect on a tax that was introduced in 1991 with the first phase of the sales tax." Little wonder that everyone was confused. No one could understand where the billions of pounds that the new tax was supposed to generate would come from if neither merchants nor consumers were going to pay it. The rhetoric was not only conflicting; it was weak and irresolute. When the head of the sales tax authority had promised merchants that his department would not pass on information about them to the income tax authorities, not only had he failed to persuade them, but he had simultaneously issued a public pledge to collude with them in the concealment of their true incomes. In other words, he would facilitate tax fraud. It is one thing for banks to offer a pledge of confidentiality in accordance with which they will not impart information regarding their clients to outside parties except under exceptional, legally stipulated circumstances. It is quite another for a tax authority to promise not to pass on information to another tax authority in the hope of winning the confidence of taxpayers.

TAXING EGYPTIANS ABROAD: AN UNCONSTITUTIONAL ROUTE

One of the laws that most proclaimed the rise of the predatory state in Egypt in the late 1980s was law 228 of 1989, imposing a tax on Egyptian civil servants working abroad. Their numbers had increased tremendously during 1980s, and their remittances amounted to about $3 billion per year on the average.[23] In light of the budgetary deficit, it was only natural that these sums would make the authorities' mouths water. Law 228 was a remarkable precedent. Until then, taxation had followed the territorial principle, which is to say that only people residing within the geographical boundaries of the state were taxable. The principle rests on the fact that citizens living and working in other countries do not benefit from the services provided by the state. The state justified the new tax on the grounds that the government safeguards all their rights, such as health insurance, until they return from abroad.[24]

Opposition to the new law eventually led to the Supreme Constitutional Court. In 1993, the court ruled that imposing a tax on workers abroad was unconstitutional. The ruling was based on two considerations. The first was that the tax conflicted with the principle of equality in that it applied only to public sector and not private sector employees. The second was that the tax conflicted with the principle of the fair distribution of the tax burden in accordance with the ability to pay. Law 228 applied the same percentage across the board instead of gradating the tax according to the income brackets.[25]

The government responded that the Constitutional Court's ruling applied only to the litigants who had filed the suit and won, meaning that only they would get their money back. During the four years that it had remained in effect, law 228 raked in E£240 million. The government hastily pushed through a new law intended to avert the previous pitfalls. Law 208 of 1994 expanded the tax to include private sector workers abroad, thus meeting the principle of equality. It also introduced a gradated scale, thereby fulfilling the principle of fairness in the distribution of the tax burden. But even then, the new law did not escape litigation on the grounds of unconstitutionality, which again the Supreme Constitutional Court upheld in a ruling issued in 1998 that the law violated the principle of fairness, this time because the tax applied to salaried employees only and not to experts on special contracts.[26] The government did not try to come up with another version of the law, but it was quick to assert that the ruling applied only to those who had brought suit, as reported in the 4 January 1998 issue of *Al-Ahram*. In addition, the president, citing the need to safeguard the fundamental resources of the state, issued a decree in July 1998 stipulating that the rulings of the Supreme Constitutional Court could not be applied retroactively in the area of taxation, as reported in the *Al-Wafd* newspaper on 13 July 1998.

THE LONG-DELAYED SOLUTION: INCOME TAX REFORM

As we pointed out earlier, the regime pursued various means to resolve its fiscal straits throughout the 1980s and 1990s. It started with the inflation tax, then proceeded to tax Egyptians working abroad, and then introduced the general sales tax. When these and other means failed to halt its deteriorating financial condition, the regime finally turned to the formidable challenge that it had long been avoiding: income tax reform.

Like most developing nations, Egypt collects relatively little from taxes. It may fare better in this regard than some oil-exporting states, for example, that collect no taxes at all. But its tax revenues are still lower than those of many other developing nations. Figure 4.7 depicts how Egypt compares to other developing and industrialized countries in this domain.

Only two decades after coming into power, the Mubarak regime gave serious consideration to income tax reform. In 2000, Medhat Hassanein was appointed minister of finance, and it was not long before he declared his intent to issue a new law for the comprehensive reform of the income tax system, which everyone felt had long since reached obsolescence. The government acknowledged that the system was incapable of collecting the revenues it needed. Other sectors of society felt that it was inefficient and unjust. Salaried employees, for example, felt that they were the only sector of society that was compelled to pay taxes because these were deducted at source. Businessmen regarded the system as cumbersome and the tax authority itself as a vestige of the Middle Ages. More important, they felt the tax rates of 40 percent on commercial profits and 32 percent on manufactures and exports were outrageous. Each group had its own reasons for condemning the existing tax system, but all were unanimous in their conviction that it desperately needed a total overhaul.

Figure 4.7. Tax Revenues as a Percentage of Public Revenues in Selected Countries, 1988

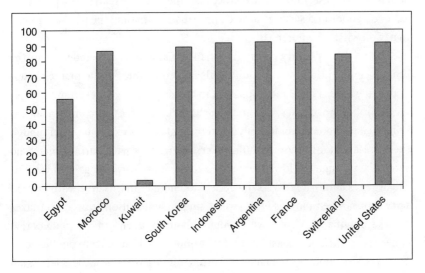

SOURCE: IMF, *Government Finance Statistics Yearbook*, 1991.

The Flaws in the Egyptian Tax System

When a newly appointed minister of finance announces, within moments of assuming office, his intention to issue a new tax law, he is clearly voicing the government's resolve to increase its revenues from taxes. Yet, if the primary impetus behind the new law was the regime's desperation in the face of a chronic and increasingly severe budgetary deficit, the underlying philosophy of the law was a response, at a certain level, to the balance of forces in society. It also reflected the internationally dominant neoliberal economic ideology. By the philosophy of the law, here, we refer to the ideological framework that delineates the goals of the tax structure and how the burden is to be distributed across the various sectors of society.

Before proceeding to this philosophy, it is useful to first look at certain characteristics of the Egyptian tax system: its bias in favor of the rich and against salaried employees, the extraordinarily high rates of tax evasion, and its rising transaction costs. Table 4.2 lists the sources of tax revenues in Egypt.

The Egyptian tax system is not socially equitable. As we can see in the table, it is heavily dependent on indirect taxes, the most important being the sales tax. More than 60 percent of total tax revenues are derived from indirect taxes. The reliance on indirect taxes has become a virtually universal rule due to profound economic and political developments. We return to this point later, but it is sufficient to note here that classical financial thinking is disinclined to over use indirect taxes because they fail to realize social equity. Taxes on goods and services provide little discrimination; the poor are forced to pay on what they purchase.

The relative inequity of the Egyptian tax system is also reflected in the limited contribution by rich individuals and companies to the financial support of the state. This is most apparent in the very low revenues from the capital and inheritance taxes, as well as in the fact that taxes on commercial and industrial profits account for only 4.4 percent of total tax revenue, even though there are about 5 million manufacturers, merchants, and businessmen who should be paying. The low revenues are all the more surprising when we consider the tax authority invests the bulk of its energies in this area, with around sixty thousand employees. The largest single contribution from direct taxes comes from financial firms, which supply about 30 percent of the total tax revenues. Nevertheless, at least a half of this amount is derived from public sector organizations, notably the General Petroleum Organization, the Suez Canal Company, and the Central Bank. Doctors, lawyers, consultants, and other

Table 4.2. Sources of Tax Revenues, 2001

Tax	Income in E£ Million	Percentage of Total Tax Revenue
Direct Taxes		
Capital Tax	75.5	0.100
Commercial and Industrial Tax	2,320.1	4.400
Tax on Salaried Employees	2,109.8	4.000
Tax on Liberal Professions	109.6	0.200
Real Estate Taxes	2.0	0.003
Social Solidarity Tax	81.9	0.100
General Income Tax	68.7	0.100
Tax on Financial Firms	15,773.0	30.000
Inheritance Tax	3.6	0.017
Total Direct Taxes	**20,538.8**	**39.100**
Indirect Taxes		
Customs Taxes	9,183.8	17.500
General Sales Taxes	16,524.6	31.500
Duties	2,889.3	5.300
Gas Tax	705.9	1.300
Suez Canal Tax	75.0	0.140
Resource Development Fees	825.4	1.500
Municipal Taxes	663.5	1.100
Other Duties	952.3	1.800
Total Indirect Taxes	**31,819.8**	**60.900**
Total Tax Revenues	**52,358.6**	**100.00**

SOURCE: Egyptian Ministry of Finance, *Closing Account of the Budget*, 2002.

practitioners of the liberal professions contribute a mere 0.2 percent of the total revenues, which is to say practically nothing at all, despite their relatively high incomes. Meanwhile, salaried employees contribute 4 percent to the total revenues, or nearly the same amount derived from the profits of commerce and industry.

On tax evasion, the second major characteristic of the Egyptian tax system, estimates placed it between E£14 billion and E£20 billion a year in 1998.[27] The penalty for tax evasion is prison, but that penalty has never been executed.[28] The tax authority would rather reach an understanding with tax evaders and collect fines equivalent to the amount of money they owe. Tax evasion thus makes sound business sense, especially for businessmen and merchants who feel that the taxes are excessive. If the tax evader is caught, the cost is no more than he would have had to pay by being honest. If successful, which the odds seem to favor, his bank account is all the more robust. At the same time, the authorities' reluctance to invoke the penalty of prison against tax evaders conveys weakness. It suggests that the government that tells society that it expects people to pay a certain percentage of their income in taxes is not serious. In fact, a regime that lacks legitimacy is in an awkward position to be strict about collecting taxes, all the more so in view of society's considerable suspicions with regard to how tax revenues are funneled. We return to this point in Chapter 5.

The third property of the Egyptian tax system is its high transaction costs. The chief indicator in this regard is the bitter legal disputes between the state and members of society over taxes. In 1998, Egyptians brought about five hundred thousand suits a year against the state, half of them against the Ministry of Finance, according to *Al-Wafd* newspaper on 13 July 1998. This volume of litigation tells us that the taxation system is riddled with holes and that it is not popular or widely respected. The percentage of tax-related suits against the state rose from 32.2 percent in 1995 to 42 percent in 2000.[29] All this intensive and lengthy litigation indicates that the costs of operating the tax system are high.

The increasing volume of litigation over taxes is also indicative of how weak the political domain in Egypt is. It suggests that there are few, if any, effective political channels for fighting the predatory state. It also reflects the ability of the courts to check the tyranny of the state, as demonstrated in the case of the taxation of Egyptians working abroad. Still, it is important to bear in mind that the significance of taking the state to court extends beyond the realm of the taxation system. It is the most salient characteristic of the struggle against the regime in the Mubarak era, a point to which we return in Chapter 5.

The Rise of the Neoclassical Outlook in Taxation Policies

The evolution of taxation systems in the industrialized world reflected four major developments: the two world wars, democratization, the modernization of the state, and the emergence of Keynesian theory. The twentieth century saw the outbreak of many wars, the most important being the First and Second World Wars. Warfare drove governments to turn more and more to their citizens for financial resources, which they obtained by increasing existing taxes and levying new ones. Meanwhile, democratization in industrialized nations vastly increased the political clout of the middle and working classes, and as their influence grew capital became subject to taxes it had never known before. War affected the volume of tax revenues—their growth in relation to the GDP—while democratization essentially affected the distribution of the tax burden, which gradually shifted away from wage earners and toward the rich.

The expansion of taxation was intrinsically connected with the modernization of the state and, specifically, its ability to keep track of people's incomes with an eye toward exacting a certain amount in taxes. The very concept of an income tax is relatively new and is associated with the rise of the industrialized state. Before this, governments relied primarily on the taxation of agricultural land and real estate. In Britain, for example, taxes were once levied on the basis of the number of windows in a home on the grounds that the more windows a house had, the wealthier its owners. A visitor to Britain today can still come across some older homes whose erstwhile masters had bricked over the windows.[30]

The factors of war, democratization, and industrialization received a powerful ideological boost from John Maynard Keynes, whose economic theory first made its mark in the 1930s and continued to hold sway over Western economic and fiscal thought until the 1970s. The most salient feature of Keynesian theory is the strong central role accorded to the state in the management of the economy and the redistribution of income through taxes in favor of the middle and working classes. The theory held that this redistribution was not only morally desirable in order to meet the principle of social justice, but also practically desirable because it would serve to stimulate economic growth. The theory contributed to the realization of a historic compromise between the political right and left, in accordance with which the right accepted state intervention in the economy and the mainstream left conceded private ownership of the means of production.[31] The compromise worked and continued to hold largely due to the prosperity of the global economy in the 1950s and 1960s. Taxation policy in the post–World War II period was an integral part of the general economic policies adopted by industrialized nations in light of the interplay between several economic, political, and ideological factors: prosperity, the historic compromise between the left and right, and Keynesian philosophy.

The situation changed dramatically in the 1980s. Countries around the world began to introduce sweeping reforms in their taxation systems. The list includes, among many others, the United States, the United Kingdom, Canada, and Sweden in the north and Jamaica, Indonesia, and Gabon in the south. The major feature of these reforms was that they reduced taxes on the rich and on company profits and compensated with sales taxes.[32] The only industrialized country that went against the flow was France. President François Mitterrand, who had just come to power at the head of a socialist-communist coalition, decided to apply Keynesian theory and, therefore, upped taxes on company profits. In the face of the sudden flight of capital from France, he quickly reversed his policy and joined the rest of the industrialized nations in applying a neoclassical tax policy.[33] A powerful force must have been pushing all these countries in the same direction. Some experts have suggested it was economic globalization. Dwight and McKenzie summed up the view as follows:

> The recent revolution in computer and information technology has enabled firms to move assets around the world at the touch of a button. It has also caused an explosion of competition not only among business, but among national governments seeking to attract new business and to keep existing businesses within their borders. This competition has forced governments to reduce tax rates, spending, and regulations and to lower trade barriers. The resulting loss of fiscal and regulatory power has put a severe crimp in the very ability of these governments to govern.[34]

Not only leftist analysts maintain that the new tax policies are less equitable. According to Vito Tanzi, an IMF expert and economic adviser to Italian Prime Minister Silvio Berlusconi, for example, "The increasing harmonization of tax policy across countries—resulting from tax competition to attract investment—will place downward pressure on tax rates and further restrict governments' ability to use tax policy for social protection. A survey of corporate tax rates in 14 major industrialized [countries] in recent years, from an average of about 46 percent in 1985 to 33 percent in 1999."[35]

Although the globalization of capital—which is to say, its freedom of movement around the world—has undoubtedly put governments under heavy pressure to reduce taxes on profits, we must not ignore the role of political and ideological factors. The 1980s and 1990s brought a sharp universal decline of the influence of the left. This trend was not only reflected in the electoral losses of left-wing politicians but also in their espousal of liberal economic policies. The global swing to the right helped the spread of the new tax policies, which was further aided by an ideological factor, namely the rise of neoclassical economic thought, which superseded Keynesian thought in academic circles and the international financial agencies that set the ideological agenda for the global economy. As a consequence, the thinking on taxes was completely reversed. Whereas Keynesians favor relatively higher taxes on companies in order to redistribute income, the neoclassicists hold that the less that companies are taxed, the more investment, which stimulates the generation of new jobs, is encouraged.

The transformations that occurred in taxation policies in the third world were affected by the same factors as those in the industrialized world. However, in the third world, yet another highly instrumental factor came into play: the international financial institutions with which developing countries had to cooperate in order to reschedule their debts after the international debt crisis in the 1980s. These institutions, which had advocated neoclassical economic principles since the 1970s, played a definitive role in shaping the tax policies of developing countries.

Thus we find in the wave of tax reforms that swept the third world in the 1980s a growing emphasis on indirect taxes and a de-emphasis on taxes on company profits. In his study of Latin American tax trends, Shome found that taxes on company profits dropped from 43.3 percent in 1986 to 36 percent in 1992 and to 27.6 percent in 1998.[36] Asher observed the same trend in Southeast Asia.[37] He noted one exception: South Korea went in precisely the opposite direction, which was largely a product of the democratic transition in that country. Following the fall of the dictatorship, the new democratically elected government instituted tax reforms that favored direct over indirect taxation as a means to promote social justice. Thus, while everywhere else the rate of revenues from direct taxes was declining, in South Korea it rose from 41.1 percent of total tax revenues in 1987 to 53.8 percent in 1994.[38]

The New Egyptian Income Tax Law: A Model
of Neoclassicism

The foregoing global trends in tax policy help put Egyptian trends into perspective. As observed above, since the 1980s countries around the world had been moving to increase their revenues by means of indirect taxes. Egypt followed suit with the implementation of the first phase of the general sales tax in 1991, in accordance with its economic reform agreement with the World Bank, and it stayed on course with the introduction of the second phase in 2001. The new tax law introduced during Medhat Hassanein's tenure as minister of finance also bore a clear stamp of neoclassical economics.

At its heart, the law had that neoclassicist magic formula: "To increase tax revenues you have to lower taxes." The rationale was that lower taxes increase the amount of money that companies can reinvest. Reinvestment will inevitably create new jobs and generate more income. Hence, tax revenues will increase. The high rates of tax evasion in Egypt lent extra force to this argument. Everyone knew that tax evasion was in good part a reaction to high tax rates on profits, which made nonpayment worth the risk. Table 4.3 shows how tax rates in 2000 were higher in Egypt than in some emerging countries.

Table 4.3. Tax Rates on Companies in Selected Middle Eastern and Third World Countries, 2000

Country	Tax Rate Percentages on Company Profits
Argentina	35
Brazil	37
Chile	15
Egypt	32–40
Hong Kong	16
Indonesia	30
Israel	36
Mexico	35
Morocco	35
Peru	30
Singapore	26
South Korea	31
Tunisia	35
Turkey	33

SOURCE: KPMG, *KPMG Corporate Tax Rate Survey*, 2000, cited in Samiha Fawzi, Hanaa Kheir el-Dine, and Amâl Rafa'at, *Marginal Effective Tax Rates and Investment Decisions in Egypt*. Working Paper No. 45 (Cairo: The Egyptian Center for Economic Studies, 2000).

It was therefore argued that lower taxes would encourage businessmen to obey the law and hand over what they owed to the government. The same logic was applied to the practitioners of the liberal professions. So it was that the new law reduced the maximum tax on commercial profits from 40 to 30 percent, on industrial profits from 32 to 30 percent, and on profits in the liberal professions from 40 to 30 percent.[39] With these reductions, Egypt's income tax policy was now on par with the policies of other developing countries.

Although the primary goal of the new tax bill was to reduce company taxes in order to improve Egypt's competitiveness in attracting investment, the government simultaneously hoped to give the impression that it was bringing benefits to all. Therefore, it was proclaimed that the new law offered exemptions to the poorest segments of the populace. Accordingly, it raised the minimum taxable salary from E£2,000 to E£2,580 per year for unmarried persons, from E£2,500 to E£3,360 for married persons, and from E£3,000 to E£4,200 for married persons with dependants.

During the debate over the bill, several social sectors aired their disappointment at the reductions it offered. Retailers felt that the reduction on commercial profits from 40 to 30 percent was not enough. Manufacturers and exporters complained that they would not be much better off under the new law because it would only reduce their tax rate from 32 to 30 percent.[40] Others maintained that the increase in the minimum taxable income levels fell far short of the increase in the daily costs of living.[41]

One point that the bill overlooked was tax exemptions. Law 42 of 1974 and its amendments and law 59 of 1979 on the industrial cities offered a huge ten-year income tax exemption for enterprises operating in the new cities. The idea was to encourage foreign and domestic investment. However, it had been apparent since the 1980s that this incentive failed to bear the desired fruit and, in fact, that it had resulted in huge losses in tax revenues. To make matters worse, once their exemption period expired, some companies dissolved themselves and registered under new names in order to benefit from another ten years of tax-free profits. Until the 1980s, criticism of the tax exemption system came almost exclusively from the left. By the 1990s, the criticism was also coming from liberal economic academic circles and even from some groups of businessmen. Some surveys carried out at the time found that businessmen tended to prefer lower taxes over an exemption period followed by high taxes.[42] This finding accords with the view of such international financial institutions as the IMF and World Bank, which also disapprove of total exemption periods. On the whole, then, there is a general agreement that exemptions are not productive. Moreover, as businessmen come to the end of their exemption period, they realize that it is more in their interests to settle for lower tax rates than for exemptions. The Federation of Industries, for example, has adopted this position, according to the *Al-Ahram* newspaper on 4 July 1999.

Despite the general consensus over the need to abolish the exemptions or at least to regulate them better, the tax bill left them untouched. Some entrepreneurs still benefiting from the exemptions sanctioned by the old laws would kick up quite a fuss if they were abolished. Perhaps the government feared that abolishing exemptions would create a climate inimical to investment. But this alone does not explain the problem. The tax exemptions system has a powerful protector in the government: the General Investment Organization. Established in the mid-1970s to stimulate investment, this organization supervises exemptions. Eliminating those exemptions is a direct threat to its jurisdiction.

The tug-of-war over the tax bill continued throughout Medhat Hassanein's term as minister of finance, which ended in June 2004. His successor, Youssef Boutros Ghali, reintroduced Hassanein's bill with some modifications. Perhaps the most important modification was the reduction of the maximum tax on commercial profits to 20 percent, half of the existing maximum rate. The new finance minister was making a very risky gamble, and he is reported to have said that the new law would be like a roulette game—win all or lose all. Success would reverse the deterioration in government revenues; failure would plunge the state into crisis. It all depended on how businessmen would respond. If they paid their taxes, that would compensate for the reduction in the rates. But what if they continued to evade taxes?

Ghali based his gamble on a seemingly logical argument. Businessmen had been evading taxes because the taxes were so high that evasion was worth the risk. Lowering taxes would therefore inspire them to abide by the tax laws. Unfortunately, there was a hole in the premise. The problem was much deeper and more complex. It was not only high taxes that encouraged tax evasion, but also how easy it was to do it. The taxation bureaucracy in Egypt is notoriously corrupt. In addition, there was an important political factor. When a ruling regime lacks legitimacy and the prevalent conviction is that tax revenues are used to finance a corrupt bureaucracy, and when there is little transparency in how the government spends its money, the motivation for tax evasion remains high. These are the problems that the minister of finance could not remedy, because they are connected to the entire political order and affect every aspect of government.

The new tax law went into effect in June 2005. Two years later, the Ministry of Finance boasted that the new law has been highly successful; as proof it reported that revenues rose from 7.1 percent of the GDP in 2004–5 to 9 percent in 2005–6 and remained at 9 percent the following year. Sadly, the devil always lurks in the details. When we look at the small print, we find that the rise in income tax revenues derived primarily from the gas tax and the Suez Canal Company. Meanwhile, tax revenues from private sector companies (financial firms) actually fell in the first year from 1.7 percent to 1.4 percent of the GDP and then returned to 1.7 percent of the GDP the following year.[43] Only in 2008–9 they increased to reach 2 percent of the GDP.[44] In other words, the new tax law has not so far been successful in generating an important increase in tax revenues.

THE APPEAL TO CAPITALISTS AND THE SOCIAL ROLE OF THE BUSINESS COMMUNITY

Another stratagem the regime used to make up for the decline in rentier revenues was to appeal to businessmen's philanthropic spirit. We are not talking here about alms to the poor or other charitable donations from wealthy individuals to the disadvantaged. We are talking about the state soliciting donations from private individuals or organizations for their help in performing certain functions of the state, such as urban beautification or building schools. In a sense, we are confronted with a form of privatization of the tax system. Instead of businessmen paying their taxes to the state for the construction of schools, they would do the job. Although no figures are available for this phenomenon, there is plenty of tangible evidence of its growth. It can be found, for example, in many beautified city squares where the names of the individuals or companies that undertook the projects are engraved on commemorative plaques. In Chapter 3, we saw how the cost of the recent urban development of Alexandria was footed by contributions from the business community. The spread of this phenomenon has been documented in several studies.[45]

It was only natural that the state would have to compensate these donors in some way. The compensation could be material, in the form of exemptions from certain fees or duties, for example, or the awarding of construction or supply contracts. But the compensation could also be moral or symbolic, as is the case with the plaques listing the names of the contributors to the beautification of public squares in Cairo and Alexandria. By and large, this moral reward is granted to the actual individuals, but in one instance the state granted a generous moral award to the entire class of businessmen: Until the 1990s, the government's primary ideological apparatus, national television, had traditionally portrayed the average entrepreneur as a member of the class of dissolute playboys and/or con men. Gradually, during the 1990s, television serials began to cast the spotlight on "good" businessmen, businessmen with a social conscience.

Does recourse to donations from the business community weaken the state's control over society? Béatrice Hiboux holds that it does not.[46] She posits that the ability of a regime to mobilize money from businessmen is a manifestation of its control over society and evidence of a considerable ability to strengthen the central authority. In support of her theory, she cites the Tunisian National Solidarity Fund, founded by President Ben Ali in 1992, which is funded by donations from the business community. In her view, this fund, which controls vast assets, is a financial system parallel to that of the state. Yet, the president alone has the final say on how the assets are spent, and he spends them on public welfare projects in order to enhance his popularity. Since such income and expenditures are not listed in the national budget, the state is, in a strong sense, being privatized. Nevertheless, Hiboux maintains, this has not diminished the influence and authority of President Ben Ali.

Paul Veyne echoes this view in *Le Pain et le Cirque*, which looks at the question from a historical perspective.[47] Veyne, too, does not think that contributions by the rich to public welfare projects threaten the authority of the state. There are no functions that must be performed exclusively by the state or, conversely, that must be relegated in their entirety to the private sector, he argues. The functions that are monopolized by the state vary from one society to another and from one era to the next. Some governments engage in what were once considered private sector functions, such as providing health insurance and patronizing arts and literature. In other countries, we find private sector agencies performing functions that are conventionally the preserve of the state. In some cultures, individuals outside the ruling authority undertook the function of the judiciary. Therefore, the fact that private entities engage in the functions of government does not necessarily imply a deterioration of the state's authority; rather it implies a redefinition of authority.

While acknowledging that the Egyptian regime's recourse to soliciting help from the private sector will not necessarily undermine its authority, the matter still merits attention. The Tunisian experience that Hiboux cited is based on the president's absolute control of the mobilization of resources from the business community, which minimizes its dangers. In Egypt, however, there is not such a high degree of centralization. Indeed, as observed in Chapter 3, there is decentralization in the mustering and deployment of private donations. Governors are prime agents in this process, as was the case in the development of Alexandria. Moreover, the decentralization extends beyond governorates to include many public institutions, including universities and colleges. As a consequence, many public institutions have been subordinated to the private interests that finance a portion of their needs and, hence, partially freed from the restrictions of central authorities that can no longer meet these institutions' basic needs.

That political authorities were compelled to grant private entities the right to participate in public welfare projects or to come to the state's aid in times of crisis indicates the risk of the coalescence of independent centers of influence. Outflows of money inevitably generate loyalties. The Egyptian regime has attempted to reduce this risk through the application of security measures. For example, when the earthquake struck in 1992, the Muslim Brothers quickly mobilized relief for the hardest hit areas. Within days, the regime's security mentality clicked into gear, and the government issued a military decree prohibiting the collection and distribution of aid outside of official channels. The regime has long shut its eyes to the Muslim Brothers' social service activities, through which the Islamist organization has built up vast networks of support. But when crisis strikes, as it did in 1992, the regime does not want the Muslim Brothers to appear to be society's rescuer. Only the army can assume that profile, which it did through the widely televised distribution of tents and blankets to disaster victims.

The regime may have turned more and more to the private sector for help in the 1990s, but it ensured that this help remained under its control and came from quarters it felt it could trust. Returning to the example of relief in the wake of the earthquake, the president's wife championed a campaign to collect donations to repair the schools that had been destroyed and to build new ones. The appeal was directed primarily to the regime's loyal base in the business community. As part of the campaign, the names of donors were announced on television immediately after they had made their contributions—the state paid its debt of recognition upon receipt.

So far, the regime has largely succeeded in containing the potential dangers of soliciting help from the business community, which seems to conform to Hiboux's observations regarding Tunisia. Yet, while the Tunisian and

Egyptian recourse to the social role of businessmen has not jeopardized the regimes' power, it has contributed to undermining the state as a normative order based on the rule of law. Hiboux could not reach this conclusion because she equates the regime and even the president to the state. The distinction that we draw between the state and the regime allows us to observe how the appeal to private philanthropy could serve authoritarianism while weakening the state. That the Tunisian president has a free hand with the Tunisian National Solidarity Fund, outside the scrutiny of the government's monitoring institutions, is a flagrant attack on the basic principles of public finance. The same applies in the Egyptian case. The more public officials control money in special funds outside the formal channels of the state, the more this debilitates the state, even if it does not necessarily diminish the power of the officials.

COMPULSORY SUPPLY OF HARD CURRENCY: REVERTING TO BUREAUCRATIC DICTATES TO MARSHAL RESOURCES

In March 2003, Prime Minister Atef Obeid issued edict 506 compelling exporters to convert 75 percent of their hard currency earnings into Egyptian pounds through Egyptian banks.[48] The official exchange rate at the time was about six Egyptian pounds to the U.S. dollar, and the unofficial exchange rate was seven pounds. For every dollar that importers brought in through the banks, they were losing one Egyptian pound. That pound went into the national treasury. In other words, the compulsory conversion of hard currency was a masked tax on exporters.

Ministerial edict 506 was justified on the grounds of the need to halt the slide of the Egyptian pound against the dollar at the time. After having held its ground throughout the 1990s, the pound began to plummet following the turn of the millennium. But even if the edict's immediate objective was related to monetary policy, it yielded certain fiscal results, namely the influx into the national treasury of revenues derived from the obligatory exchange of hard currency gains.

Some quarters of the business community regarded edict 506 as a reversion to the government decree approach to economic management and a huge backward step in the economic liberalization that had begun in 1990.[49] Independent business organizations, such as the Association of Egyptian Businessmen (EBA), were more critical than such corporate state-controlled organizations as the General Federation of Trade Unions. As reported in the 13 December 2003 issue of *Al-Ahram*, the EBA wrote a letter to the prime minister warning of the grave damage that would afflict the Egyptian economy and export trade as a consequence of the edict. The Federation of Chambers of Commerce, in contrast, avoided a clear stance. Nevertheless, its president, Khaled Abu Ismail, who was also a member of the Council on Agricultural Commodities, announced that the council was drawing up a blacklist of exporters of agricultural goods who did not exchange their foreign currency earnings into pounds in Egyptian banks (cited by Al-Akhbar on 20 December 2003).

The Ministry of Foreign Trade, which is presumably close to exporters and which was headed at the time by one of the most economically liberal-minded officials, apparently also had to participate in the campaign against exporters. An information exchange link was established between the ministry and the Customs Authority to ensure that the Ministry of Commerce received accurate information on exporters and their volumes of exports. On the basis of this information, the Ministry of Foreign Trade suspended the activities of some exporters who had failed to comply with edict 506, according to *Al-Ahram Hebdo* newspaper on 4 February 2004.

It was not long before the edict was brought before the courts. On 13 December 2004, the Administrative Court in the Council of State ruled to abolish the prime ministerial edict obliging all private and public agencies and individuals to sell 75 percent of their foreign currency payments to Egyptian banks within a week of receiving them, pronouncing the edict to be aggressive and unlawful.

REGULATING THE UNREGULATED SECTOR

Like all other developing nations, Egypt has a sector of the economy that operates outside the official legal and institutional edifice. The informal sector, as it is called, engages in legitimate and socially acceptable commercial activities, but, for many reasons, its members have preferred not to register their activities with the government or to establish relations with many of its institutions. The entities of the unregulated sector are estimated to account for 40 percent of all entities operating in the economy and to employ more than 40 percent of the Egyptian labor force.[50] The governing institution that takes the most exception to being snubbed by the entities of the unregulated sector is the Ministry of Finance. Those entities do not pay taxes. Not surprisingly, therefore, after having exhausted many other avenues for increasing state revenues, fiscal authorities homed in on that sector.

The first step was taken in 2000 when the newly appointed minister of finance, Medhat Hassanein, began to form a perception of and to create a database on this sector. He relied on the services of two economic research centers. The first was the Egyptian Center for Economic Studies, a private research institute that during the past fifteen years has developed into an influential liberal economic think tank in Egypt. The second was the Peruvian Center for Liberty and Democracy, headed by Hernando de Soto, an economist who has recently gained widespread repute for his thesis on "dead capital." In *The Mystery of Capital*, de Soto attributes the economic lag of the third world to the spread of untapped economic resources that consist of unregistered and unofficially owned economic and financial assets, such as property and workshops that operate in the black.[51] Because of the unofficial nature of this ownership, the assets cannot be leveraged into capital. A homeowner with an officially registered deed, for example, can use his property as collateral in order to obtain a loan, whereas this option is not available to a squatter in a shantytown. In addition, entities in the unregulated sector cannot obtain other forms of support from the state. Regulating the unregulated sector would breathe life into the dead capital.

De Soto's theory has a developmental aim, which is to stimulate a sector of the economy whose growth is currently hampered because it does not enjoy official recognition. But one of the side effects of the theory is that the unregulated entities would then fall into the clutches of the tax regime. It was precisely this side effect that attracted the attention of the Ministry of Finance and inspired it to enlist de Soto's help.

The results of the study, which was jointly undertaken by the Egyptian Center for Economic Studies and the Peruvian Center for Liberty and Democracy, were unveiled in a press conference in January 2004. At that conference, reported *Al-Ahram* newspaper on 19 January 2004, de Soto claimed that the unofficial sector owned assets worth some $240 billion, which, he said, exceeded the amount of all foreign investments that had entered Egypt since the end of the Napoleonic expedition in Egypt in 1801!

Bear in mind that it was the Ministry of Finance that was pushing the idea of regulating the unregulated sector. Nothing could be more indicative of the fact that the regime's priority was to tap an untapped source of tax revenues and that the notion of empowering dead capital was little more than an ideological cover. But even taking the notion at face value, it could not succeed on its own in persuading the unregulated sector to come under the umbrella of the economic rules and regulations of the country. De Soto, in his study, found that loans to entities in the informal sector in Egypt cost 40 percent more than loans to entities in the formal sector.[52] But while there may have been some incentive to join the regulated sector, there were still incentives not to join. Remaining in the unregulated sector offered distinct advantages that extended beyond nonpayment of taxes. Otherwise put, if entities in the informal sector perceived it in their interest to deal officially with government institutions, they would have gone along with the idea.

Since the carrot of low-cost loans was clearly not sufficiently enticing, the government tried another carrot: reducing the fees for registering assets with the notary public. These had already been declining. Until the end of the 1980s, the fees came to 12 percent of the value of the property to be registered. In 1991, it was reduced by half to 6 percent, a significant decrease. But since that, apparently, was not low enough to encourage people to officially register their property, in 2003 it was reduced to 4.5 percent. The following year, the minister of justice announced that registration fees revenues had increased by E£19 million over the previous year. Interpreting this as a sign of the desire among entities in the unregulated sector to make their property ownership official, the ministry of justice reduced the fee once more to only 3 percent of the value of the asset, according to *Al-Ahram* on 24 February 2004.

These successive reductions of title registration fees are indicative of how determined the government is to regulate the unregulated sector. Still, it will take more than this carrot to win over more of the unregulated sector. The common wisdom in the business community is that the further away from the government you are, the less you have to lose, not just because of taxes but also because of the many commissions that have to be paid to government functionaries.

SLOW INSTITUTIONAL CHANGES: THE RISE OF THE MINISTRY OF FINANCE AND THE DECLINE OF THE MINISTRY OF PLANNING

The regime's major dilemma since the mid-1980s has been how to raise more revenues and control public spending in order to reduce the budget deficit. It has largely failed in this resolve. In this section we explain why this failure is in considerable measure due to the regime's incapacity to introduce the institutional changes needed to accomplish its goal.

For public revenues to increase and public expenditures to be reined in, the influence of the institutions responsible for the former must increase, and the influence of the institutions responsible for disbursing funds must decrease. The foremost agency charged with collecting revenues for the state is the Ministry of Finance. It is one of the oldest ministries in the modern Egyptian state founded by Mohammed Ali in the nineteenth century. But in spite of its long pedigree, it has not taken deep root in society. Circumstances seem to have always intervened to keep it from playing a strong role. Foreign influence and the British occupation in the nineteenth century hampered the ability of this ministry to perform its function.[53] Under the capitulations system that Egypt inherited from the Ottoman Empire and that became more extensive under British occupation, the Egyptian government could not extract income taxes from the subjects of foreign powers. This made it too awkward for the government to impose an income tax on Egyptians, because it would be perceived as biased against its own citizens.[54] Therefore, during this period, the Ministry of Finance levied revenues only by means of indirect taxes, customs duties in particular. That type of tax was far easier to obtain, unlike income taxes, which require a sophisticated tax apparatus. It was not until the Montreux conference in 1937 that Egypt finally managed to free itself from the capitulations system. And it was not until the end of the 1930s that the Ministry of Finance began to levy income taxes, which means that the Egyptian tax apparatus began to evolve and develop relatively recently. With the end of capitulations, when the Ministry of Finance could finally flex its muscles, it became one of the most important cabinet posts. Proof of this is that the secretary-general of the powerful pre-1952 Wafd Party, Mukram Ebeid, had served as minister of finance.

In the Nasserist era, the role and influence of the Ministry of Finance faded again. Taxes were not the Nasser regime's way of generating revenues; it simply seized control over capitalist assets through nationalization. With the creation of the Ministry of Planning in 1962, the Ministry of Finance received a debilitating blow. The new ministry moved in on some of the Finance Ministry's areas of jurisdiction, one of which was to "prepare and administer the investment expenditures of the state." This Egyptian bureaucratese meant that the Ministry of Planning was now responsible for purchasing equipment and assets for productive and nonproductive purposes, from air conditioners and cars for government officials to machinery and materials for public sector companies. The Ministry of Planning was the clearest institutional embodiment of the Nasserist era, with its centralized state-planned and -driven approach to economic development. From 1962 to 2004, the public expenditure budget was split between the Ministries of Planning and Finance, with the former, as noted, in charge of "investment" expenditures and the latter responsible for current expenditures (such as salaries) in addition to the administration of taxes and duties.

In 1974, the Sadat regime ushered in a new era in Egypt's economic history with the Open Door policy. The policy did nothing to diminish the role of the Ministry of Planning. Even though the domestic and foreign private sectors now began to play the field, the increase in the revenues of the state pumped huge resources into the coffers of the Ministry of Planning, which continued to administer and disburse development allocations. In 1980 the ministry received a powerful new instrument for performing this task: the National Investment Bank, discussed earlier in this chapter, whose board of directors was chaired by the minister of planning.

The powers of the Ministry of Planning remained undiminished by the economic deregulation policy introduced by the Mubarak regime in 1990, and it continued its role of managing state investment outlays. The perpetuation of the ministry's operations rested on the argument that a market economy, like a centralized economy, required planning. However, the ministry did not have the authority or the means for planning in a market economy. In such an economy, planning entails two chief procedures: the formulation of fiscal policy (lowering or raising taxes, for example) and the formulation of monetary policy (such as setting interest or currency exchange rates). In Egypt, these were undertaken, respectively, by the Ministry of Finance and the Central Bank. The only instrument that the Ministry of Planning had at its disposal was a portion of public spending, namely investments outlays.

Dividing the public outlays budget between the Ministries of Finance and Planning was not an Egyptian invention. The Nasserist regime imported the idea from socialist countries. However, the persistence of that division of labor beyond the 1970s created a major budgetary problem. The separation between the mindset for mobilizing resources and the mindset for administering expenses, as embodied in the different functions of the two ministries, makes it difficult if not impossible to achieve a balanced budget. Balancing the income and expenditures columns is easier when a single institution oversees financial policy and avoids outlays unless it can ensure that it has the funds to cover them. The Ministry of Planning tends to increase public spending with little concern for budgetary balances. If, for example, it decides upon a construction project, it will earmark money for construction from the resources it controls. Once construction begins and workers need to be paid, the Ministry of Finance has to be called in because it is in charge of paying current expenses. Suddenly, the Ministry of Finance finds itself footing a large part of the bill for a project it had no say in approving.

The Ministry of Planning, then, presents a problem with regard to balancing the national budget. The problem is not just that this ministry managed to survive and adapt to the economic liberalization espoused by the regime in the 1990s. In 1997, it was even given a moral boost with the elevation of then Minister of Planning Kamal Al-Ganzouri to prime minister. This appointment stirred no small amount of surprise in light of Al-Ganzouri's well-known inclination toward a centrally steered economy, a tendency acquired over many years of service in the Ministry of Planning even before heading that ministry.

Retaining the Ministry of Planning without redefining its role and elevating its chief to prime minister was a sign that economic liberalization would not touch the heart of the organizational and institutional composition of the state. This ministry, which does not possess the means for planning in a market economy, continues to draw up national economic and social plans. This situation is also certain to persist, for it is constitutionally stipulated. Article 24 of the Constitution of 1971 states, "The people shall control all means of production and direct their surplus in accordance with development plan laid down by the State." Article 86 states, "The People's Assembly shall exercise the legislative power, and shall approve the general policy of the state, the general plan of economic and social development, and the general budget of the state."[55]

Moreover, the plan drawn up by the Ministry of Planning covers more than just state expenditures for economic and social development. It also lays the general guidelines for both the public and private sectors. Not only does it indicate how much money should be allocated to each sector of the economy; it also indicates how large a share the private sector should shoulder. We thus find ourselves faced with a very curious paradox: The legislative authority of a state that is officially based on a market economy is required to approve a plan that tells the private sector how much it has to invest in certain areas of the economy. The situation of the Ministry of Planning is a flagrant example of the institutional rigidity that has plagued the Egyptian state in the Mubarak era.

Al-Ganzouri was suddenly forced to resign in 2000 (the circumstances surrounding this event remain a mystery), after which the Ministry of Planning's star began to fade in favor of that of the Ministry of Finance. In 2002, the government moved to transfer supervision of the National Investment Bank to the Minister of Finance who, in turn, automatically became the chairman of the bank's board of directors, as mentioned by *Al-Ahram* on 1 December 2004. With this, the Ministry of Finance took its first step toward resuming full responsibility for designing and implementing the fiscal policy of the state. The completion of this process is essential if the state is ever to bring its budget under control. As observed above, balancing the books necessitates bringing the mentality of levying resources together with the mentality of regulating spending so as to ensure that money is not spent without the resources to cover it.

Although the institutional adjustment to the demands imposed by the need to balance the national budget has been set into motion, this did not begin until 2002, twelve years after the inauguration of economic liberalization and twenty-eight years after the introduction of the Open Door economic policy.

CONCLUSION

As we have seen in this chapter, in its struggle to find new sources of revenue to compensate for the decline in rentier resources, the regime almost instinctively resorted to the most surreptitious and least politically costly means. This was what we termed the inflation tax. Eventually, however, it was forced to turn to more open and more politically costly means, such as the sales tax and, finally, the income tax. The regime kept trying, but it failed to generate the revenues it needed. Figure 4.8 depicts the steady decline of national revenues as a percentage of GDP throughout the 1990s and into the new millennium. The downward trajectory came to a halt in 2003–4, after which revenues showed a slight increase. The improvement, as usual, was mainly due to the rise of petroleum and natural gas prices and the consequent marked rise in Suez Canal revenues, which is to say that it was not due to higher tax yields from the private sector.

The decline in state revenues would not be a sign of failure if the individuals in charge had actually decided to reduce the taxes they levy on society, as has occurred in many countries. However, it is a sign of failure when they had their minds set on increasing tax revenues, which is the case in Egypt, and the

Figure 4.8. Public Revenues as a Percentage of GDP, 1993–2009

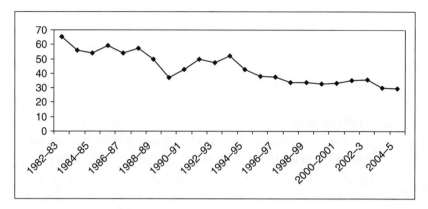

SOURCE: Computed by the author from Ministry of Finance, *Closing Account of the Budget*, various years; *The Financial Monthly*, various years.

increasing trend toward levying taxes persistently refused to offset the decline in revenues as a portion of the GDP. But not only did the state fail to increase revenues, but it simultaneously refused to keep spending within the bounds of its limited resources. The national deficit, naturally, continued to climb. Measured as a ratio of the GDP, it reached 10.5 percent in 2002–3 and 6.9 percent in 2008–9.[56] This ratio was just 6 percent in 1989–90 before the implementation of the economic reform program, which had reduction of the fiscal deficit as one of its main aims.

There are many reasons that the government has failed in its attempts to tap new sources of revenues. Sometimes it resorted to illegitimate means, as with the tax that was levied on Egyptians working abroad and the edict compelling exporters to change 75 percent of their hard currency earnings into Egyptian pounds. Both measures were condemned by the courts as unconstitutional. Sometimes, the regime acted with insufficient resolve and was unable to rally political support, both in government and among the public, for its revenue development projects. A case in point is the income tax bill that the regime began to formulate in 2000 and finally passed and implemented in 2005.

In general, then, the government has been slow to come to terms with the decline in revenues and equally slow to come to terms with the need to adjust to the demands of bringing the deficit under control. In large measure, the regime could only fumble its way forward because it had failed to obtain true popular support for its efforts to secure new resources. It had some support, of course, from the corporatist organizations it controlled, such as the General Federation of Chambers of Commerce. However, such support was artificially orchestrated and almost worthless, derived as it was from organizations that nominally represented certain sectors of society but that actually functioned to control those social sectors on behalf of the regime.

That the state has proved itself weak in terms of its attempts to secure the support of society by no means implies that society has been strong in its resistance to the state. The prevalent modes of resistance to taxes are indirect and apolitical, such as tax evasion and litigation. The intensive appeal to the judiciary against the excesses of the executive is one of the most salient traits of the political order in the Mubarak era. Under this regime, the judiciary has acquired a certain degree of autonomy, which has made it the only agency capable of countermanding some executive decrees. The Supreme Constitutional Court managed to dissolve the People's Assembly twice on the grounds of a ruling that the electoral laws were unconstitutional. As we saw in this chapter, that court also issued two rulings on the unconstitutionality of imposing an income tax on Egyptians working abroad, while an administrative court abolished prime ministerial edict 506 regarding hard currency earnings.

This is not to say that such relative autonomy has prevented the executive from meddling in the affairs of the judiciary at times, or from refusing to respect its rulings at other times. Yet, the judiciary has proved to be the chief agency capable of checking the excesses of the executive. This reputation has inspired virtually everyone with almost any problem to turn to the courts. The phenomenon has occasionally attained absurd proportions, such as in suits against works of art that ostensibly corrupt public taste or against the prime minister of Israel for crimes committed against the Palestinians. The spread of this phenomenon reflects, perhaps, the trend among unknown lawyers to make a name for themselves. However, its true significance resides in the fact that, in the absence of an effective political domain, the courts have become the only available channel for pressing for change. Clearly, the role that the regime has relegated to the courts is part of its strategy of depoliticization. The judiciary serves as a vent. Instead of airing their opposition in political forums and modes of expression, people take their battle to the courts. Apparently the strategy has succeeded in reducing some of the political costs of the growth of the predatory state in the 1990s. This said, the fiscal crisis of the state and the regime's strategies for dealing with it are having profound political repercussions, which is the subject of Chapter 5.

5 THE END OF THE RENTIER/CARETAKER STATE AND THE RISE OF EGYPTIAN CAPITALISM
A Fiscal Infrastructure for Democracy?

EGYPT'S AUTHORITARIAN REGIME was heavily dependent on the state's financial assets to sustain its monopoly on power. These resources were dwindling, and, in order to compensate, the regime was forced to turn increasingly to more politically risky economic policies. But to what extent does the drain in revenues jeopardize the stability of the regime? To what extent will the regime's growing reliance on society to finance the state tilt the balance in the relationship between the government and the public in favor of the latter?

In this chapter, we attempt to demonstrate that the regime's current struggle to emerge from its fiscal straits presents a wider window for political change. As the regime's control mechanisms that depend upon money ease their grip, and as the relative power of the capitalist class and portions of the middle class increases with respect to the state, society acquires greater leverage for change. We have already seen this dynamic in progress in Egyptian politics in recent years, especially in the parliamentary elections. However, before presenting a portrait of the political scene and how it reflects major transformations in Egyptian political economy, we turn to a brief discussion of the theories on the relationship of the economic system and the system of governance.

RENTIER ECONOMY EQUALS AUTHORITARIANISM; TAXES EQUAL DEMOCRACY

In their study of the rentier state in the Arab world, Hazem Beblawi and Giacomo Luciani demonstrate a direct causal relationship between the nature of state revenues and the political character of the state.[1] Rentier revenues generate an authoritarian state; tax revenues create a democratic one. Why? According to the theory, the rentier state is rich and does not have to depend on society for tax revenues. Instead, society depends on the state for just about everything: income, jobs, education, health care, and other social services. The enormous financial resources of such states, as of the Persian Gulf countries, place them in a position of strength with respect to their citizens, allowing them to dominate in an authoritarian manner. Conversely, where the state depends on society as a major source of funds, society is elevated to a position of partnership and insists upon forms of public supervision and control. The formula is straightforward: Those who have the power to give, have power over those who take. It applies just as much to the relationship between state and society as it does between individuals in society.

So what happens when the rentier state grows poor and when its revenues dwindle and its deficit climbs? Government will have little choice but to levy taxes, and at this point society can insist that government listen to society, show society some respect, and account for how it plans to spend or has spent the funds it has collected from the public. In other words, this is when the public can force government to become democratic. Beblawi's and Luciani's simple yet very logical thesis on the connection between the rentier economy and authoritarianism is, perhaps, the most important contribution of Middle East studies to the field of political economy in that it focuses attention on state revenues as a major variable in the making or breaking of democratic transformation.

The theory of rentier revenues as a producer of authoritarianism has spread beyond the field of Arab and Middle Eastern studies. Mick Moore echoes the theory in his contention that the rentier nature of the state leads to political underdevelopment because the state does not have to depend on a bureaucracy of professionals other than in such areas as security.[2] States that survive on taxation, on the other hand, require sophisticated proficiency-based bureaucracies. They also need to be thoroughly informed on economic activities in society in order to levy taxes effectively and design appropriate development policies. Moreover, the interests of the state will be intrinsically bound to economic growth and a thriving production sector, which would inherently augment revenues.[3]

We encounter the notion of taxes as a generator of democracy in historical sociology. The evolution of democracy in Europe and the United States was strongly connected with conflicts between certain classes and the state over taxes. The idea is epitomized in the famous cry of the American Revolution, "No taxation without representation." Charles Tilly expounded on this concept in a study of the role of wars in the formation of the modern state in Europe.[4] Waging war costs a lot of money. If the state needs to turn to society to procure this money, it is forced into a negotiating situation with groups or segments of the population who insist on concessions from the state in exchange for sacrificing a portion of their fortunes. Tilly further argues that the need to levy taxes and the consequent need to manage revenues were instrumental in the rise of modern state bureaucracies founded upon the principle of meritocracy.[5]

Criticism and Refinement of the Rentier State Theory

If rentier revenues spell authoritarian rule, how do we explain the existence of authoritarian states that do not have rentier economies? This is precisely the objection that Michael Herb registers against Beblawi's and Luciani's theory.[6] He points out that Arab states in general are authoritarian, regardless of whether or not their economies are rentier. Other experts on the Arab world, such as Nazih Ayubi and Alan Richards and John Waterbury hold similar opinions.[7] For his part, Yasuyuki Matsunaga rejects all general theories that hold that rentier revenues produce authoritarianism.[8] The fiscal foundation of the state explains nothing, in and of itself, he states. If we want to know the extent to which it obstructs democratic development, we must probe in detail the circumstances surrounding the fiscal foundation and how it is used to reproduce despotism. Philippe Cardin offers tangible evidence in support of Matsunaga's argument. In his comparative examination of three rentier states— Saudi Arabia, Iran, and Venezuela—he demonstrates that the countries have very different systems of government and concludes that there is no such thing as a rentier model of government.[9]

It is true that the Arab state in general is authoritarian, regardless of whether or not it has an essentially rentier economy. However, it is equally true that petroleum-based rentierism has affected all Arab countries, even the non-oil-producing states. Whether this took place through aid from wealthy Arab nations to poorer ones or through labor migrations to oil-rich states, rentier oil revenues became critical to political stability. In the first case, financial aid helped prop up non-rentier authoritarian regimes; in the second, employment opportunities abroad opened avenues for individual solutions to economic and social difficulties, providing a vent to prevent the buildup of domestic pressures against the regimes.

Even so, the criticisms mentioned above still diminish the validity of the rentier state theory, compelling us to look beyond state revenues for possible sources of authoritarian rule. Why should there not be more than one cause? After all, the rise of democracy was not solely the product of the clash between state and society over taxes. Attempts to explain authoritarianism solely on the basis of the fiscal foundation of the state have been taken to absurd lengths. For example, the statistical comparative study undertaken by Wantchekon and Jenson not only established a direct causal relationship between rentier incomes and authoritarian government, but also pinned this relationship down to a precise mathematical formula: For every 1 percent increase in the ratio of rentier income to GDP, there is an 8 percent increase in the authoritarian propensity of the state. This blinkered approach to a very complex evolutionary process ignores untold variables.[10]

As the foregoing example suggests, the rentier theory is prone to the same reductionist syndrome that affects all theories that attempt to furnish blanket explanations for political economic phenomena. We can hardly contend that poverty, unemployment, and marginalization necessarily lead to revolution or that economic development inherently leads to democratic transformation. Such claims rob purely political dynamics of all independent force. Therefore, why not trim the explanatory ambition of the rentier theory? How about restating it as "rentier revenues are conducive to authoritarian government," while simultaneously acknowledging that authoritarianism has causes other than money? Then we should simultaneously be able to hold that the drying up of rentier revenues and the growth of taxation are conducive to democratization, while stressing that the desire to control the public purse is one of several potential sources of democracy.

In addition to the above-mentioned criticisms, the Egyptian case offers some concrete evidence against the rentier state theory. The theory implicitly presumes that as rentier revenues decline, the state must inevitably turn to taxes. Egypt's authoritarian regime has provided some tangible refutation of this. As we saw in Chapter 4, it turned to other means to compensate for the falloff of rentier revenues, such as encouraging the business community to share in state finances through donations or to undertake municipal projects or functions that had previously been performed by the state. Also, as the Egyptian case has shown, when the state is forced to tax, it will not necessarily resort to the income tax, the type that stirs the strongest resistance and that is the most likely to trigger democratic demands. Income taxes are the hardest to obtain because income is less transparent than property or than consumption that can be subjected to sales taxes. Consequently, income taxes require a minimum degree of acceptance and consensus between society and the state. As we have seen, when the Egyptian regime found itself forced to turn to taxation, it resorted first to sales taxes and various fees and charges. It took a long time before it summoned the resolve to increase its revenues through income taxes. This occurred in 2001, when then Minister of Finance Medhat Hassanein drafted a new law to reform the income tax structure, a law that was finally implemented in 2005.

The rentier state theory also presumes that mounting tensions over taxes between society and the state will stimulate a grassroots movement to either force the government to curtail its taxation ambitions or to insist upon public supervision and scrutiny of revenues derived from the public. As logical as the assumption is, it fails to give sufficient weight to the powers of authoritarian regimes to contain the opposition and divert its energies into nonpolitical channels. The Egyptian regime has proven relatively successful at choking off avenues for political protest while opening a vent through the judiciary as a means to curb government excesses. The vent diverts the public from the political struggle to the litigation struggle, which inherently diffuses the opposition (recourse to the courts does not demand mobilizing, organizing, and sustaining a movement; it only requires consultations with a competent lawyer).

A final problem with the rentier state theory is that it posits a certain evolutionary progression: The decline of the rentier state → imposition of taxes → mounting democratic pressures. The implication is that the rentier state is brought down by an uprising of the taxpaying public. However, one could conceive of a different progression: The decline of the rentier state → weakening regime control → emerging social forces → growing possibilities for political change. In this second model, the primary impetus for change derives not from opposition to taxes but from the mounting power and influence of social classes as the regime begins to crumble.

An Alternative Model for the Relationship Between Rentierism and Democracy

The reductionism in the rentier state theory compels us to consider other theoretical possibilities to account for how the rentier state affects democratic transformation. We therefore need to broaden our scope to political economy theories that offer more general conceptions of the relationship be-

tween socioeconomic transformations and political change. I suggest applying the class-structural model proposed by Huber and Rueschemeyer, which
attempts to investigate the origins of democracy in the evolution of the relationships between various classes and social groups, and between these and
the state.[11] Democracy, according to these theorists, entails a redistribution of
power between society and the state as the consequence of several factors.

The first factor is the balance of power between the state and civil society.
Civil society is used here in its broader sense as referring to all organizations of
interest representation, such as labor unions, occupational syndicates, and
business associations. Civil society's power needs to grow strong enough to
counter the power of the state. Conversely, a state that is not dependent on
civil society for its material and human resources and is, consequently, independently powerful is unlikely to back down in the face of democratic forces.

The second factor pertains to the state's control of the religious sphere. An
alliance between the state and the religious establishment inherently bolsters
the power of the state. It follows that freeing the religious sphere from state
control is conducive to democratic transformation.

The third factor is the global economic and political order, which affects
both of the previous factors and delineates the scope of the options available
to players at the national level.

Here we focus solely on the first factor, as the other two are not directly
relevant to our subject and require separate and extensive studies. In the following section, we examine how the waning of the rentier/caretaker state affects the balance of power between the state and social classes.

THE EGYPTIAN CASE: MORE AUTHORITARIANISM
WITH A LOOSENING GRIP

In *A Grand Delusion*, Eberhard Kienle enumerates several indications of a
trend toward greater authoritarianism in Egypt in the 1990s.[12] The most salient was the clampdown on press freedoms, which reached its height in 1995
in the attempt to pass law 94 on the press; the military trials of Muslim Brothers members, whom the regime had allowed a relatively large scope of freedom in the 1980s; the rescinding of mayoral elections and reinstatement of the
mayoral appointment system; and the 1998 amendment of the Supreme Constitutional Court law to prevent the retroactive enforcement of its rulings (as
mentioned in Chapter 4, this was related to the tax on incomes of Egyptians
working abroad).

This tendency toward tightening security controls is characteristic of authoritarian regimes as they decline, and it reflects their decreasing power with respect to the rising power of certain social classes. The dwindling resources of the state are catalysts for this shift in the relationship between the regime and society in Egypt, in particular the entrepreneurial, middle, and working classes of society. The process of readjusting the power relationships between these sectors of society and the regime paves the way for political change.

Egyptian Capitalism: An Emerging Class

As rentier revenues declined, the balance of power between the regime and capitalist forces shifted in favor of the latter. With the exception of the opening years of the 1990s, when there was a brief spike in state revenues (and, hence, outlays), the weight of the state in the economy has steadily declined since the mid-1980s. In tandem, the private sector has acquired a steadily growing share of control over the country's material and human resources. Financial and human resources are the two most important ingredients in Egyptian politics. Businessmen succeed in politics by buying supporters and votes and, also, by buying the cooperation of the government bureaucracy.

The regime, too, depends on money and the provision of services to buy political support. This is the pith of the Nasserist legacy: securing political support through the redistribution of material gains in the form of jobs and social services. An NDP candidate wins parliamentary elections if not by outright fraud, then by dint of his close connections with government, which enable him to furnish services to his constituency. The NDP cannot mount a demonstration unless it pays participants in advance. Take, for example, the demonstration it organized to protest the American war against Iraq in 2003. It had to bus government functionaries and workers to Cairo stadium, give them a day's paid leave plus a cash reward, and supply lunch.

As the state's revenues declined so did the regime's political purchasing power. The state could no longer afford to expand the government payroll, except by creating jobs with few responsibilities and even less pay, and it could not afford to purchase new supporters. The most it could do was to try to hold on to the support base it has: some 5 million state employees. The bulk of these support the regime passively, which is to say by remaining submissive, and only a relative handful are prepared to support it actively because they have vested interests in the status quo.

Meanwhile, the political purchasing power of the emerging capitalist class was rising. The regime succeeded in persuading members of this class to fill part of the growing gap in the provision of social services as the result of the state's dwindling resources. However, it ended up paying a price in the form of the unraveling of centralized control over these services. The People's Assembly elections of 2000 and 2005 testify to this development.

Parliamentary Elections 2000: Money Talks

The People's Assembly elections in 2000 featured a precedent in Egypt as the result of a Supreme Constitutional Court ruling ordering judicial supervision of the polls. Judicial supervision was not total, as it did not cover the preliminary electoral committees. However, even partial judicial supervision reduced the opportunities for rigging the elections. It is therefore possible to maintain that these elections furnished a fairly clear reflection of the political map of Egypt at the outset of the twenty-first century.[13]

Perhaps what most hit home in these elections was exactly how frail all Egyptian political parties were, including the NDP. For the first time in its history, the ruling party failed to obtain at least two-thirds of the seats in the People's Assembly. It received less than 40 percent of the vote and could only secure a majority in the house by including independents in its ranks. But the NDP's poor showing did not work in favor of the official opposition parties. These together won only sixteen seats, barely 3.6 percent of the house.

The regime had lost some of its power to secure the victory of its candidates in the polls, which was a remarkable turn in Egyptian politics. That most of the independents who had won were originally NDP members and that the vast majority of them rejoined the party after the elections does not detract from the significance of the development. The same applies to the reports that internal divisions in the NDP created tensions that hampered a consensus over the selection of candidates. What counts here is that a large number of independents won even though they were not official candidates of the ruling party. This fact alone should give pause for thought.

Another group that scored a major success in these elections was businessmen, who garnered seventy-seven seats, more than double the thirty-seven they had won in the 1995 elections.[14] In 2000, money had been lavished on the campaigns as never before. Money had clearly made considerable inroads against government connections as a source of power. The case of Rami Lakah, who competed for the seat of the Daher constituency, is illustrative.

Lakah had two disadvantages. First, he belonged to a minority within a minority—he was not only Christian, but Catholic. Second, he had nowhere near the political clout of his rival, Abdul-Ahad Gamel El-Din, the official NDP candidate for that constituency and former head of the Supreme Council for Youth and Sports. But Lakah had a major edge over his rival. He was a business tycoon worth well over a billion pounds, from which he spent liberally on his campaign and on the voters in Daher, who ushered him into the People's Assembly.

The presence of big business in the People's Assembly went beyond the quantitative. For the first time since the Free Officer's coup in 1952, businessmen headed parliamentary committees, the most important being the Planning and Budgetary Committee headed by Ahmed Ezz, the country's leading steel magnate. The committees are not that influential in formulating public policy, but this stems from the weakness of parliament itself. The executive branch almost totally dominates the decision-making process. Economic policy is formulated by the minister of economy, not by the parliament's Planning and Budgetary Committee. Nevertheless, the chair of this committee carries an important symbolic weight, almost as symbolically significant as a ministerial post. Moreover, the actual influence of the committees is steadily increasing, now that they are dominated by politicians from the coterie of Gamal Mubarak, the son of the president, such as Hussam Badrawi and Ahmed Ezz.

Parliamentary Elections 2005: Money Talks Louder

The People's Assembly elections in 2005 confirmed the growing influence of big business in Egyptian politics. Businessmen reaped 22 percent of the parliamentary seats, up from 17 percent in 2000 and only 12 percent in the 1995 assembly.[15] One of the most striking features of these elections was the remarkable increase in electoral bribes, as noted in the reports by the agencies that monitored the polls. This had an extraordinary inflationary effect on the cost of votes. According to some reports, the price of a vote had climbed to more than E£500 in such electoral districts as Nasr City, where there was a neck-in-neck race between the business tycoons Fawzi Al-Sayyid and Mustafa Al-Sallab.[16] Parliamentary seats had become subject to the laws of supply and demand. Clearly there was a greater demand, largely due to the judicial supervision of the polls. Ballot rigging inherently undermines the price of a vote; it makes buying votes a waste of money. Why should candidates pay voters when they can control the outcome by forging ballots or falsifying the count? Curbing electoral fraud, therefore, gave the ballot a market value. On the supply side, people sensed the increased demand for their votes, and rising unemployment and the economic doldrums into which the Egyptian economy had sunk induced many to sell them. Those willing to sell naturally held out for the highest bidder. In the electoral districts where the competition was the most intense or in which business magnates were most determined to obtain a People's Assembly seat with the prospects of the parliamentary immunity that comes with it, the going price of a vote soared.

One of the most significant results of the 2005 elections was unprecedented success of the Muslim Brothers, whose candidates seized eighty-eight seats after fierce campaigns against NDP rivals. This achievement further confirmed the unprecedented role of money in the elections. The Muslim Brothers is the wealthiest political organization in Egypt. A good chunk of its wealth went into creating philanthropic service networks that enabled it to establish strong grassroots links to large voting blocs. As a report by a human rights agency that monitored the elections observed, evidence of lavish expenditures on Muslim Brothers campaigns was everywhere. It could be seen in the sleek and costly posters, billboards, and other publicity materials of various shapes and sizes that proliferated on the walls and over the streets in electoral districts. It could be seen in the campaign rallies, most of whose participants would have been bused in at no small expense. As the election was to begin soon after the end of Ramadan, that meant breakfasting banquets, handouts of cooking staples, and Ramadan gift boxes, upon which were emblazoned the name, picture, and campaign emblem of the Muslim Brothers candidate for the district, plus the Muslim Brothers campaign slogan, "Islam is the solution."[17]

While the number of businessmen in parliament increased, the representation of labor in the 2005 parliament shrank to 4 percent, down from 7.5 percent in the previous parliament.[18] The decline in proportion of workers' representatives in the People's Assembly not only reflects their more limited financial capacities; it also is the result of the decrease in the number of workers' candidates nominated by the NDP. In 2005, the ruling party fielded only four labor chiefs from the General Federation of Labor Unions. The paucity of labor representatives on the NDP lists stirred deep resentment within the federation (*Nahdat Misr*, 29 October 2005). Much of the resentment was focused on the emerging wing of businessmen in the NDP, led by Gamal Mubarak.

However, the decreasing numbers of labor federation candidates backed by the NDP mirrors the transformation that has been gradually turning the ruling party into one dominated by a number of business magnates. The transformation began many years ago, with the aim of injecting new life into the ruling party by bringing in prominent representatives of the business community.

The declining fortunes of the General Federation of Labor Unions in the NDP struck home vividly with the defeat of the federation's chairman, Al-Sayyid Rashed, in the electoral district of Sidi Gaber in Alexandria. The 2005 elections also saw the defeat of major syndicate figures from the previous parliament, such as Al-Badri Al-Farghali, who stood for the left-wing Progressive Nationalist Union Party (Al-Tagammu') in Port Said. Al-Farghali attributed his defeat to the "alliance of money" against him.

The "Bourgeoisification" of the NDP

The senior posts in the NDP remain in the hands of the upper echelons of the regime. President Hosni Mubarek, former air force commander, is still the party's chairman, and Safwat Al-Sherif, former intelligence chief, is still its secretary-general. Most of its other leaders are veteran politicians whose political skills were honed in the corridors of the one-party state, whether that party went by the name of the Socialist Union, the Egyptian Arab Socialist Party, or the National Democratic Party. In fact, the NDP is the natural continuation of the Socialist Union Party founded by President Gamal Abdel Nasser in the 1950s. Even if it has long since diverged from its original political, economic, and social orientations, it remains a centralized dominant party run from the top whose key figures are appointed, not elected. The party does not have a clear and cohesive ideology, though it claims to represent the interests of all sectors of society from those with limited income to the capitalist upper crust. This is reflected in its membership, which includes the businessman who joins the party to gain political support for investment projects as well the unemployed individual who hopes that party connections will procure him a license to open a cigarette kiosk. It is the organic extension of the "alliance of the working forces of the people" beneath which banner the Nasserist regime ruled in the 1960s and that encapsulated the attempt to merge a broad spectrum of social sectors led by the military-bureaucratic elite.

For several years the NDP has been undergoing a significant change. We might term this development the Gamal Mubarak policy portfolio—a collection of policies characterized by liberal economic outlooks and the determination to assimilate Egypt more strongly into the global economic order. The rise of the president's son to NDP assistant secretary-general and secretary of policies is commonly interpreted as a means to smooth the road to his succession as president. Despite President Mubarak's repeated denials, those who oppose the president and his son continue to point to evidence of a succession scenario. To this author, the Gamal Mubarak phenomenon extends beyond that issue to embrace a profound shift in the sociopolitical balances in the country. The ascendancy of the Gamal Mubarak policy portfolio in the NDP reflects not only the emerging force of Egyptian capitalism, but also an attempt to contain this force within the framework of the current regime.

The rise of Egyptian capitalism is founded not only on its control of human and financial resources, but also on its possession of vast intellectual resources. The free market ideology, which has prevailed in Egypt since the 1990s, is grounded in a worldwide political and ideological transformation that rests on a powerful arsenal of ideas and theories produced by international financial institutions. The Egyptian regime first yielded to this ideology in the 1990s, since which time the private sector has increasingly assumed the reins of the development process. The regime has two chief reservations. The first comes under the rubric of the need to observe "national security considerations," which essentially translates as preventing foreigners (notably Israelis) from owning any strategic economic enterprises. The second is the need to observe "the social dimension" in economic policies, which means that political security agencies reserve the right to veto economic decisions that could trigger sudden jolts in the standard of living of sectors of society that might exhibit their wrath as they did in January 1977, when the country was gripped by the most violent mass uprising since the 1952 coup in response to the government's decision to lift subsidies on essential commodities in accordance with an agreement with the IMF. Such social and national security considerations aside, the free market ideology now dominates the mentality of the Egyptian elite. That the official and independent media still sometimes lash out at Egyptian capitalism does not reduce the hold of the ideology. The attacks take aim at the "parasitic" nature of the entrepreneurial class, its conspicuous spending, corruption, and other such moral aspects, but when it comes to serious public discussion of economic policy, liberal economics wins hands down.

Once we place the NDP policy secretary in perspective of the growing power and influence of the capitalist class, it becomes easier to understand why more and more prominent businessmen have been occupying key political positions. The distribution of political positions in Egypt obeys a precise equation that reflects the relative weight of various groups in the regime. If army officers obtain a percentage of top posts (governorships, for example), this mirrors the weight of the armed forces. That businessmen are garnering a share of top posts reflects the regime's acknowledgement of the growing weight of this community for the first time since the inception of the 1952 order. Moreover, the process picked up pace in the summer of 2004 when the newly appointed Ahmed Nazif government brought on board three businessmen as ministers of industry, transportation, and tourism.

EGYPTIAN CAPITALISM: FROM AN OWNING TO A RULING CLASS?

The regime thus has turned to capitalism to support itself with the power of an emerging social force and, simultaneously, to contain this power. So far, businessmen remain in a subordinate position, as the regime still holds a number of important cards. The ace in the government's hand is its still considerable control over the banking system, the nerve center of the market economy, especially a market economy that has yet to develop a sophisticated stock market, as is the case with Egypt. Regardless of how strongly international financial institutions stress the importance of privatizing the banks to economic deregulation, this is where the regime has dug in its heels. The banks are its chief instrument for keeping businessmen in check. Therefore, the state still controls about half of bank deposits and bank loans.[19]

To a large extent, the regime applies a political mentality to the management of this money. Public banks can do a lot: They can raise a businessman to heaven or topple him to earth. Major loans are granted to people with close connections to the regime. This approach precipitated the banking crisis several years ago, as loans were being handed out not in accordance with sound loan approval procedures (based on actual feasibility studies) but on the basis of the applicant's ability to strike close connections in government. But what was the regime to do? If it relinquished its grip over the banking system, it would forfeit its leash on capitalist forces.

The regime has also restricted the capitalists' freedom of organization and right to representation. Although many business organizations have appeared since the 1970s, the largest remain government-controlled corporate entities, such as the Federation of Egyptian Industries (FEI) and the General Federation of Chambers of Commerce (GFCC). The Minister of Industry still appoints a third of the members of the FEI board of directors, and the Minister of Supply appoints half the members of the GFCC board of directors.[20] Granted, there are private independent business organizations, such as the Association of Egyptian Businessmen, and joint chambers of commerce with foreign governments, such as the Egyptian-American Chamber of Commerce. However, such organizations embody only a minority of the business community, and the state does not recognize them as officially representative of businessmen. Occupational and political representation of the entrepreneurial class remains closely regulated, even if this sector of society enjoys the greatest margin of organizational and political freedoms, especially when compared to workers, for example.

The very fact that the regime has means to check the political influence of businessmen is what makes the Gamal Mubarak succession project conceivable and a plausible option for some. His person embodies a compromise between the ruling bureaucracy and emerging capitalism. As the president's son, he is loyal to the former; as a business studies graduate from the American University in Cairo who worked in investment banking in London, he is close to the business community. He also epitomizes the evolution of the ruling elite from the managers of society's economic assets to the owners of these assets. The transformation is a generational phenomenon: Are not most of the sons of senior officials prominent businessmen? The Egyptian bureaucracy produced tycoons and bankers; they turned their monopoly over political resources (power, connections, and influence) into economic resources (loans, commercial deals, and capital). As this suggests, the emerging forces of Egyptian capitalism are a very special type: They are very close to the centers of power.

Maybe Gamal will succeed his father; maybe he will not. It is impossible to predict. Gamal himself may be wondering. So much depends on innumerable variables at home and abroad. What we can be fairly sure of is that the next candidate for the Egyptian presidency must have an essential trait: the ability to express in a balanced way the interests of the military-security government apparatus and the interests of big business. In the absence of a popular revolution or a coup by a group outside the current regime, both of which lack any substantive evidence of probability, Egypt will be ruled in the coming years by a marriage between the military and business establishments. The next president could come from either one or the other; what counts is that the ruling establishment consists of elements from both.

EGYPTIAN CAPITALISTS: A DEMOCRATIC CLASS?

The emergent capitalist force could augment the opportunities for democratization in Egypt if this class is democratically inclined. Some studies have pointed to the absence of any indicators that it supports democracy and human rights.[21] However, this applies equally to most sectors of society in Egypt, not just the rising capitalists. Democracy as an idea is pretty much restricted to intellectual circles, and these, too, sometimes exhibit authoritarian tendencies. No class or sector of society is inherently democratic or despotic. Social and political circumstances are what generally determine how diverse groups stand on democracy. Ultimately, attitudes are shaped by a combination of ideology and material interests. As Rueschemeyer, Stephens, and Stephens point out, capitalism inclines to democracy when democracy favors its material interests, as occurred in Europe when emerging capitalist interests clashed with despotic monarchies.[22] When democracy expanded and extended the franchise to the working class, which at the time had been radicalized, the capitalist class swung toward despotism. The Rueschemeyer, Stephens, and Stephens study, which covers thirteen European countries, questions the theory commonly held by liberals and Marxists that the bourgeoisie brought democracy to Europe. They conclude that, apart from France, Britain, and Switzerland, no other capitalist sector played an important role in the process of democratic transformation.

Our hypothesis, then, is that Egyptian capitalism will lean toward supporting authoritarianism if it fears that expanding political rights will bring to power political forces hostile to its interests. The People's Assembly elections in 2000 and 2005 indicate that when electoral fraud is curtailed, businessmen's parliamentary fortunes improve. It follows that, since Egyptian capitalism is already present in the assembly and is capable of increasing its share of seats, it would have little problem with a reduction in the powers of the executive and the establishment of a strong parliamentary order. The electoral experiences have shown that a candidate's best guarantee for securing a parliamentary seat resides in his ability to provide services for his constituents. This ability derives either from his money or his government connections; as we have seen, the former criterion has been gaining ground over the latter as a mainstay of political influence. Nor is there any practical ideological obstacle to this trend in view of the dominance of economic liberalism in Egyptian society. Even the Islamists, as has been shown in various studies, have a distinct propensity for the Protestant ethic that Max Weber argues is conducive to the growth of capitalism because of the value placed on honest wealth as a sign of divine favor.[23] Although parts of society and government harbor a certain ingrained hostility toward businessmen as a class, this sentiment has not been translated into an alternative socioeconomic program. Until now, the criticism of this class has homed in precisely on the moral character of their wealth, not on the principle of private property. In the absence of a true left opposed to capitalism on principle, free and fair elections will not jeopardize the material interests of this class.

But if capitalism has little to fear from the left at present, some capitalists are concerned by the growing popularity of the Islamist trend. They worry that if Islamists came to power through the electoral process, they would overthrow the current order, usher in a culturally and socially rigid and narrow-minded regime that would be inherently inimical to individual freedoms, and jeopardize relations with the industrialized nations with which some Egyptian capitalists now enjoy close economic relations. For non-Muslim businessmen (generally Copts), this anxiety is compounded by the fear of political Islam's antipathetic tendencies toward non-Muslims and the specter of an Islamist theocracy that would transform them into second-class citizens. One could therefore surmise that significant sectors of Egyptian capitalism will remain wary of democratic transition as long as the Islamist trend dominates the popular political culture and as long as it stands a chance of achieving an overwhelming victory in the event of free and fair elections. Conversely, their reservations would subside if the popularity of this trend ebbed, as long as it ebbs without a concomitant rise of an anticapitalist left.

There is more to democracy than free and fair elections. It also entails expanding syndicate rights, which involves loosening the government's iron grip on labor unions. Such a development would unleash an active and organized labor movement both at the workplace and in the political arena, which is a phenomenon Egyptian capitalism has not had to contend with for decades. Most private sector business establishments refuse to allow syndicate committees on their premises, for which reason a vast majority of private sector labor remains unsyndicated, and the vast majority of the members of the General Federation of Egyptian Labor Syndicates are from the public sector.

In sum, there is an emergent capitalist class that rests its growth on its accumulating economic, human, and intellectual resources, and this growth is being translated into increasing political influence at the expense of the military-technocratic establishment. However, in view of the regime's continued hold over several key instruments of control, the chief formula for political change is a political marriage between the state bureaucracy and capitalism under the umbrella of the regime and the NDP, in particular. This formula has already obtained the approval of the sector of the capitalist class that is most closely connected with the regime. Within this general framework, one can envision growing support among this class for real electoral integrity if its members feel assured that no radical political camp stands a chance of winning. At the same time, many would probably oppose a democratic order in the fuller sense of the term, which is to say an order that would guarantee a broader range of civil liberties, such as the right to syndicate and the right to organize politically, because that would strengthen the hand of labor and possibly open the door to movements opposed to or highly critical of capitalism.

THE MIDDLE CLASS: WITH GROWING AUTONOMY COMES GREATER INDEPENDENCE FROM THE REGIME

The middle class comprises widely divergent groups in terms of income level, employment conditions, level of education, and political and ideological outlook. It consists in general of two chief wings. On one side is the conventional middle class made up of people engaged independently in small enterprises, of generally limited education, and with little familiarity with modern technology. The obvious example is small merchants. On the other side is the modern middle class, whose occupations require the deployment of intellectual skills. These people could either be salaried state employees, such as civil servants or teachers; salaried employees in the private sector; or independently employed professionals, such as doctors and lawyers.

The decline of the rentier/caretaker state has had the strongest impact on the salaried modern middle class.[24] This social segment, according to some analysts, formed the social base of the Nasserist regime and was the hardest hit, economically and socially, by the onset of the economic Open Door policy. The common impression is that the middle class has collapsed, an idea encapsulated in the title of the book by the eminent economist Ramzi Zaki, *Farewell to the Middle Class*.[25] However, the notion does not apply to the whole of the middle class. The Open Door policy of the 1970s and the economic reform of the 1990s affected different parts of the middle class in completely different ways. Some parts flourished; others declined. Some of its members had levels of education and the social and political connections that paved the way to new jobs in the private sector or in the civil service. Those who lacked these advantages had to accept lower status and lower paying jobs in either the private or public sector. Yet others, more unfortunate, were forced to join the ranks of the unemployed.

Our central premise here is that the shrinking state and the growing private sector have moved the middle class toward heterogeneity, with the fortunes of some portions rising and others falling. These same factors have led to greater autonomy from the state of the prospering portions of the middle class and to marginalization of the declining portions. A major indication of the autonomy of the well-to-do middle class is that it no longer uses or needs to use services provided by the state. Its members send their children to private schools, receive medical treatment in private hospitals, and travel in private modes of transportation. Most have satellite dishes and are hooked up to the Internet, which largely frees them from the state's ideological machinery. The most popular news channel among this class is Al Jazeera, the most popular entertainment channel is Dream, and the most widely listened to radio station among the youth of this class is Nugum FM (FM Stars). The public services that the well-to-do continue to depend on are still monopolized by the state, namely infrastructural services and the justice and security services. On these matters, well-to-do middle class people have little good to say. The further they are from what they regard as an inefficient and corrupt government bureaucracy, the happier they are.

Those who now compose the lower middle class harbor a deep rancor against the regime. Those in government employ (apart from a fortunate few) are angered by the decline in their standard of living and the deterioration in their work conditions. If they manage to draw a decent income, they probably do so through commissions (baksheesh), kickbacks, or other dodgy ruses. Many have a vehement hatred for the private sector, but it is an instinctive hatred rather than one founded on belief in a possible alternative and cannot, therefore, serve as an indicator of a sense of affiliation with or faith in the state. In addition to material decline, this class also suffered deterioration in social status and moral stature, in part due to the lack of an ideology that accords a pivotal role to civil servants in the new era. As a result, the support the regime receives from this portion of the middle class is passive, in the sense that the people do not overtly oppose the regime. However, it is unlikely that their resentments will turn into outright hostility unless the regime wages disciplinary campaigns to cure corruption in government bureaucracy. It is unlikely that the regime would risk such an action unless it could expand its support outside the state bureaucracy.

The changes in the middle class have had a significant impact on political life in Egypt. The growing autonomy or alienation from the state that is affecting many segments of the middle class propels people either toward political apathy or toward support of opposition movements, especially those with an Islamist orientation. When we look at middle-class occupational syndicates in the 1980s and 1990s, we find that those in which the Islamist movement was most successful were the ones that represented the sectors of society that are the most autonomous from the state, namely the syndicates of lawyers, doctors, and engineers, most of whose members are employed in the private sector or are self-employed. Conversely, the syndicates of teachers, workers, and journalists, whose members are predominantly from the state and public sectors, have kept their distance from the Islamist trend. The Islamists have made their greatest inroads among the sectors of society that could afford to withdraw their support from the regime because of their relative independence from the state. This even applies to the pharmacists' syndicate, the occupational syndicate that has the highest ratio of Christians (around 30 percent), but that simultaneously has the highest ratio of members who are self-employed or employed in the private sector.

While the government is offering fewer and fewer services to the middle classes, it is asking them for more and more taxes and fees. The liberal professions, in particular, will be expected to bear more of the brunt of funding the state. Fiscal authorities feel that this group currently contributes the lowest share.[26] In 2009, tax revenues from individual private professions were only E£292 million, compared to E£8 billion from wage earners.[27] Therefore, the new tax law discussed in Chapter 4 both reduces the tax rates for the liberal professions and toughens the penalty for evasion. The carrot-and-stick approach aims to break this sector's relative autonomy and draw the sector into a closer relationship with the state as a financer. Presumably this development will encourage this class to take a greater interest in public affairs and to become more politically involved. People who pay out money are generally keen to follow up on the fruits it yields. It is sufficient to note that for the first time in the history of the July 1952 order, pharmacists went on strike to protest a government-ordered tax hike. On 16 February 2009, the General Syndicate of Egyptian Pharmacists called on all pharmacies to close shop until the Ministry of Finance backed down on its decision to place them in a higher tax bracket and apply this retroactively (*Al-Masri Al-Youm*, 18 February 2009). Regardless of how divided public opinion was over this incident, the pharmacists' strike indisputably marks a qualitative shift in the political behavior within the liberal professions, which have long constituted one of the most important politically uninvolved segments of the middle class. The same applies to the conventional middle class, which is also being affected by income tax reforms. As we saw in Chapter 4, when the government tried to move to the second phase of the sales tax, merchants declared a strike and organized protest marches.

THE WORKING CLASS: FROM EBBING STATE CONTROL
TO GROWING PRIVATE SECTOR CONTROL

The influx of rentier incomes from the mid-1970s to mid-1980s allowed the regime to manage resources so that it could satisfy the public sector working class. Therefore, as the country made the transition to the market economy the government could adhere to the social contract Gamal Abdel Nasser had struck with this class. The contract read that in exchange for job security and a wage high enough to keep a roof over their heads and food on the table, the members of this class would remain loyal to the regime or at least not rebel. When facing the severe strains of the fiscal crisis of the mid-1980s, the regime knew it would have to terminate the contract or at least amend some of its articles. Above all, it realized that it would have to drastically cut the public sector labor force, an action that it would never have dared to perform until it obtained another huge injection of income following the outbreak of the Persian Gulf War and the signing of an economic reform deal with the IMF and World Bank. With these revenues, it could institute an early retirement scheme whereby workers would receive financial rewards for handing in their resignations. The scheme proved popular, despite the criticism leveled against it for handing out a large lump sum of money at once and for thereby enticing workers into sacrificing their long-term interests for short-term gain.

The scheme helps explain the relative calm that prevailed on the labor front in the 1990s. Contrary to the commonly held expectation, economic deregulation did not precipitate workers' protests. In fact, labor proved more tranquil than in the previous decade. But economic factors alone are not sufficient to explain this. This period also brought a dramatic increase in Islamist militancy. The Egyptian al-Gama'a al-Islamiya and the Gihad declared all-out war against the regime, and their violence targeted political and security officials, tourists, secularists, and Christians. Ordinary citizens were also victims of the crossfire between the Islamist extremists and the security forces, and some were targeted for opposing the laws Islamist groups were trying to impose on the public space. Against this delicate and perilous backdrop, many sectors of society were concerned first and foremost with defeating the militant Islamist groups. Left-wing activists in the labor movement, for example, opted for calm so as not to distract the regime from fighting what some on the left termed "religious fascism."

The relative calm that prevailed on the labor front in the 1990s cracked following the turn of the century. By the middle of the first decade of the new millennium, labor activism had attained such an unprecedented level as to compel Joel Beinin, a prominent expert on the Egyptian labor movement and coauthor with Zachary Lockman of *Workers on the Nile*,[28] to observe, "This constitutes the largest and most sustained social movement in Egypt since the campaign to oust the British occupiers after World War II."[29]

To an extent, the same economic and political factors that explain the relative calm of labor in the 1990s also explain, albeit in the reverse, the resurgence of a charged labor climate the following decade. By now, the boom in Gulf War revenues had petered out, and the government was facing economic straits again. The defeat of Islamist militants removed the priority that had inspired other political forces to strike a tacit truce with the regime. At the same time, however, the resurgence of labor activism was part of a general resurgence in political activism triggered by various regional and domestic developments. On the one hand, there was mounting discontent against foreign policies that the opposition believed supported or abetted the American-led invasion and occupation of Iraq and Israeli injustices against the Palestinian people. On the other hand, the succession crisis reached a new peak as President Mubarak turned seventy-seven in 2005, and the ruling elite became sharply split between supporters of passing the presidency to his son and supporters of keeping the presidency in the armed forces. Such rifts and tensions paved the way for a wave of opposition activism, epitomized by many groups such as the Kifaya (Enough) Movement, which campaigned against the president's nomination for another term of office and against the alleged scheme of hereditary succession. The growing impetus of this movement and the general mood of opposition to the regime helped fire labor activism.

Public sector workers played the most important role in the protest activities at the outset of the new millennium, even though the majority of the working class is now employed in the private sector. In large measure, this is due to the fact that political expertise is still concentrated among public sector workers, who make up the bulk of the membership of the Federation of Egyptian Workers Syndicates. As mentioned above, most private sector firms do not allow syndicate committees on their premises.

This concentration of labor activism in the public sector should not blind us to the profound change that the Egyptian working class has undergone as the consequence of the wane of the rentier/caretaker state. As more and more workers have joined the private sector, the private sector labor vote has become increasingly pivotal. To this voting bloc businessmen owe their increased presence in the People's Assembly, where they held 22 percent of the seats in 2005. According to available statistics on the parliamentary elections in 2000, voter turnout in traditional working-class districts in Greater Cairo was low: 11.5 percent in Helwan, 12.3 percent in al-Weili, and 22.5 percent in Shobra al-Kheima. Overall voter turnout that year was around 28 percent. Meanwhile, in the new satellite cities inhabited by private sector labor, turnout was considerably higher, with 30 percent in Tenth of Ramadan and 67.5 percent in Six October, which scored the highest voter turnout in the country in the 2000 elections. Such voting trends suggest a withdrawal from political participation among public sector labor and a powerful trend toward political participation among private sector labor. Reports on the 2005 elections indicate a continuation of this trajectory. In Six October City, voter turnout rates were extraordinarily high, with some polling stations registering up to 90 percent.[30]

We are seeing the waning of state control of the working class and the waxing of private sector business control over this class. That is, Egyptian politics is shifting from public clientelism to private clientelism. This fact helps us understand the steady drop in workers' representation in parliament, which fell from 7.5 percent in 2000 to 4 percent in 2005. The regime is fielding fewer and fewer public sector workers for the People's Assembly. As mentioned above, the fact that the NDP nominated only four candidates from the General Federation of Labor Unions stirred considerable bitterness in labor syndicate circles, and that the rancor is focused primarily on the new wing in the ruling party led by Gamal Mubarak. The shrinking number of labor leader candidates backed by the NDP reflects the gradual transformation of the NDP into a businessmen's party.

Although public sector labor continues to monopolize the representation of workers in the General Federation of Labor Unions and in parliament, this situation clearly can not persist for long. Granted, private sector labor is strongly controlled by private businessmen, as is reflected in its voting patterns. But this does not obviate the rise from the ranks of private sector labor of new leaders capable of assuming the mantle of leadership from public sector labor, which carried the torch for the Egyptian working class for nearly half a century.

Without a doubt, the growing political profile of the working class will contribute greatly to democratic transformation. Democracy is built on a strong balance between various parts of society. As the power of workers grows with respect to the regime and to business bosses, and as their autonomy and organizational capacities increase, the prospects for democratization in Egypt will also increase.

CONCLUSION

This chapter examined the impact of the ebb of the rentier/caretaker state on political change in Egypt. We opened with a discussion of the rentier state theory, which posits a causal relationship between the availability of rentier incomes and the state's ability to exercise authoritarian control over society and between a sharp reduction in such incomes and the prospects of political change. While acknowledging the validity of this logic, we argued that it made no allowance for intermediate variables that link the collapse of state revenues to political change. We demonstrated that the relationship is not as straightforward as it appeared to some theorists and that a variety of other factors enter the equation. We therefore opted for the Rueschemeyer, Stephens, and Stephens model for democratic transformation, which, unlike the rentier state theory, reaches beyond an analysis of the balance of power between the state and society by disaggregating society into various classes and sectors so as to permit for a closer inspection of these groups' varying attitudes and practices with regard to democracy.

We have seen how the state's fiscal straits and the regime's attempts to overcome them helped augment the power of the capitalist class with respect to the regime. This development induced the regime to expand its social base into that community and incorporate businessmen into government, thereby co-opting a significant portion of the capitalist class and, simultaneously, bolstering itself through access to new sources of finance. The result is that the

Egyptian regime today rests on an alliance forged between the top bureaucracy and some capitalist elements. Although, according to our analysis, it is
unlikely that capitalist forces will oppose the regime or contribute even indi-
rectly to its fall, their growing control over economic resources is reshaping
the Egyptian political arena. First, it is propelling society toward a plurality in
power centers. While the politicization of businessmen benefits the regime by
expanding its social support base, it simultaneously increases internal rifts
because of the tensions between the established government elites and the
capitalist elements that have recently come on board. Second, the politicization of businessmen inevitably politicizes other classes. When businessmen
get into politics, others get involved too, as we have seen with the emergence
of private sector labor as a critical voting bloc in the 2000 and 2005 parliamentary elections. Many businessmen actively promoted the participation of
their employees by helping them obtain their voter registration cards. Still,
as we pointed out, while this sector of labor remains subordinate to the
bosses, there is no guarantee that this will remain the case. Those whose
votes today are determined by a free meal and a day's paid leave may vote
completely differently tomorrow on the prospect of larger gains or longer-
term considerations.

The growing political influence of businessmen sparked resentment
among the intelligentsia and some segments of the middle class who were
feeling increasingly marginalized. The emergence and success of the Kifaya
Movement was one of the manifestations of mounting anger against both the
regime and the growing role of the capitalist class in the regime. Two of the
major weak points of Gamal Mubarak, the bête noire of the opposition, are
his close connections to big business and his neoliberal political economic
leanings.

That the growing political clout of businessmen has worked to spread political involvement among other sectors of the public can only enhance the
prospects of democratic transition in Egypt. There can be no democracy
without participation. In fact, one of the gravest challenges to democracy in
Egypt in recent decades has been the high levels of political apathy, as demonstrated by voter turnout of only 28 percent in the 2005 elections (the actual
ratio is lower if we take into consideration electoral fraud) compared with, say,
60 percent in the 1951 elections, the last to be held in the quasi-liberal period
that preceded the coup of 23 July 1952 that established the militarist regime
that still holds the reins of power in Egypt today.[31]

If the growing power of businessmen as a consequence of the fiscal straits of the state has fired the anger of some segments of the middle class and fueled their political activism, businessmen per se are not necessarily the original source of their frustration and discontent. As we observed in this chapter, dwindling state revenues caused public services to the middle class to dwindle, while causing the state to increase its demands on this class. The government is especially keen to harvest higher tax returns from the middle class and from the practitioners of the liberal professions in particular. This is certain to lead to more and more clashes between taxpayers and the state.

Perhaps it would be appropriate before closing this chapter to underscore the major impact of the socioeconomic sphere on politics and the extent to which such factors determine the possibilities. Nevertheless, the chances that any one possibility will prevail are contingent upon any number of political and ideological variables both at home and abroad. We have seen in this chapter that opportunities for democracy in Egypt have increased as the result of the end of the rentier/caretaker state and the rise of the tax-levying state. Yet, it should be clear that our discussion has focused solely on what we might term the "fiscal infrastructure" for democracy. This structure might shape the realm of possibilities, but the actual fate of democracy will depend on a number of other factors, not least of which is the power and role of political Islam. Such factors are outside the scope of this study.

CONCLUSION

AUTHORITARIAN REGIMES do not only resort to repressive means to perpetuate themselves; they also use money. Money can buy the loyalty of some segments of society and placate others. The money factor is even more important for rentier or quasi-rentier states. It is impossible to understand the evolution of these types of regimes without placing state revenues and expenditures at the center of the analysis. The political economy perspective is, in short, greatly advantageous to an investigation of these regimes.

Since the mid-1970s, Egypt has been ruled by an authoritarian regime whose stability has depended on a quasi-rentier state that obtained large influxes of money from oil, Suez Canal revenues, and foreign aid. How has the Mubarak regime managed to perpetuate its stability despite a sharp drop in rentier revenues since the mid-1980s, and how has Egyptian politics changed as a consequence? These were the central questions that prompted this study.

The obvious starting point was to examine the evolution of Egypt's national revenues since the 1970s with an eye to demonstrating how these revenues formed the most salient factor in explaining changes in the size of state expenditures. Chapter 1 showed that the best approach to investigating these changes was not an ideological vantage point (the socialist or capitalist orientation of the regime) or the perspective of official economic policy (interventionist or laissez-faire). As we saw, the regime twice swung to the right on economic policy, toward the promotion of a free market economy and a reduction of the role of the state in steering the economic process, first in the 1970s, and again in the 1990s. On both occasions, the state propaganda machine blazoned the advantages of a free market and the private sector, and assailed the ills of a planned economy and the public sector, while the opposition within and outside the regime roared against "the state's withdrawal from the economy." Such ideological commotion could not hide the palpable fact that public expenditures increased in the 1970s and in the early 1990s. We therefore concluded that the primary driving force behind the size and evolution of the rentier or quasi-rentier state had little to do with ideological slogans and declared economic policies and everything to do with rentier revenues. When these increased, the size of state bureaucracy followed; when they shrank, so too did the state bureaucracy.

Accordingly, it is not difficult to perceive why the Egyptian regime appears to be incapable of carrying out fiscal policy. A large chunk of its revenues comes from rentier income, that "gift from the heavens," as Alfred Marshall put it, so the regime in Egypt is strongly inclined to look heavenward in the hope that it will rain gold. Petroleum and Suez Canal revenues are heavily influenced by external factors over which the regime has little control. The revenue that it can most influence comes from foreign aid, which is why soliciting foreign aid is one of the Egyptian regime's major activities. Hence, the persistent refrain that the regime pitches to external audiences—Egypt is the political cornerstone of the Middle East; it has the power to lead the Arabs to war against Israel, and it is the only power that can bring the Arabs to make peace with Israel—and Mubarak's revelation that 70 percent of his time is devoted to the Palestinian question. Aid-related revenues are why Egypt's image abroad is one of the foremost obsessions in Egyptian foreign policy and why the regime can tolerate opponents apart from those it sees as jeopardizing the influx of foreign aid, such as sociology professor Saad Eddin Ibrahim, who was sentenced to two years in prison in 2008 on the charges of "tainting Egypt's image abroad" and asking Washington to link aid to Egypt with the Egyptian government's performance on human rights.

If, as suggested throughout this book, spending is one of the most important instruments of political control for the authoritarian regime in Egypt, how did the regime accommodate the sharp decline in its revenues and, hence, its spending power? Our study of developments in the composition of public expenditures found that the regime reordered its priorities, trimming allocations here so as to make higher allocations there. For example, it reduced outlays on the army in exchange for granting the military establishment greater financial autonomy, which is to say that the army could now generate its own resources through extensive investment in various areas of civil production. The regime also cut back outlays on subsidies, enabling it to concentrate more resources on the police, domestic security, and the state's cultural and media propaganda machinery. In tandem with the reprioritization of allocations to government agencies, there was a shift in the distribution of resources within the various agencies in favor of the upper echelons of the bureaucracy. In other words, under the pressure of the fiscal crisis, remuneration of government employees became less equitable. Simultaneously, turning a blind eye to bribery, kickbacks, and other forms of increasingly widespread corruption enabled the government employees to compensate for the shrinkage of their official salaries. In short, Egypt perpetuated its political control despite financial straits by reordering spending priorities while providing unofficial vents to those adversely affected.

The process of accommodating to declining revenues also affected how resources were distributed between central government and local government agencies. The Egyptian state bureaucracy is highly centralized, which becomes tangibly evident from a glance at the national budget. The governorates are heavily dependent upon central government for most of their financial needs. They are not entitled to levy taxes, only to collect certain municipal fees and charges. As the regime reduced allocations to the governorates, the governorates were forced to depend more and more on their own resources. This development was paraded beneath the rhetorical gloss of "decentralization," a banner the regime embraced upon the advice of international financial institutions and USAID. However, real decentralization requires a reformulation of the relationship between central government and local government in the direction of increasing the powers of the latter. Such a process never took place in Egypt at the institutional level, and the constitutional and legal framework governing the relations between the institutions of government has remained essentially unchanged. One of the most salient traits of the Mubarak era is flexibility within the confines of institutional rigidity. It is little wonder, then, that under the so-called decentralization process local government did not acquire the right to levy taxes, which would have reflected an institutional change. Instead, governorates were granted permission to create special funds derived from municipal fees and charges and from the donations of businessmen. This solution proved costly. The funds were infested by a particularly high level of corruption, so far removed were they from central government oversight and public scrutiny (as represented by the municipal councils), which can only flourish under a democratic system. In addition, the funds violated one of the most important principles of public finance: the all-embracing unity of the public budget. Their revenues and outlays were not recorded in national budget accounts even though they were an integral part of public finance.

In light of the foregoing, the evolution of the relationship between central government and the governorates is indicative not of the decentralization but of the fragmentation of the state. Perhaps this was inevitable, given the regime's disinclination to move toward political decentralization, which is difficult to reconcile with the political control exercised by an authoritarian government.

The Mubarak regime's resistance to change in its attempts to alleviate crisis was amply demonstrated in our study of its attempts to develop state revenues. The succession of measures that the regime took betray a particular logic: Start with the measures that entail the least possible political cost, even if they come at a high economic cost, before proceeding to politically costlier measures, such as income taxes. Thus, the regime began with the "inflation tax," which is to say that it issued new banknotes. Then it turned to the more transparent and politically costlier sales tax. When this proved insufficient to generate enough revenue, it was forced to resort to the most unpopular measure and the most likely to stir public resistance: reform of the income tax structure in the hope of curtailing tax evasion and fraud. It is perhaps premature to judge whether this reform has proved capable of generating a tangible increase in state revenues. However, the latest figures on tax revenues cited in this study indicate that tax reform has so far had limited success and that the regime therefore failed to raise the ratio of public revenues with respect to GDP.

A decrease in state revenues is not a sign of failure when officials decide to lower tax rates, as has happened in many countries. But it is a sign of failure when they resolve to increase tax revenues and fail to attain the desired objective, as occurred in Egypt, where increased taxation has not offset the shortage of revenues with respect to GDP. The regime has also failed to trim its expenditures to match the decline in revenues, and the budgetary deficit has continued at a high level.

The Egyptian experience illustrates the difficulty of instituting tax reform under an authoritarian regime. Reforming tax structures entails a commensurate restructuring of the relationship between the state and the citizens whereby the latter undertake their obligations to pay taxes in exchange for the assurance that the former undertakes its obligation to spend tax revenues wisely and honestly and commits itself to a transparent accounting of how it handles the public purse. It is difficult for authoritarian regimes to bring themselves to make these kinds of changes. A related problem is that tax reform requires the state to make compromises and reach understandings with representatives of different sectors of society. The Ministry of Finance has signed a number of agreements with business organizations and has entered into negotiations with organizations that represent groups from the middle class, such as physicians and pharmacists, and it met with considerable success in obtaining their approval of its tax reform policies. However, these organizations are weak and marginal due to the deterioration of civil society in general after more than half a century of authoritarian rule. The support that the government obtains from these organizations is for the most part meaningless, since they are semi-governmental or corporatist entities subordinate to the will of the regime rather than to the sectors of society they are meant to represent.

The state's inability to raise the amount of tax revenues it collects from society does not necessarily indicate that society has mobilized itself effectively against the power of the state. In Egypt, the most prevalent resistance to taxation is indirect and apolitical. Intensive litigation to counter an overbearing executive is a salient trait of the Mubarak era; the regime has granted a degree of autonomy to the judiciary, and on several occasions, measures introduced by the regime to increase tax revenues have been overturned. It is our belief that the primary function of this relative autonomy is to depoliticize the opposition by drawing it into judicial processes. This is not to suggest that the regime has refrained from meddling in judicial affairs or has refused to respect judicial rulings from time to time. But even so, the judiciary has served as the primary vehicle for checking the excesses of the executive authority in the Mubarak era.

Tax fraud is another common apolitical means of resisting taxation in Egypt. The prevalence of these two forms of resistance shed light on the relationship of the state and society in Egypt. It is a relationship in which both sides are weak. The state makes policies and laws that it is unable to persuade or force society to respect, and society neither openly fights these policies and laws nor feels obliged to abide by them. This reality challenges the notion that the relationship between the state and society is a zero-sum game. The weakness of one side is not evidence of the strength of the other. If strength of the state is taken to mean its ability to enforce the law by winning popular consent or by coercion, the Egyptian state is weak.

The quasi-rentier state in Egypt has waned or, at least, is on the wane. As the end of the Mubarak era nears, Egypt is living on about half of the revenues (in terms of GDP) as it did when Mubarak first came to power. This hard reality must have a profound effect on the nature of political life in Egypt. For example, will the waning of the rentier state necessarily propel Egypt toward the club of democratic nations? The rentier state theory discussed in Chapter 5 suggests that it will in that the end of rentier income and the need to levy taxes renders the state vulnerable to pressures from society. However, the Egyptian case demonstrates that the end of rentier income does not necessarily propel the state to impose taxes. As seen in Chapter 4, rather than leading the rise of a tax-levying state, the end of the quasi-rentier state led to the rise of a predatory state inclined to inveigle money out of society through such indirect and nontransparent routes as the mint. The ruling elite turned to taxation and income tax reform only after some twenty years of grueling financial troubles. Also, as discussed in Chapter 3, the financial pressures that forced the state to reduce its allocations to local government propelled it toward fragmentation, not toward decentralization.

Thus, the end of rentierism does not necessarily lead to democratic transformation. However, it has generated important changes in the Egyptian political sphere, opening new realms that can be exploited democratically. For example, the regime's attempts to extricate itself from financial difficulties led to the rising power of the capitalist class with respect to the ruling elite, a development that drove the latter to embrace or contain elements of this class in order to expand its social base and bolster itself with fresh economic and human resources. As a consequence, the ruling elite today is founded on an alliance between the upper echelons of the government establishment (the army and the security agencies, above all) and some sectors of the business class. While we can rule out the possibility that this class will oppose the regime or contribute in a direct way overthrowing it, the fact that it controls vast economic resources reorders the political equation in Egypt. First, it has given rise to a plurality of power centers. The politicization of businessmen may have helped the regime expand its social support base, but it simultaneously created tensions between the traditional ruling establishment and the new capitalist elements that have been taken on board. In addition, the politicization of businessmen led to the politicization of other segments of society. The 2000 and 2005 parliamentary elections saw the rise of a powerful new voting bloc— private sector workers sent to the polls in large numbers by businessmen candidates who obtained voter registration cards for them. Granted, these new voters entered the electoral game through the gateway of political clientelism, but that does not eliminate the prospect of their electoral independence under conditions of greater political freedom. The Egyptian political regime is still based on clientelism, a relationship between political patrons and clients. What is new today is that the patrons are no longer the bureaucratic and military elites; businessmen are now swelling their ranks. Although the growing diversity of patrons has nothing to do with democracy or democratic plurality, it does provide clients with a greater margin of maneuverability.

The politicization of businessmen has sent waves through other sectors of society. In particular, it has stirred considerable rancor among intellectuals and segments of the middle class who feel increasingly marginalized by the growing hold of private capital over politics and government in Egypt. The rise of the Kifaya (Enough) movement that is opposed to the scheme to secure the heredity succession of Gamal Mubarak, who is closely connected to powerful circles in the business community, is a symptom of the mounting anger among the intelligentsia about the growing political clout of business magnates.

Clearly, the growing political involvement of businessmen has galvanized other sectors of society into political participation, increasing the prospects for democratization in Egypt. There can be no democracy without political participation. The state's increasing recourse to taxation may also be moving society in this direction. The recent attempt to obtain greater revenues from an important segment of the middle class—the liberal professions— precipitated clashes between this sector of society and the state. As observed in Chapter 5, in 2009, for the first time since the July 1952 revolution, one group within this class—pharmacists—went on strike to protest a government decision to put them into a higher tax bracket.

Observers of the Egyptian political scene today can not fail to notice a major phenomenon: a dramatic increase in protest that has been described by Joel Beinin as the most powerful social movement in Egypt since the 1940s.[1] Nor will it escape observers that social conflict over economic resources has occupied a central position in the Egyptian public realm in recent years, which augurs an important political transformation in which class politics will play a crucial role. We could go so far as to hold that class politics may eventually overshadow identity politics, in which realm Islamist and fundamentalist trends have reigned, placing such issues as women's attire at the center of public debate. Some scholars, such as Asef Bayat, Olivier Roy, and Patrick Haenni, have suggested that Egypt has entered the post-Islamist era.[2] The notion may seem odd during a time of flaring tensions between the

United States and many Islamist factions in the wake of the events of 11 September 2001, but perhaps the saying "wars intensify as they near an end" applies here. Although it is probably precipitous to assert that Egypt has entered the post-Islamic era, it is certain that Egypt is in the process of a profound transition whereby the waning of the rentier state and the growing conflict over economic resources is opening possibilities for breaking the hold of identity politics over the Egyptian public sphere and, hence, weakening the sway of the Islamist movement.

This study has attempted to shed light on one of the most important dilemmas facing the Egyptian state, which is how to ensure stable and reasonable levels of revenue to enable it to perform its functions effectively. The central object of the study was the problem of the state in Egypt, and its fiscal crisis, we believed, would be a fruitful avenue of inquiry. As mentioned in the introduction, we were greatly influenced by works that stressed the importance of studying the state from the fiscal perspective, and we remain convinced that the problem of the weak state in Egypt is and will continue to be one of the major challenges facing its political elite. The liberal conceptual framework has failed to comprehend the dilemma of the Egyptian state, as it does not differentiate between the regime and the state or between the repressive power of the state and its developmental power. As a consequence, there prevailed the erroneous belief that the problem in Egypt is that a powerful authoritarian state dominates a weak and submissive society, whereas, in fact, the problem is that both the state and its civil society are weak, and the solution is to strengthen both.

Egypt is not an exception in the third world. The dilemma of how to strengthen the state is more severe in most other Arab countries, where the nation-state is still under construction, as in Lebanon, or where the state has collapsed entirely or is on the verge of collapse, as in Somalia and Sudan, respectively. The chief challenge, then, is not solely to democratize their forms of government, but also to build and secure the authority of the state. This book is an attempt to assess the problem of authoritarianism and its relationship to the weak state. It is simultaneously an attempt to study the question of democracy and its relationship to the strength of the state. One of the most important conclusions is that authoritarian rule is not a prerequisite for building a strong state. On the contrary, the Egyptian case demonstrates that the authoritarian character of the regime can be one of the more formidable obstacles to the establishment of a strong state.

EPILOGUE
The Political Economy of Egypt's 2011 Uprising

THE EGYPTIAN UPRISING of 2011 erupted just as the book was going to print. This epilogue provides a political economy reading of the uprising in line with the analysis presented earlier in the chapters.

In early February 2011, as I looked out on the crowds in Tahrir Square, the symbolic center in the struggle for democracy, the site now known as the "Square of Freedom," it seemed evident that this uprising was the extension of a longstanding, ongoing conflict among a number of parties: the corrupt authoritarian ruling group headed by President Mubarak, trying to maintain power; the millions of people across nearly all the major cities of Egypt, now occupying the streets; and the various political groups, each trying to steer the events toward their own aims and political preferences. But it was equally clear that something new had been achieved—a new spirit of courage, sacrifice, and solidarity among the common people who took to the streets, as well as some political gains. Hosni Mubarak, the old "patriarch," has promised to leave his post in September 2011 after the completion of his sixth mandate, declaring on television that his only wish now was just to die in Egypt! His son Gamal and some of his allies were expelled from the National Democratic Party, the ruling party, which had seen most of its offices destroyed by furious demonstrators. The Central Security Forces, composed of hundreds of thousands of men who have repressed demonstrations and opposition since the rules of Nasser and Sadat and generally imposed terror across the country for decades, were defeated. Their forces were observed taking off their uniforms while escaping the rage of the masses. Many state security headquarters (the offices of the political police) were set ablaze. After three days of the uprising, the ruling group recognized the legitimacy of the uprising's demands. It took yet more days before the regime sought to negotiate with the opposition, still maneuvering all the time to find ways to continue the Mubarak regime, just without Mubarak himself.

The Egyptian uprising has so far lost more than 300 martyrs, caused thousands of injuries, and seen hundreds disappeared and arrested—the highest price paid by the Egyptian democratic movement in many decades. But the strength of today's opposition groups and the willingness of the democratic movement to pay this ultimate price for regime change is not merely a coincidence of events. Indeed, it is a natural outcome of long-term structural changes in Egyptian political economy. As shown throughout this book, the exhaustion of the semi-rentier/caretaker state is fundamentally altering the contours of Egyptian politics.

The Egyptian state today functions on roughly half the revenues (in terms of percentage of GDP) as it did when Mubarak first came to power in 1981. Oil and gas revenues, Suez Canal returns, and foreign aid are no longer sufficient to feed the state coffers and make up for low tax revenues. Fiscal crisis is a dilemma for any authoritarian regime, as its stability depends not only on political repression, but also on buying the loyalty of segments of the population. For a quarter century, the Mubarak regime endeavored to stop the dwindling rentier revenues and reorganize public expenditures in an attempt to reduce the political costs of the financial decline. Ultimately, the story of the Mubarak regime is simply one of a proven ability to delay, a limited success at forestalling the inevitable political outcomes of fiscal crisis and a changing political economy. The regime's strategies to adapt to the crisis over the years, as well as the high cost to the state and economy were detailed in the first three chapters of this book. But a regime can delay the political consequences of fiscal crises only so long. In the end, public will makes its wishes known. The possibility for rule beyond the Mubarak regime and the opportunities for political mobilization were discussed in Chapters 4 and 5 and in the Conclusion.

The Egyptian uprising of 2011 is the largest upheaval since the 1919 revolution against the British occupation, but it is not without precedent. Eighteenth and nineteenth January 1977 saw the explosion of an uprising that also included most of the cities of Egypt. The differences between these two uprisings, however, lie not only in their respective durations—two days versus over two weeks as of this writing and quite possibly longer—but in three distinctive features. First, the 1977 uprising came as an immediate reaction to an increase in prices of basic food items, which at that time were controlled by a central authority, declared by government media on 18 January 1977. The 2011 events were not directly linked to any specific government policy. The starting date for the 2011 protests—25 January, a "Day of Anger"—was announced weeks in advance by new political groups. In other words, in 2011, the uprising was an action, while in 1977, it was a reaction.

The second difference is the nature of the people's demands. In 1977, the demand was purely economic: mainly reversing the increase in prices, which the regime immediately accepted. But today, in 2011, the demands are mostly political: the resignation of the president, the end to the entire regime of Hosni Mubarak, and democratization, including removing the state of emergency that has been imposed on the country for the thirty years of Mubarak's rule.

The third difference is the social composition of the protests. In 1977, mostly students and state employees, white and blue collar, initiated the protests. They were joined by some of the very poor and unemployed. In 2011, it is a wider swath of the population in the streets—middle class citizens, the self-employed, and employees in the private sector have joined the protests, alongside students, public sector workers, the extremely poor, and the unemployed.

Ultimately, the differences between the two events can be explained by the changing Egyptian political economy. The uprising of 1977 came after three years of economic liberalization (*infitah*), a process that created a new class of *nouveau riche* and generated deep resentment among state employees and the poor. As for the 2011 uprising, it takes place after now twenty years of Mubarak's open economy initiative and after a long process of decline in state services and an increasing recourse to taxing the Egyptian population. Today, Egypt has a relatively important new middle class: financially autonomous vis-à-vis the state, relatively well educated, well connected to the external world, acquiring organizational skills and capacities via the Internet and the new modes of communication. This middle class has grown increasingly worried by the deterioration of state institutions and the incapacity of the state to stimulate successful economic development, while at the same time turning to ask for more money, such as the newly imposed property tax. In the end, a new balance of power is being forged between the government and the middle class.

It is too early to predict the outcomes of the 2011 Egyptian uprising, but it is evident that we are now observing the autumn of Mubarak's dictatorship. This uprising is not the product of euphoria among the youth, as the official media sometimes try to claim, but rather the outcome of a lengthy structural transformation in the political economy of Egypt. May the future bring democracy to this country, not a new form of authoritarianism.

REFERENCE MATTER

ACKNOWLEDGMENTS

THIS BOOK IS the distillation of about ten years of research effort first initiated at Lausanne University and continued at the Institute of Political Studies (IEP) in Paris. The work was translated and adapted for the Egyptian and Arab reader and published in 2004 by Merit, again in 2006 and 2007 by al-Dar, and finally in its current translation and updated version for the English reader.

Many people helped me throughout that long journey. First are my parents, who supported me financially and morally during my postgraduate studies. My friend and fellow researcher Patrick Haenni supported me throughout my years in France, most particularly in obtaining my fellowship and by his work editing my French dissertation. Soheir Fahmi, Najat Belhatem, Dina Heshmat, and Véronique Danis also helped in editing and proofreading my various writings. Rafaat Abou Seif and Mary Youssef were my key supporters in obtaining the bulk of the budgetary data on which the book is mainly based.

Thanks also are due to Marwa Farouk who helped in the gathering of judicial information, Tamer Makram who helped in the statistical analysis, Professor Jean Leca at the IEP who accorded me the chance to work under his supervision, Alain Roussillon, the distinguished researcher of Egyptian politics, who introduced and recommended me to Jean Leca and Professor Clement Moore. Alain's memory will always be alive in my heart.

The Arabic version of *The Autumn of Dictatorship* has been the main gate that allowed my entry into Egyptian intellectual and political life. I am indebted to all the researchers and journalists who have helped review and spread the word about the book and extend its main message through the Egyptian media that a distinction should be made between the Egyptian state and the ruling group governing that state, and that an urgent reform of the political regime is necessary in order to reverse the weakening and fragmenting process of the Egyptian state. I am especially indebted to the novelist Bahaa Taher and the journalist Ibrahim Eissa.

I am particularly indebted to the friends and colleagues who encouraged and supported me in compiling and publishing the English version. My profound thanks are due to Joel Beinin, who connected me with Stanford University Press and enabled the fund that partially paid the English translator. My deepest gratitude I owe to Mary Mourad who helped in the editing and whose entry in my life has changed the course of my being. To Mary, my life companion, I dedicate this book.

NOTES

Preface

1. Samer Soliman, "L'Argent de l'État et Politique: La Sortie difficile de l'État Rentier en Egypte sous Moubarak," PhD diss., l'Institut d'Etudes Politiques de Paris, 2004.

2. Samer Soliman, *Al-Nizam al-Qawi wa al-Dawla al-Da'ifa : Al-Azma al-Maliyya wa al-Taghyîr al-Syasi fi Misr fi 'Ahd Mubarak* [Strong Regime, Weak State: The Fiscal Crisis and Political Change Under Mubarak] (Cairo: Merit, 2004).

3. Samer Soliman, *Al-Nizam al-Qawi wa al-Dawla al-Da'ifa: Al-Azma al-Maliyya wa al-Taghyîr al-Syasi fi Misr fi 'Ahd Mubarak* [Strong Regime, Weak State: The Fiscal Crisis and Political Change under Mubarak], 3rd edition (Cairo: al-Dâr, 2006).

4. "Egyptian Researcher Asks Questions About the Future of His Country After the Departure of the Ruling Regime," Reuters, 1 May 2006.

Introduction

1. Cited in Sébastien Guex, *L'Argent de l'État* (Lausanne: Éditions Réalités Sociales, 1998).

2. Robert Springborg, *Mubarak's Egypt: Fragmentation of the Political Order* (Boulder, CO: Westview, 1989).

3. Reuters, 17 July 1990.

4. American Embassy in Cairo, *Economic Trends Report* (Cairo: The American Embassy in Cairo, 2003), p. 1.

5. Calculation based on data from Ministry of Finance, *Closing Account of the Budget*, various issues, and Ministry of Economy, *The Monthly Economic Bulletin*, various issues.

6. For more details on the political deliberalization of the 1990s, see Eberhard Kienle, *A Grand Delusion: Democracy and Economic Reform in Egypt* (London: I.B. Tauris Publishers, 2000).

7. Alfred Marshall, *Principles of Economics: An Introductory Volume* (London: Macmillan, 1920, reprinted 1988).

8. See, for example, Theda Skocpol et al., *Bringing the State Back In* (New York: Cambridge University Press, 1985).

9. Michael Mann, *The Sources of Social Power,* Volume II: *The Rise of Classes and Nation-States, 1760–1914* (New York: Cambridge University Press, 1993), p. 59; and "The Autonomous Power of the State: Its Origins, Mechanisms and Results," in *States in History*, ed. John Hall (New York: Basil Blackwell, 1986), pp. 113–119.

10. Joel Migdal, *Strong Societies and Weak States* (Princeton, NJ: Princeton University Press, 1988).

11. Joseph Schumpter, "The Crisis of the Tax State," *International Economic Papers* 4, no. 4 (1918): 5–38.

12. Karl Marx and Frederick Engels, *The Communist Manifesto* (London: Electric Book Co., 2001).

13. Karl Marx, *Eighteenth Brumaire of Louis Bonaparte* (New York: International Publishers, 1991).

14. Nicos Poulantzas, *Political Power and Social Class* (London: Verso, 1969).

15. Ibid.

16. James O'Connor, *The Fiscal Crisis of the State* (New York: St. Martin Press, 1973), p. 6.

17. Ibid., p. 7.

18. Ibid., p. 8.

19. Ibid., p. 9.

20. Ibid., p. 8.

21. Anthony Giddens, *A Contemporary Critique of Historical Marxism* (London: Macmillan, 1981), p. 18.

22. James O'Connor, *The Fiscal Crisis of the State* (London/New Brunswick, NJ: Transactions Publishers, 2002, with a new introduction by the author).

23. Ian Gough, "State Expenditure in Advanced Capitalism," *New Left Review* 92, no. 1 (1975): 53–92.

24. Ibid.

25. Ibid., p. 76.

26. Margaret Levi, *Of Rule and Revenue* (Berkeley: University of California Press, 1988).

27. Ibid., p. 2.

28. Ibid., p. 3.

29. See Skocpol, *Bringing the State Back In.*

30. Levi, *Of Rule and Revenue*, p. 3.

31. Ibid.

32. Ibid., pp. 11, 12, 17, 23, 32, 33.

33. Ibid., pp. 35–37.

34. Ibid., p. 139.

35. Ibid., p. 7.

36. Peter Hall, "Political Science and the Three New Institutionalisms," *Political Studies* 44, no. 5 (1996): 936–957.

37. Sven Steinmo et al., *Structuring Politics: Historical Institutionalism in Comparative Analysis* (New York: Cambridge University Press, 1992).

38. Ibid, p. 8.

39. Ibid.

40. Sven Steinmo, *Taxation and Democracy: Swedish, British and American Approaches to Financing the Modern State* (New Haven, CT: Yale University Press, 1993).

41. Sven Steinmo et al., *Structuring Politics: Historical Institutionalism in Comparative Analysis* (New York: Cambridge University Press, 1992).

42. Richard Musgrave, "Taxation and Democracy," *Journal of Economic Literature* 3, no. 2 (1995): 854–855.

43. Jonas Pontusson, "From Comparative Public Policy to Political Economy," *Comparative Political Studies* 28, no. 3 (1995): 353–378.

44. Hazem Beblawi and Giacomo Luciani, *The Rentier State in the Arab World* (London: Croom Helm, 1987).

45. Ibid., p. 12.

46. Hazem Beblawi, "The Rentier State in the Arab World," in *The Arab State,* ed. Giacomo Luciani (London: Routledge, 1990).

47. Giacomo Luciani, "Resources, Revenues and Authoritarianism in the Arab World: Beyond the Rentier State," in *Political Liberalization and Democratization in the Arab World,* ed. Bahgat Korany, Rex Brynen, and Paul Nobel (London: Lynne Rienner Publishers, 1999).

48. Ibid., p. 73.

49. Galal Amin, *Egypt's Economic Predicament* (New York: E.J. Brill, 1995).

50. Hélène Cottonet, "Ressources Exogènes, Performances Industrielles et Croissance: Le Cas de l'Égypte, 1970–1997," PhD diss., Clemont-Ferrand University, 2003; and Marie-France Vernier, "Essor des Recettes en Devises et Intervention de l'État: Le Syndrome Rentier, Approches dans le Cas Egyptien," PhD diss., Paris XIII University, 1999.

51. Poulantzas, *Political Power and Social Class.*

52. Stephen Krasner, "Approaches to the State," *Comparative Politics* 16, no. 2 (1984): 223–246.

53. Colin Hay, Michael Lister, and David Marsh, eds., *The State: Theories and Issues* (Basingstoke, UK: Palgrave Macmillan, 2006), pp. 10–11.

54. Ibid., pp. 12–13.

55. Evelyne Huber and Dietrich Rueschemeyer, "The Impact of Economic Development on Democracy," *Journal of Economic Perspective* 7, no. 3 (1993): 71–86.

56. See, for example, John Waterbury, *The Egypt of Nasser and Sadat: The Political Economy of Two Regimes* (Princeton, NJ: Princeton University Press, 1983).

57. Transparency International, Annual Report, 2008, www.transparency.org/publications/publications, p. 51.

58. The state public budget law 53 of 1973 modified by law 11 of 1979 stipulated that the public budget include all utilizations and resources and exempted special accounts and funds from the entire budget. Its article 20 made it possible by presidential decree to establish specialized funds for limited utilization of certain resources.

59. Egyptian Constitution, 1971.

60. Cited in Guex, *L'Argent de l'État*.

Chapter 1

1. The Open Door policy, or *Infitah*, was initiated in 1974 by President Sadat and activated by law 43 that year. It was intended to move Egypt away from its centralized economy to a more liberal economy by encouraging foreign and domestic private investment.

2. For further detail on the growth of industrial capitalism in the Mubarak era, see Samer Soliman, *State and Industrial Capitalism in Egypt,* Cairo Papers in Social Science (Cairo: American University in Cairo Press, 1998).

3. Ministry of Planning, *Follow-up Report*, 1980–81 and 1990–91.

4. Ibid.

5. Ibid.

6. Sadiq Ahmed, *Public Finance in Egypt: Its Structure and Trends* (Washington, DC: World Bank, 1984).

7. Hans Löfgren, "Economic Policy in Egypt: A Breakdown in Reform Resistance?" *International Journal of Middle East Studies* 25, no. 3 (1993): 407–421.

8. Ministry of Finance, *Balance Sheet for the Budget*, 1986–87 and 1987–88.

9. Ibid.

10. Löfgren, "Economic Policy in Egypt."

11. Ibid.

12. Peter Allum et al., *Egypt Beyond Stabilization* (Washington, DC: IMF, 1998).

13. World Bank, *Report and Recommendation of the President of the International Bank for Reconstruction and Development to the Executive Directors on a Proposed Structural Adjustment Loan to Egypt* (Washington, DC: World Bank, 1991).

14. These figures are based on calculations by the author of figures from the Ministry of Finance's closing accounts for the national budget for several years and from the Egyptian Central Bank's annual reports, also for several years.

15. Center for Economic and Financial Studies, Faculty of Economics and Political Science, *Report on International Finance in Egypt,* 1999.

16. USAID/Egypt, http://egypt.usaid.gov.

17. Alan Richards, "The Political Economy of Dilatory Reform: Egypt in the 1980s," *World Development* 19, no. 12 (1991): 1721–1730.

18. Nazih Ayubi, *Overstating the Arab State* (London: IB Tauris & Co. Ltd, 1995), p. 326.

19. For further details on his opinion, see Henry Moore Clement, "Money and Power: The Dilemma of Egyptian Infitah," *Middle East Journal* 40, no. 4 (1986): 634–650.

20. Alfred Marshall, *Principles of Economics* (London: Macmillan and Co., Ltd, 1920).

Chapter 2

1. James O'Connor, *The Fiscal Crisis of the State* (New York: St. Martin's Press, 1973).

2. International Monetary Fund, *Arab Republic of Egypt: Economic Readjustment with Growth*, Country Economic memorandum (Washington, DC: IMF, 1990).

3. Perhaps the best work on this subject is Robert Springborg, *Mubarak's Egypt: Fragmentation of the Political Order* (Boulder, CO: Westview, 1989).

4. Hussein Abdel Razeq, *Misr fi 18 wa 19 yanayir* [Egypt during 18 and 19 January] (Cairo: Shuhdi, 1985).

5. Daniel Brumberg, "Survival Strategies vs. Democratic Bargains: The Politics of Economic Reform in Contemporary Egypt," in *The Politics of Economic Reform in the Middle East*, ed. Henri J. Barkey (New York: St. Martin's Press, 1992), p. 85.

6. See Springborg, *Mubarak's Egypt*.

7. Ibid.

8. Abu Ghazala's pro-American sympathies were well-known, to the degree that the Egyptian novelist Son'allah Ibrahim devoted whole passages to the field marshal's statements to this effect in his novel *Zat* (Self). Son'allah Ibrahim, *Zat*, 2nd ed. (Cairo: Dar al-Mustaqbal al-Arabi, 1998).

9. Springborg, *Mubarak's Egypt*.

10. *Al-Qahira*, a magazine founded in the early 1990s, is an example.

11. Ministry of Planning, *The Annual Economic and Social Plan*, 1998, p. 35.

12. Unfortunately, we have no figures testifying to the extent of such contributions. That the official press emphasised their importance does not necessarily mean that they were considerable. The media play given to them could merely have been part of the campaign to improve the entrepreneurial class that supported the regime or to enhance the popularity of Suzanne Mubarak.

13. Adel Badr, a teacher and scholar on educational affairs.

14. Centre for Political and Strategic Studies, *Report on Strategic Economic Directions*, 2000.

15. Abdel Khaleq Farouq, *Iqtsadiyât al Idâra al 'Amma* [The Economies of Government Administration] (Cairo: Dar al-Kalima, 2003).

16. Hassanein made frequent references to this categorization in his speeches in conferences on the budget, which I had the opportunity to attend.

17. Mustafa Al-Fiqi, chairman of the People's Assembly Foreign Relations Committee, during the deliberations over the 2001–2 budget, 12 May 2001.

18. See, for example, Central Accounting Agency, *Report on the Closing Account of the Budget*, 1997–98.

19. According to Ra'fat Abu Seif, former first deputy of the Ministry of Planning.

Chapter 3

1. Karl Wittfogel, *Oriental Despotism* (New Haven, CT: Yale University Press, 1957).

2. James Mayfield, *Local Government in Egypt: Structures, Process and the Challenges of Reform* (Cairo: AUC Press, 1996).

3. Sarah Bein Nafisa, researcher and expert in Egyptian local politics, interview, 24 March 2001.

4. Ibid.

5. See for example, Larry Schoeder, *Intergovernmental Fiscal Relations in Egypt* (Cairo: USAID, 1991).

6. Ministry of Finance, *Closing Account of the Budget*, 1980–81 and 1989–90.

7. Samir Abdel Wahab, *Maglis al-Sha'b wa qadâya al-Nizâm al-Mahhali al-Misri* [The People's Assembly and the Problems of the Egyptian Local System] (Cairo: The Center for Public Administration Studies and Consultancy, 1998).

8. The funds continue to worry the ministry, as was revealed in my interview with Abdel Fattah al-Gabali, adviser to the minister of finance.

9. Patrick Haenni, "Banlieues Indociles? Sur la Politisation des Quartiers Périurbains du Caire," PhD diss., Paris Institute for Political Studies, 2001.

10. Diaa' Rashwan, interview, 15 June 2001.

11. Eberhard Kienle, *A Grand Delusion: Democracy and Economic Reform in Egypt* (London: IB Tauris & Co. Ltd, 2000).

12. Computed by the author on the basis of statistics from Ministry of Finance, *Closing Account of the Budget*, various years.

13. Ministry of Finance, *Closing Account of the Budget*, various years.

14. Ibid.

15. Ibid.

16. See, for example, the report that this department submitted to the People's Assembly: Central Accounting Authority, *Report on the Closing Account of the Budget of 1996–97*.

17. Al-Dotur, 5 January 2010, www.dostor.org/politics/alexandria/10/january/4/1937.

18. Adviser to the Minister of Finance Abdel Fattah Al-Gabali, interview, 30 September 2000.

19. Supreme Constitutional Court ruling 36 for 1998.

20. Constitution of the Arab Republic of Egypt, 1971.

21. Prime Ministerial Decree 25 of 1998.

22. Ministry of Planning, *Annual Economic and Social Development Plan*, 1997–98.

23. Abul-Ezz Al-Hariri, the People's Assembly representative from Alexandria.

24. Minutes of the meeting of the Alexandrian Chamber of Commerce, 22 February 2003.

25. UNDP and Institute of National Planning, *Human Development Report*, 1998.

26. Ministry of Planning, *Annual Economic and Social Development Plan*, 1997–98.

27. Secretary-general of Qina, interview, 5 June 2001.

Chapter 4

1. The term *predatory state* comes from Margaret Levi, *Of Rule and Revenue* (Berkeley: University of California Press, 1988).

2. Hinh Dinh and Marcelo Giugale, *Inflation Tax and Deficit Financing in Egypt*, Working Paper 668 (Washington, DC: World Bank, 1991).

3. Graham Bird, "Exchange Rate Policy in Developing Counties," *Third World Quarterly* 19, no. 2 (1998): 255–276.

4. Ibid.

5. See, for example, the economic reports issued by the U.S. Embassy in Cairo.

6. Marie-France Vernier, "Essor des Recettes en Devises et Intervention de l'État: Le Syndrome Rentier, Approches dans le Cas Egyptien," PhD diss., Paris XIII University, 1999, p. 41.

7. Ibid.

8. Ibid.

9. Ministry of Finance, *The Financial Monthly Report*, March 2010, p. 35.

10. Ibid.

11. The Ministry for Social Affairs is now called the Ministry of Social Solidarity.

12. Ministry of Economy, *The Monthly Economic Bulletin*, various issues.

13. Ibid.

14. Egypt State Information Service, www.sis.gov.eg/Ar/Story.aspx?sid=26038.

15. Mervat Tallawy, "Government plans to seize pension funds," www.masrawy.com/News/Egypt/Politics/2010/may/7/telawy.aspx.

16. Central Bank of Egypt, *Annual Report*, 2003.

17. Jean-Claude Ducros, *Sociologie Financière* (Paris: Presse Universitaire de France, 1982), p. 77.

18. Mahmoud Mohammed Ali, Director of Sales Tax Authority, *Al-Ahram*, 8 May 1995.

19. Ministry of Finance, *Closing Account of the Budget*, various issues.

20. Ministry of Finance, *The Financial Monthly Report*, June 2008, p. 26.

21. This was corroborated by the president of the Chamber of Commerce of Cairo, Mahmoud Al-Arabi, in an interview on 15 June 2003.

22. Mahmoud Mohammed Ali, *Al-Ahram*, 8 May 1995.

23. Central Bank of Egypt, *Annual Report*, various issues.

24. Ramadan Sadiq Mohammed, "al-Darâ'b bayna al-Fikr al-Mâlî wa al-Qadâ' a-Dostôri: Dirâsa Taliliyya li Aham al-Ahkâm bi 'Adam al-Dostôriyya wa Athâriha" [Taxes Between Fiscal Thought and Constitutional Justice: An Analytical Study of the Most Important Rulings of Unconstitutionality and Their Consequences], Ph.D diss., Faculty of Law, University of Helwan, Cairo, 1997.

25. Ibid.

26. Ibid.

27. Ibid.

28. Husni Gad, former director of research in the General Tax Authority and current director of the General Tax Authority, interview, 13 February 2001.

29. I would like to express my deepest gratitude to Marwa Farouq for her help in collecting and analyzing the data in this section.

30. "A Brief History of Tax," *The Economist* 354, no. 8155 (January 2000): 9.

31. Sven Steinmo, "The End of Redistribution? International Pressures and Domestic Tax Policy Choices," in *Tax Policy*, ed. Sven Steinmo (Cheltenham UK: Elgar Publishing, 1998).

32. Ibid.

33. Guy Peters, *The Politics of Taxation: A Comparative Perspective* (Oxford: Basil Blackwell, 1991), p. 275.

34. Lee Dwight and Richard McKenzie, "The International Political Economy of Declining Tax Rates," in *Tax Policy*, ed. Sven Steinmo (Cheltenham, UK: Elgar Publishing, 1998).

35. Vito Tanzi, "Globalization Without a Net," *Foreign Policy* 125 (July–August 2001): 78–79.

36. Parthasarathi Shome, *Taxation in Latin America: Structural Trends and the Effect of Administration* (Washington, DC: IMF Working Papers, 1999).

37. Mukul Asher, "Globalization and Tax Systems," *ASEAN Economic Bulletin* 18, no. 1 (2001): 119–140.

38. Ibid.

39. Ministry of Finance, *General Features of the New Income Tax Law*, undated.

40. See the report submitted by the American Chamber of Commerce in Cairo to the Minister of Finance, referred to in *Al-Ahram Al-Iqtisadi*, 22 October 2001.

41. Former Minister of Finance Abdel Hamid Ata, Progressive Rally Party expert on tax affairs, interview, 21 January 2001.

42. See the studies carried out by the Egyptian Center for Economic Studies, particularly interest Samiha Fawzi, Hanaa Kheir el-Dine, and Amâl Rafa'at, *Marginal Effective Tax Rates and Investment Decisions in Egypt*, Working Paper no. 45 (Cairo: The Egyptian Center for Economic Studies, 2000).

43. Ministry of Finance, *The Financial Monthly*, June 2008, p. 28.

44. Ministry of Finance, *The Financial Monthly*, March 2010, p. 28.

45. See the many studies undertaken by Patrick Haenni, especially "Banlieues Indociles? Sur la Politisation des Quartiers Périurbains du Caire," PhD diss., Paris Institute for Political Studies, 2001.

46. Béatrice Hiboux, "De la Privatisation des Economies à la Privatisation des États," in *La Privatisation des États*, ed. Béatrice Hiboux (Paris: Karthala, 1999), p. 25.

47. Paul Veyne, *Le Pain et le Cirque* [Bread and the Circus] (Paris: Seuil, 1976), p. 23.

48. Egyptian Regulations, www.aba.org.eg/arabic/regulation/regulations.htm.

49. This was the opinion of the Association of Egyptian Businessmen as voiced on several occasions by Ashraf Al-Atal, Vice-Chairman of the Exports Committee of the Association of Egyptian Businessmen. See, for example, *Al-Ahram Al-Iqtisadi*, 19 January 2004.

50. *Business Today*, March 2004.

51. Hernando de Soto, *The Mystery of Capital: Why Capitalism Triumphs in the West and Fails Everywhere Else* (New York: Basic Books, 2000).

52. *Business Today*, March 2004.

53. Under the system of Dual Control imposed on Egypt in the 1880s, the British and French intervened to manage Egyptian fiscal policy.

54. Abdel Hakim Al-Refai, *Le Mouvement de Reforme des Impôts* (Paris: Librairie Général de Droit et de Jurisprudence, 1929).

55. The Constitution of the Republic of Egypt, www.misr.gov.eg/arabic/laws/constitution/index.asp.

56. Ministry of Finance, *The Financial Monthly*, March 2010, p. 26.

Chapter 5

1. Hazem Beblawi and Giacomo Luciana, *The Rentier State in the Arab World* (London: Croom Helm, 1987).

2. Mick Moore, "Political Underdevelopment. What Causes 'Bad Governance.'" *Public Management Review* 3, no. 3 (2001): 385–418.

3. Ibid.

4. Charles Tilly, *Coercion, Capital and European States: AD 990–1992* (Cambridge, MA: Basil Blackwell, 1992).

5. Ibid.

6. Michael Herb, "Taxation and Representation," *Studies in Comparative International Development* 38, no. 3 (2003): 3–31.

7. Nazih Ayubi, *Over Stating the Arab State* (London: IB Tauris & Co. Ltd, 1995), pp. 454–455; and Alan Richards and John Waterbury, *A Political Economy of the Middle East* (Boulder, CO: West Review, 1996).

8. Yasuyuki Matsunaga, "L'État Rentier Est-Il Réfractaire à la Démocratie?" *Critique Internationale* 8, no. 8 (2000): 46–58.

9. Philippe Cardin, "Rentierism and the Rentier State: A Comparative Examination," MA diss., McGill University, Montreal, Canada, 1993.

10. Leonard Wantchekon and Nathan Jensen, *Resource Wealth and Political Regimes in Africa* (New Haven, CT: Yale University Press, 2000).

11. Evelyne Huber and Dietrich Rueschemeyer, "The Impact of Economic Development on Democracy," *Journal of Economic Perspective* 7, no. 3 (1993): 71–86.

12. Eberhard Kienle, *A Grand Delusion: Democracy and Economic Reform in Egypt* (London: IB Tauris & Co. Ltd, 2000).

13. Sarah Ben Néfissa and Alâ' Eddine Arafât, *Al-Intikhabât wa Al-Zabâ'niya Al-Siyâsiyya fi Misr* [Elections and Political Clientelism in Egypt] (Cairo: Cairo Center for Human Rights, 2005).

14. Ibid.

15. Samer Soliman, *Al-Mosharaka al-Siyasiya fi Al-Intikhabât al-Niyâbiyya 2005: Al-'awâ'iq wa al-Mutatallabât* [Political Participation in the 2005 Parliamentary Elections: Obstacles and Requirements] (Cairo: The Egyptian Society for the Promotion of Social Participation, EU Commission, 2006).

16. Ibid.

17. Ibid.

18. Ibid.

19. Elias Abou-Haidar, *Libéralisme et Capitalisme d'État en Egypte: L'impossible Privatisation des Banques Publiques* (Paris: Harmattan, 2000).

20. Federation of Egyptian Industries, www.fei.org.eg; and Federation of Egyptian Chambers of Commerce, www.fedcoc.org.eg/ChamberPortal/AboutUnion/.

21. Eric Gobe, *Les Hommes d'Affaires Égyptiens—Démocratisation et Secteur Privé dans l'Egypte de l'Infitâh* (Paris: Khartala, 1999).

22. Dietrich Rueschemeyer, Evelyne Huber Stephens, and John D. Stephens, *Capitalist Development and Democracy* (Chicago: University of Chicago Press, 1992).

23. See Patrick Haenni, "L'islam Branché de la Bourgeoisie Égyptienne," *Le Monde Diplomatique*, September 2003; and "Mondaines Spiritualités: Amr Khâlid, Shaykh Branché de la Jeunesse Dorée Cairote," *Politique Africaine* 87, no. 1 (2002): 45–68.

24. See Baher Shawqi and Samer Soliman, "Tashrih Iqtisadi Igtimâ'i li al-Tabaqa al-Wusta al-Misriya" [A Socioeconomic Dissection of the Egyptian Middle Class], *Ahwal Misriya* 1, no. 1 (1998): 35–57.

25. Ramzi Zaki, *Wada'an Lil-Tabaqa al-Wusta: ta'Ammulât fi al-Thawra al-Sinâ'iyya al-Thaniya wa al-Libirâliyya al-Gadîda* [Farewell to the Middle Class: Thoughts on the Second Industrial Revolution and Neoliberalism] (Cairo: Dar Al-Mustaqbal al-Arabi, 1997).

26. Former Minister of Finance Medhat Hassanein, interview, 23 August 2002.

27. Ministry of Finance, *The Financial Monthly*, May 2010.

28. Joel Beinin and Zachary Lockman, *Workers on the Nile: Nationalism, Communism, Islam, and the Egyptian Working Class, 1882–1954* (Princeton, NJ: Princeton, University Press, 1987).

29. Joel Beinin, "The Egyptian Workers Movement in 2007," *Chroniques du CEDEJ* (Centre d'Études et de Documentations Économiques, Juridiques et Sociales), 2007.

30. Soliman, *Al-Mosharaka al-Siyasiya fi Al-Intikhabât al-Niyâbiyya 2005* [Political Participation in the 2005 Parliamentary Elections].

31. Ibid.

Conclusion

1. Joel Beinin, "The Egyptian Workers Movement in 2007," in *Chroniques du CEDEJ* (Cairo: Centre d'Études et de Documentations Économiques, Juridiques et Sociales, 2007).

2. Asef Bayat, "The Coming of a Post-Islamist Society," *Critique: Journal for the Critical Studies of the Middle East* 5, no. 9 (1996): 43–52; and Olivier Roy and Patrick Haenni, eds., "Le Poste Islamisme," *Revue du Monde Musulman et de la Méditerranée* 85–86 (1999): 11–30.

BIBLIOGRAPHY

Abd Al-Fattah, Nabil. *Veiled Violence: Islamic Fundamentalism in Egyptian Politics in the 1990s.* Beirut: Dar Sechat, 1994.

Abdel Razeq, Hussein. *Misr fi 18 wa 19 yanayir* [Egypt during 18 and 19 January]. Cairo: Shuhdi, 1985.

Abdel Wahab, Samir. *Maglis al-Sha'b wa qadâya al-Nizâm al-Mahhali al-Misri* [The People's Assembly and the Problems of the Egyptian Local System]. Cairo: The Center for Public Administration Studies and Consultancy, 1998.

Abdel Wahab, Samir, and Mamdouh Mostafa Ismail. *Siyâsat Tanmiyat al-Mawârid al-Mâliyya al-Mahaliyya* [The Politics of Increasing Local Financial Revenues]. Cairo: Center for Public Administration Studies and Consultancy, 2001.

Abou-Haidar, Elias. *Libéralisme et Capitalisme d'État en Egypte: L'impossible Privatisation des Banques Publiques.* Paris: Harmattan, 2000.

Ahmed, Sadiq. *Public Finance in Egypt: Its Structure and Trends.* Washington, DC: World Bank, 1984.

Al-Faris, Abdel Razzaq. *Al-Hokuma wal Foqara' wal Infâq al-'Am: Dirâsa li Zahira 'Agz al-Mowâzana wa Athariha al-Iqtisâdiyya wal Igtimâ'iya fi al-Boldân al-'Arabiyya* [The Government, the Poor, and Public Spending: A Study of the Phenomenon of Budget Deficit and Its Economic and Social Effects in Arab Countries]. Beirut: Center for Arab Unity, 1997.

Al-Gibali, Abdel Fattah. *Al-Dayn al-'Am al-Mahalli fi Misr. Al-Asbâb wa al-Holôl* [The Public Debt in Egypt: The Causes and the Solutions]. Cairo: Al-Ahram Center for Political and Strategic Studies, 1999.

Al-Hakim, Ola Sulayman. *Al-Tawzi' al-Iqlîmi lil Infâq al-Igtimâ'i* [The Regional Distribution of Social Spending]. Research Papers Series 98. Cairo: National Institute for Planning, 1997.

Allum, Peter et al. *Egypt Beyond Stabilization.* Washington, DC: IMF, 1998.

Al-Refai, Abdel Hakim. *Le Mouvement de Reforme des Impôts.* Paris: Librairie Général de Droit et de Jurisprudence, 1929.

Al-Saidi, Abdallah. *Al-Darâ'b wa al-Tanmiya: Dirassa Lidawr al-Darâ'b ala al-Dakhl fi Tamwîl al-Infâq al-âm bi Misr* [Taxes and Development: A Study of the Role of Income Taxes in Financing Public Expenditures in Egypt]. Cairo: Dar al-Nahda al-Arabiyya, 1990.

Alt, James. "The Evolution of Tax Structures." In *Tax policy*, ed. Sven Steinmo. Cheltenham UK: Elgar Publishing, 1998.

Althusser, Louis. *Lire le Capital.* Paris: Maspéro, 1968.

American Embassy in Cairo. *Economic Trends Report.* Cairo: American Embassy in Cairo, 2003.

Amin, Galal. *Egypt's Economic Predicament.* New York: E.J. Brill, 1995.

Amin, Samir. "The State and Development." In *Political Theory Today*, ed. David Held. Cambridge, UK: Polity Press, 1991.

Amsden, A. H. "The State and Taiwan's Economic Development." In *Bringing the State Back*, ed. P. B. Evans and Theda Skocpol. New York: Cambridge University Press, 1985.

Asher, Mukul. "Globalization and Tax Systems." *ASEAN Economic Bulletin* 18, no. 1 (2001): 119–140.

Askari, Hossein, John Cummings, and Michael Glover. *Taxation and Tax Policies in the Middle East.* London: Butterworth Scientific, 1982.

Auty, Richard. *Resource Abundance and Economic Development: Improving the Performance of Resource-Rich Countries.* Helsinki: UN University/World Institute for Development Economics Research, 1998.

Ayubi, Nazih. "The Fiscal Crisis and the Washington Consensus: Towards an Explanation of Middle East Liberalization." In *L'Économie Égyptienne: Libéralisation et Insertion dans le Marché Mondial*, ed. Louis Blain. Paris: l'Harmattan, 1993.

———. *Overstating the Arab State.* London: IB Tauris & Co. Ltd, 1995.

Badie, Bertrand. "État, Légitimité et Contestation en Culture Islamique." In *L'Etat au Pluriel*, ed. Ali Kazacigil. Paris: Economica, 1985.

Bailey, Kenneth. *Methods of Social Research.* New York: Free Press, 1987.

Bates, Robert. *Political and Economic Interaction in Economic Policy Reform.* Oxford: Blackwell, 1993.

Bates, Robert, and Donald Lien Da-Hasinang. "A Note on Taxation, Development, and Representative Government." *Politics and Society* 14, no. 1 (1985): 53–70.

Bayart, Jean-François. *La Greffe de l'État.* Paris: Karthala, 1996.

———. *La Réinvention du Capitalisme.* Paris: Karthala, 1994.

Bayat, Asef. "The Coming of a Post-Islamist Society." *Critique: Journal for the Critical Studies of the Middle East* 5, no. 9 (1996): 43–52.

Beblawi, Hazem. *Dawr al-Dawla fi al-Iqtisâd* [The Role of the State in the Economy]. Cairo: al-Hay'a al-'Amma lil Kitâb, 1999.

———. "The Rentier State in the Arab World." In *The Arab State,* ed. Giacomo Luciani. London: Routledge, 1990.

Beblawi, Hazem, and Giacomo Luciani. *The Rentier State in the Arab World.* London: Croom Helm, 1987.

Beinin, Joel. "The Egyptian Workers Movement in 2007." In *Chroniques du CEDEJ.* Cairo: Centre d'Études et de Documentations Économiques, Juridiques et Sociales, 2007.

Beinin, Joel, and Zachary Lockman. *Workers on the Nile: Nationalism, Communism, Islam, and the Egyptian Working Class, 1882–1954.* Princeton, NJ: Princeton University Press, 1987.

Bell, Daniel. *The Cultural Contradictions of Capitalism.* London: Heinemann, 1976.

Ben Néfissa, Sarah, and Alâ' Eddine Arafât. *Al-Intikhabât wa Al-Zabâ'niya Al-Siyâsiyya fi Misr* [Elections and Political Clientelism in Egypt]. Cairo: Cairo Center for Human Rights, 2005.

Bennett, Robert. *Decentralization, Local Government and Markets.* Oxford: Clarendon Press, 1990.

Berger, Mark. "Old State and New Empire in Indonesia: Debating the Rise and Decline of Suharto's New Order." *Third World Quarterly* 17, no. 2 (1997): 321–362.

Bird, Graham. "Exchange Rate Policy in Developing Counties." *Third World Quarterly* 19, no. 2 (1998): 255–276.

Block, Fred. "The Fiscal Crisis of the Capitalist State." *Annual Review of Sociology* 7, no. 1 (1981): 1–27.

Bourdieu, Pierre, et al. *The Craft of Sociology.* New York: Walter de Gruyter, 1991.

Brumberg, Daniel. "Survival Strategies vs. Democratic Bargains: The Politics of Economic Reform in Contemporary Egypt." In *The Politics of Economic Reform in the Middle East,* ed. Henri J. Barkey. New York: St. Martin's Press, 1992.

Buchanan, James, and Richard Wagner. *Democracy in Deficit.* New York: Academic Press, 1977.

Cardin, Philippe. "Rentierism and the Rentier State: A Comparative Examination." MA diss., McGill University, Montreal, 1993.

Central Bank of Egypt. *Annual Report.* 2003.

Chan, S. *East Asian Dynamism: Growth, Order, and Security in the Pacific Region.* Boulder, CO: Westview, 1993.

Chibber, Vivek. "Bureaucratic Rationality and the Developmental State." *American Journal of Sociology* 107, no. 4 (2002): 87–111.

Clark, C., and K. C. Roy. *Comparing Development Patterns in Asia.* Boulder, CO: Lynne Rienner, 1997.

Clement, Henry Moore. "Money and Power: The Dilemma of Egyptian Infitah." *Middle East Journal* 40, no. 4 (1986): 634–650.

Cottonet, Hélène. "Ressources Exogènes, Performances Industrielles et Croissance: Le Cas de l'Égypte, 1970–1997." PhD diss., Clemont-Ferrand University, 2003.

Crozier, Michel, and Erhard Freiderg. *L'acteur et le Système*. Paris: Éditions de Seuil, 1977.

De Soto, Hernando. *The Mystery of Capital: Why Capitalism Triumphs in the West and Fails Everywhere Else*. New York: Basic Books, 2000.

Dinh, Hinh, and Marcelo Giugale. *Inflation Tax and Deficit Financing in Egypt*. Working Paper 668. Washington, DC: World Bank, 1991.

Downs, Anthony. "Why the Government Budget Is Too Small in a Democracy." In *Tax Policy*, ed. Sven Steinmo. Cheltenham, UK: Elgar Publishing, 1998.

Ducros, Jean-Claude. *Sociologie Financière*. Paris: Presse Universitaire de France, 1982.

Ebeid, Mona Makram. "Egypt's 2000 Parliamentary Elections." *Middle East Policy* 8, no. 2 (2001): 32–44.

El-Ktiri, Mustafa, and Najib Akesbi. *La Réforme de la Fiscalité Marocaine à l'Heure de l'Ajustement Structurel*. Casablanca: Toubkal, 1987.

El-Samalouty, Gannat. *Corporate Tax Investment Decisions in Egypt*. Cairo: Egyptian Center for Economic Studies, 1999.

Fandy, Mamoun. "Egypt's Islamic Groups: Regional Revenge?" *Middle East Journal* 48, no. 4 (1994): 607–625.

Farouq, Abdel Khaleq. *Al-Mowâzana al-'Amma lil Dawla wa Hoquq al-Insân* [The National Budget and Human Rights]. Cairo: Association for Legal Help and Human Rights, 2002.

———. *Iqtsadiyât al Idâra al 'Amma* [The Economies of Government Administration]. Cairo: Dar Al-Kalima, 2003.

Fauvelle-Aymar, Christin. "The Political and Tax Capacity of Government in Developing Countries." *Kyklos* 52, no. 3 (1999): 391–413.

Fawzi, Samiha, Hanaa Kheir el-Dine, and Amâl Rafa'at. *Marginal Effective Tax Rates and Investment Decisions in Egypt*. Working Paper 45. Cairo: Egyptian Center for Economic Studies, 2000.

Fine, Ben, and Colin Stoneman. "Introduction: State and Development." *Journal of Southern African Studies* 22, no. 1 (1996): 5–25.

Fontveille, Louis. "Évolution et Croissance de l'État Français de 1815–1970." PhD diss., Paris University, 1976.

Gallo, Carmenza. *Taxes and State Power: Political Instability in Bolivia 1900–1950*. Philadelphia: Temple University Press, 1991.

Gibert, Alain, and Gilbert Gugler. *Urbanization in the Third World*. Oxford: Oxford University Press, 1992.

Giddens, Anthony. *A Contemporary Critique of Historical Marxism*. London: Macmillan, 1981.

Goldscheid, Rudolf. "A Sociological Approach to Problems of Public Finance." In *Classics in the Theory of Public Finance*, ed. Richard Musgrave. London: Macmillan, 1958.

Gough, Ian. "State Expenditure in Advanced Capitalism." *New Left Review* 92, no. 1 (1975): 53–92.

Guex, Sébastien. *L'Argent de l'État*. Lausanne: Éditions Réalités Sociales, 1998.

Ha, Yeon-Seob. "Public Finance and Budgeting in Korea Under Democracy: A Critical Appraisal." *Public Budgeting and Finance* 17, no. 1 (1997): 56–74.

Haenni, Patrick. "Banlieues Indociles? Sur la Politisation des Quartiers Périurbains du Caire." PhD diss., Paris Institute for Political Studies, 2001.

———. "L'Islam Branché de la Bourgeoisie Égyptienne." *Le Monde Diplomatique*, September 2003.

———. "Mondaines Spiritualités: Amr Khâlid, Shaykh Branché de la Jeunesse Dorée Cairote." *Politique Africaine* 87, no. 1 (2002): 45–68.

Hall, Peter. "Political Science and the Three New Institutionalisms." *Political Studies* 44, no. 5 (1996): 936–957.

Hamel, Jacques. *Case Study Methods*. London: Sage Publications, 1993.

Hansen, Susan. *The Politics of Taxation: Revenue Without Representation*. New York: Prager, 1996.

Hay, Colin, Michael Lister, and David Marsh, eds. *The State: Theories and Issues*. Basingstoke, UK: Palgrave Macmillan, 2006.

Held, David. *Public Expenditure*. Oxford: Roberston, 1983.

Henry, Clement, and Robert Springborg. *Globalization and the Politics of Development in the Middle East*. Cambridge, UK: Cambridge University Press, 2001.

Herb, Michael. "Does Rentierism Prevent Democracy?" Paper Presented at the Annual Meeting of the American Political Science Association, Boston, 21 August–1 September 2002.

———. "Taxation and Representation." *Studies in Comparative International Development* 38, no. 3 (2003): 3–31.

Hiboux, Béatrice. "De la Privatisation des Economies à la Privatisation des États." In *La Privatisation des États*, ed. Béatrice Hiboux. Paris: Karthala, 1999.

Hill, Enid. *Modes of Political Economy Research and Egypt: Studies in Egyptian Political Economy*. Cairo Papers in Social Science 2. Cairo: The American University in Cairo Press, 1979.

Hinnebusch, Raymond. "The Politics of Economic Reform in Egypt." *Third World Quarterly* 14, no. 1 (1993): 159–172.

Huber, Evelyne, and Dietrich Rueschemeyer. "The Impact of Economic Development on Democracy." *Journal of Economic Perspective* 7, no. 3 (1993): 71–86.

Huntington, Samuel. *Political Order in Changing Societies*. New Haven, CT: Yale University Press, 1968.

Hussein, Abdallah. *Osloub Tanmiyat wa Idârat al-Mawarid al-Maliyya bi al-Mahaliyât* [The Means for Developing and Managing Financial Resources in Municipalities].

Cairo: The Conference for Developing and Managing Financial Revenues in Municipalities, 1982.

Ibrahim, Son'allah. *Zat.* 2nd ed. Cairo: Dar al-Mustaqbal al-Arabi, 1998.

Immergut, Ellen M. "The Theoretical Core of the New Institutionalism." *Politics and Society* 26, no. 1 (1998): 5–34.

Institute of National Planning and UNDP. *Human Development Report.* Various issues, 1994–2002.

International Monetary Fund. *Arab Republic of Egypt: Economic Readjustment with Growth.* Country Economic Memorandum. Washington, DC: IMF, 1990.

Kesselman, Mark. "How Should One Study Economic Policy-Making?" *World Politics* 44, no. 4 (1998): 645–672.

Khallaf, Hussein. *Tatawor al-Irâdât al-'Amma fi Misr al-Hadîtha* [The Evolution of Public Revenues in Modern Egypt]. Cairo: Institute for Arabic Research and Studies, 1966.

Kheir El-Din, Hanaa, et al. *Marginal Effective Tax Rates and Investment Decisions in Egypt.* Working Paper 45. Cairo: Egyptian Center for Economic Studies. 2000.

Kienle, Eberhard. *A Grand Delusion, Democracy and Economic Reform in Egypt.* London: IB Tauris & Co. Ltd, 2000.

Krasner, Stephen. "Approaches to the State." *Comparative Politics* 16, no. 2 (1984): 223–246.

Kugler, Arbetman, and William Domke. "Comparing the Strength of Nations." *Comparative Political Studies* 19, no. 1 (1986): 39–69.

Kugler, Jacek, and Marina Arbetman. *Political Capacity and Economic Behavior.* Oxford: Westview Press, 1997.

Kuran, Timur. "The Vulnerability of the Arab State: Reflections." *Independent Review* 3, no. 1 (1998): 111–113.

Kwass, Michael. *Privilege and the Politics of Taxation in Eighteenth-Century France.* Cambridge, UK: Cambridge University Press, 2000.

Lamborn, Alan. "Power and the Politics of Extraction." *International Studies Quarterly* 27, no. 2 (1983): 125–146.

Leca, Jean. "Democratization in the Arab World: Uncertainty, Vulnerability and Legitimacy. A Tentative Conceptualization and Some Hypotheses." In *Democracy Without Democrats: The Renewal of Politics in the Muslim World,* ed. Ghassan Salamé. London: IB Tauris & Co. Ltd, 1994.

Lee, Dwight, and Richard Mckenzie. "The International Political Economy of Declining Tax Rates." In *Tax Policy,* ed. Sven Steinmo. Cheltenham UK: Elgar Publishing, 1998.

Leftwich, Adrian. "Bringing Politics Back In: Towards a Model of the Developmental State." *Journal of Development Studies* 31, no. 3 (1995): 400–427.

———. *Democracy and Development.* Cambridge: Polity Press, 1996.

Levi, Margaret. *Of Rule and Revenue*. Berkeley: University of California Press, 1988.

Löfgren, Hans. "Economic Policy in Egypt: A Breakdown in Reform Resistance?" *International Journal of Middle East Studies* 25, no. 3 (1993): 407–421.

Luciani, Giacomo. "Resources, Revenues and Authoritarianism in the Arab World: Beyond the Rentier State." In *Political Liberalization and Democratization in the Arab World*, ed. Bahgat Korany, Rex Brynen, and Paul Nobel. London: Lynne Rienner Publishers, 1999.

Mann, Michael. "The Autonomous Power of the State: Its Origins, Mechanisms and Results." In *States in History*, ed. John Hall. New York: Basil Blackwell, 1986.

———. *The Sources of Social Power, Volume II: The Rise of Classes and Nation-States, 1760–1914*. New York: Cambridge University Press, 1993.

Marshall, Alfred. *Principles of Economics: An Introductory Volume*. London: Macmillan and Co., Ltd, 1920, reprinted 1988.

Marx, Karl. *Eighteenth Brumaire of Louis Bonaparte*. New York: International Publishers, 1991.

Marx, Karl, and Frederick Engels. *The Communist Manifesto*. London: Electric Book Co., 2001.

Mascarenhas, R. C. *Comparative Political Economy of East and South Asia: A Critique of Development Policy and Management*. London: Macmillan, 1999.

Matsunaga, Yasuyuki. "L'État Rentier Est-Il Réfractaire à la Démocratie?" *Critique Internationale* 8, no. 8 (2000): 46–58.

Mayfield, James. *Local Government in Egypt: Structures, Process and the Challenges of Reform*. Cairo: AUC Press, 1996.

McCarney, Patricia. *The Changing Nature of Local Governments in Developing Countries*. Toronto: Center for Urban and Community Studies, University of Toronto, 1996.

Michael, L. "Does Oil Hinder Democracy?" *World Politics* 53 (2001): 3–325-61.

Migdal, Joel. *Strong Societies and Weak States*. Princeton, NJ: Princeton University Press, 1988.

———. "Studying the State." In *Comparative Politics*, ed. Mark Lichbach et al. Cambridge, UK: Cambridge University Press, 1997.

Milliband, Ralph. *The State in Capitalist Society*. New York: Basic Books, 1969.

Ministry of Economy. *The Monthly Economic Bulletin*. Various issues.

Ministry of Finance. *Closing Account of the Budget*. 1980–81 and 1989–90.

———. *The Financial Monthly Report*. Various issues.

———. *General Features of the New Income Tax Law*, undated.

Ministry of Planning. *Annual Economic and Social Development Plan*, 1997–98.

Mitchell, Timothy. "The Limits of the State: Beyond Statist Approaches and Their Critics." *American Political Science Review* 85, no. 1 (1991): 77–96.

————. "No Factories, No Problems: The Logic of Neo-liberalism in Egypt." *Review of African Political Economy* 82, no. 6 (1999): 455–469.

Mohammed, Ramadan Sadiq. "Al-Darâ'b bayna al-Fikr al-Mâlî wa al-Qadâ' a-Dostôri: Dirâsa Taliliyya li Aham al-Ahkâm bi 'Adam al-Dostôriyya wa Athâriha" [Taxes Between Fiscal Thought and Constitutional Justice: An Analytical Study of the Most Important Rulings of Unconstitutionality and Their Consequences]. PhD diss., Faculty of Law, University of Helwan, Cairo, 1997.

Moharram, Ibrahim. *Al-Ru'ya al-Mustaqbaliyya Liltanmiya fi Misr* [The Long-Term Perspective for Development in Egypt]. Cairo: National Institute for Planning, 2002.

Moore, Barrington. *The Social Origins of Dictatorship and Democracy: Lord and Peasant in the Making of the Modern World*. Boston: Beacon Press, 1996.

Moore, Mick. "Political Underdevelopment: What Causes 'Bad Governance'?" *Public Management Review* 3, no. 3 (2001): 385–418.

Musgrave, Richard. "Taxation and Democracy." *Journal of Economic Literature* 3, no. 2 (1995): 854–855.

Muten, Leif. "Leading Issues of Tax Policy in Developing Countries: The Administrative Problems." In *The Political Economy of Taxation*, ed. Alan Peacock and Francesco Forte. Oxford: Basil Blackwell, 1981.

O'Connor, James. *The Fiscal Crisis of the State*. New York: St. Martin Press, 1973.

————. *The Fiscal Crisis of the State*. London/New Brunswick, NJ: Transactions Publishers, 2002.

————. *The Meaning of Crisis: A Theoretical Introduction*. New York: Basil Blackwell, 1987.

Owen, Roger. "The Middle Eastern State: Repositioning Not Retreat?" In *The State and Global Change,* ed. Hassan Hakimian and Ziba Moshaver. London: Curzon Press, 2001.

Peters, Guy. *The Politics of Taxation: A Comparative Perspective*. Oxford: Basil Blackwell, 1991.

Peterson, Paul. "The New Politics of Deficits." *Political Science Quarterly* 100, no. 4 (1985): 575–601.

Pontusson, Jonas. "From Comparative Public Policy to Political Economy." *Comparative Political Studies* 28, no. 3 (1995): 353–378.

Poulantzas, Nicos. *Political Power and Social Class*. London: Verso, 1969.

Prseworski, Adam. "Problems in the Study of Transition to Democracy." In *Transition from Authoritarian Rule: Comparative Perspectives,* ed. Guillermo O'Donnell, Philippe Schmitter, and Laurence Whitehead. London: Johns Hopkins University Press, 1986.

Richards, Alan. "The Political Economy of Dilatory Reform: Egypt in the 1980s." *World Development* 19, no. 12 (1991): 1721–1730.

Richards, Alan, and John Waterbury. *A Political Economy of the Middle East.* Boulder, CO: West Review, 1996.

Roussillion, Alain. *L'Égypte et l'Algérie au Péril de la Libéralisation.* Les Dossiers du CEDEJ. Cairo: Centre d'Études et de Documentation Économique, Juridique et Sociale, 1996.

Roy, Olivier, and Patrick Haenni, eds. "Le Poste Islamisme." *Revue du Monde Musulman et de la Méditerranée* 85–86 (1999): 11–30.

Rueschemeyer, Dietrich, Evelyne Huber Stephens, and Johns D. Stephens. *Capitalist Development and Democracy.* Chicago: University of Chicago Press, 1992.

Sachs, Jeffrey, and M. Bruno. "Energy and Resource Allocation: A Dynamic Model of the 'Dutch disease.'" *Review of Economic Studies* 49, no. 5 (1982): 845–859.

Sadowski, Yehya. *Political Vegetables: Businessman and Bureaucrat in the Development of Egyptian Agriculture.* Washington, DC: Brookings Institution, 1991.

Salamé, Ghassan. *Democracy Without Democrats: The Renewal of Politics in the Muslim World.* London: IB Tauris & Co. Ltd, 1994.

Schoeder, Larry. *Intergovernmental Fiscal Relations in Egypt.* Cairo: USAID, 1991.

Schumpter, Joseph. "The Crisis of the Tax State." *International Economic Papers* 4, no. 4 (1918): 5–38.

Shawqi, Baher, and Samer Soliman. *"Tashrih Iqtisadi Igtimâ'i li al-Tabaqa al-Wusta al-Misriya"* [A Socioeconomic Dissection of the Egyptian Middle Class]. *Ahwal Misriya* 1, no. 1 (1998): 35–57.

Shome, Parthasarathi. *Taxation in Latin America: Structural Trends and the Effect of Administration.* Washington, DC: IMF Working Papers, 1999.

Skocpol, Theda, et al. *Bringing the State Back In.* New York: Cambridge University Press, 1985.

Smith, B. C. *Decentralization: The Territorial Dimension of the State.* London: George Allen and Unwin, 1985.

Snider, Lewis W. "The Political Performance of Third World Governments and the Debt Crisis." *The American Political Science Review* 84, no. 4 (1990): 1263–1280.

Soliman, Samer. *Al-Mosharaka al-Siyasiya fi Al-Intikhabât al-Niyâbiyya 2005: Al-'awâ'q wa al-Mutatallabât* [Political Participation in the 2005 Parliamentary Elections: Obstacles and Requirements]. Cairo: Egyptian Society for the Promotion of Social Participation, EU Commission, 2006.

———. *Al-Nizam al-Qawi wa al-Dawla al-Da'ifa: Al-Azma al-Maliyya wa al-Taghyîr al-Syasi fi Misr fi 'Ahd Mubarak* [Strong Regime, Weak State: The Fiscal Crisis and Political Change Under Mubarak]. Cairo: Merit, 2004.

———. *Al-Nizam al-Qawi wa al-Dawla al-Da'ifa: Al-Azma al-Maliyya wa al-Taghyîr al-Syasi fi Misr fi 'Ahd Mubarak* [Strong Regime, Weak State: The Fiscal Crisis and Political Change Under Mubarak]. 3rd ed. Cairo: al-Dâr, 2006.

———. *State and Industrial Capitalism in Egypt.* Cairo Papers in Social Science, 21, n. 2. Cairo: The American University in Cairo Press, 1998.

Springborg, Robert. *Mubarak's Egypt: Fragmentation of the Political Order.* Boulder, CO: Westview, 1989.

Steinmo, Sven. "The End of Redistribution? International Pressures and Domestic Tax Policy Choices." In *Tax Policy,* ed. Sven Steinmo. Cheltenham, UK: Elgar Publishing, 1998.

———. *Taxation and Democracy: Swedish, British and American Approaches to Financing the Modern State.* New Haven, CT: Yale University Press, 1993.

Steinmo, Sven, Kathleen Ann Thelen, and Frank Longstreth. *Structuring Politics: Historical Institutionalism in Comparative Analysis.* New York: Cambridge University Press, 1992.

Steinmo, Sven, and Caroline Tolbert. "Do Institutions Really Matter?" *Comparative Political Studies* 31, no. 2 (1998): 165–178.

Swank, Duane. "Funding the Welfare State: Globalization and the Taxation of Business in Advanced Market Economies." *Political Studies* 46, no. 4 (1998): 671–693.

Tanzani, Vito, and Zee Howell. *Tax Policy for Emerging Markets: Developing Countries.* IMF Working Paper 35. Washington, DC: IMF, 2000.

———. "Tax Policy for Emerging Markets: Developing Countries." *National Tax Journal* 53, no. 2 (2000): 299–323.

Tanzi, Vito. "Globalization Without a Net." *Foreign Policy* 125 (July–August 2001): 78–79.

———. *Public Finance in Developing Countries.* Cheltenham, UK: Elgar Publishing, 1991.

Tilly, Charles. *Big Structures, Large Processes, Huge Comparisons.* New York: Russell Sage Foundation, 1984.

———. *Coercion, Capital and European States: AD990–1992.* Cambridge, MA: Basil Blackwell, 1992.

Tohamy, Sahar. *Tax Administration and Transaction Costs in Egypt.* Working Paper 33. Cairo: Egyptian Center for Economic Studie, 1998.

Transparency International. Annual Report, 2008. www.transparency.org/publications/publications.

Tripp, Charles. "States, Elites and the Management of Change." In *The State and Global Change,* ed. Hassan Hakiman and Ziba Moshaver. London: Curzon Press, 2001.

Tschirgi, Dan. "Marginalized Violent Internal Conflict in the Age of Globalization: Mexico and Egypt." *Arab Studies Quarterly* 21, no. 3 (1999): 13–25.

UNDP and Institute of National Planning. *Human Development Report.* Cairo, 1998.

Veltmeyer, Henry, et al. *Neoliberalism and Class Conflict in Latin America: A Comparative Perspective on the Political Economy of Structural Adjustment.* London Macmillan, 1997.

Vernier, Marie-France. "Essor des Recettes en Devises et Intervention de l'État: Le Syndrome Rentier. Approches dans le Cas Egyptien." PhD diss., Paris XIII University, 1999.

Veyne, Paul. *Le Pain et le Cirque* [Bread and the Circus]. Paris: Seuil, 1976.

Vivek, Chibber. "Bureaucratic Rationality and the Developmental State." *American Journal of Sociology* 107, no. 4 (2002): 951–989.

Wahba, Mourad. "Private and Public Economic Bases: The Egyptian Case." In *Development in the Age of Liberalization: Egypt and Mexico*, ed. Dan Tschergi. Cairo: American University in Cairo Press, 1996.

———. *The Role of the State in the Egyptian Economy, 1945–1981*. New York: Ithaca Press, 1994.

Wantchekon, Leonard, and Nathan Jensen. *Resource Wealth and Political Regimes in Africa*. New Haven, CT: Yale University, 2000.

Waterbury, John. *The Egypt of Nasser and Sadat: The Political Economy of Two Regimes*. Princeton, NJ: Princeton University Press, 1983.

White, Gordon. "Developmental States and Socialist Industrialization in the Third World." *Journal of Development Studies* 21, no. 1 (1984): 97–121.

Wildavsky, Aaron. *The New Politics of the Budgetary Process*. New York: Harper Collins Publishers, 1992.

Willis, Eliza, Garma Garman, et al. "The Politics of Decentralization in Latin America." *Latin American Research Review* 34, no. 1 (1999): 7–57.

Wittfogel, Karl. *Oriental Despotism*. New Haven, CT: Yale University Press, 1957.

World Bank. *Egypt into the Next Century*. Washington, DC: World Bank, 1995.

———. *Report and Recommendation of the President of the International Bank for Reconstruction and Development to the Executive Directors on a Proposed Structural Adjustment Loan to Egypt*. Washington, DC: World Bank, 1991.

———. *The State in a Changing World*. Washington, DC: World Bank, 1997.

World Bank and Egyptian Ministry of Planning. *Poverty Reduction in Egypt: Diagnosis and Strategy*. Cairo: World Bank and Egyptian Ministry of Planning, 2002.

Zaki, Ramzi. *Wada'an lil-Tabaqa al-wusta: ta'Ammulât fi al-Thawra al-Sinâ'iyya al-Thaniya wa al-Llibirâliyya al-Gadîda* [Farewell to the Middle Class: Thoughts on the Second Industrial Revolution and Neoliberalism]. Cairo: Dar Al-Mustaqbal al-Arabi, 1997.

Zaytoun, Moyaha. *Al-Infâq al-'Am al-Igtimâ'i wa Madâ Istifâdat al-Foqarâ'* [Social Public Spending and How It Benefits the Poor]. Cairo: Kitâb al-Ahram al-Iqtisadi, 1998.

Zein Eddin, Salah Eddin. *Al-Islâh al-Daribi* [Tax Reform]. Cairo: al-Nahda al-Arabiyya, 2000.

INDEX

aid, 2, 23, 27, 40, 42, 43, 47, 48, 52, 57, 127, 140, 164

Al-Ahram, 36, 37, 98, 107, 108, 110, 114, 124, 128–131, 135

Al-Ahram Al-Iqtisadi, 36, 37

Alexandria, 76, 87–91, 94, 95, 125–127, 148

Al-Ganzouri, Kamal, 134, 135

Ali, Mohamed, 25

Amin, Galal, 22

army, 26, 28, 40, 61, 63–65, 127, 164, 168

Asian, 4, 6, 12, 66

authoritarianism, 6, 22, 77, 78, 128, 139–141, 143, 152, 170

Ayubi, Nazih, 50

bargaining power, 15, 16, 21

Beblawi, Hazem, 21, 138, 139, 140

Beinin, Joel, 158, 169

Ben Ali, Zein Al-Abidine, 126

bourgeoisie, 3, 7, 8, 10, 152

bread riots, 40, 41, 57, 64

Buchanan, James, 17

budget, 1, 10, 17, 68–71, 75, 79, 80, 83, 87–89, 91–93, 96, 106, 108, 126, 133, 134, 135, 165; balance sheet of the, 30, 32, 33; budgetary allocations, 63, 65, 74; deficit, 2, 8, 45, 109, 112, 113, 116, 131, 136, 139, 166

bureaucracy, 18, 27, 29, 50, 59, 74, 84, 85, 98, 100, 139, 144, 154, 156, 164; corrupt, 155; effective, 28; ruling, 3, 151; taxation, 124; top, 161, 165

business community, 50, 68, 91, 95, 97, 98, 112, 128, 131, 141, 148, 151; partnership with the government, 87, 88, 90, 94; powerful circles in the, 169; social role of the, 87, 125–127

businessmen, 87–90, 94–96, 99, 111, 112, 116, 118, 123–126, 128; Association of Egyptian, 110; political role of, 144–147, 150–153, 159–162, 165, 168, 169

Cairo, 23, 43, 73, 76, 77, 78, 85, 86, 88, 89, 90, 91, 92, 94, 111, 112, 126, 144, 151, 159

capitalism, 11, 144; Egyptian, 4, 37, 149, 151, 152, 153

capitalist development. *See* development, capitalist

capitalists, 8, 9, 10, 12, 13, 24, 27, 36, 125, 150, 152, 153

Central Accounting Agency, 70, 72

Central Bank, 42, 98, 116, 133

central government, 75, 76, 78, 79, 80, 82, 83, 84, 85, 86, 87, 91–93, 95, 165, 166

centralization, 3, 20, 25, 33, 76–78, 80, 85, 88, 127

civil servant, 59, 70

class struggle, 10, 13

clientelism, 159, 168, 169

cold war, 48, 104

constitution, 32

corruption, 30, 31, 33, 56, 72, 74, 75, 84, 85, 87, 88, 96, 149, 156, 165

Cottonet, Helene, 22

decentralization, 77, 78, 79, 80, 85, 89, 95, 96, 127, 165, 166, 168

Rochelle A. Davis, Palestinian Village Histories: Geographies
of the Displaced
2010

Haggai Ram, Iranophobia: The Logic of an Israeli Obsession
2009

John Chalcraft, The Invisible Cage: Syrian Migrant Workers
in Lebanon
2008

Rhoda Kanaaneh, Surrounded: Palestinian Soldiers in the
Israeli Military
2008

Asef Bayat, Making Islam Democratic: Social Movements
and the Post-Islamist Turn
2007

Robert Vitalis, America's Kingdom: Mythmaking
on the Saudi Oil Frontier
2006

Jessica Winegar, Creative Reckonings: The Politics of Art
and Culture in Contemporary Egypt
2006

Joel Beinin and Rebecca L. Stein, editors, The Struggle
for Sovereignty: Palestine and Israel, 1993-2005
2006